Corporate Communications for Executives

Authored and Edited by
Michael B. Goodman

STATE UNIVERSITY OF NEW YORK PRESS

Published by
State University of New York Press, Albany

For information, address State University of New York Press,
90 State Street, Suite 700, Albany NY 12207

Production by David Ford
Marketing by Fran Keneston

Library of Congress Cataloging-in-Publication Data

Goodman, Michael B.
    Corporate communications for executives / authored and edited by
Michael B. Goodman.
        p. cm.—(SUNY series, Human communication processes)
    Includes bibliographical references and index.
    ISBN 0-7914-3761-2 (hardcover : alk. paper).—ISBN 0-7914-3762-0
(pbk. : alk. paper)
    1. Communication in management. 2. Public relations—
Corporations. 3. Social responsibility of business. 4. Corporate
culture. 5. Communication in organizations. I. Title.
II. Series: SUNY series in human communication processes.
HD30.3.G656 1998
658.4'5—dc21   97-45206
                                                          CIP

10 9 8 7 6 5 4 3 2 1

bs
S.10.06

Corporate
Communications
for
Executives

University of
Chester

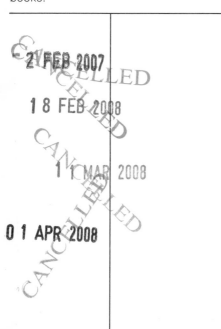

SUNY Series, Human Communication Processes
Donald P. Cushman and Ted J. Smith, III, editors

For My Friend and Mentor
Andy Kaufmann
(1932–1992)

Contents

Acknowledgments

"The Odor of Mendacity: Root Causes of Poor Corporate Communication," Edmond H. Weiss, Fordham University.

"Communication and Change," Michael B. Goodman, Fairleigh Dickinson University.

"Interpersonal Stress in the Organization: The Role of Psychological Fusion," Paul P. Baard, Fordham University.

"Corporate Culture: Add 99 Years of Seasoning," Elliott Hebert, Warner-Lambert (ret.).

"The Business Environment, Demographics and Technology: A Case Study of Florida Power and Light's Electronic Employee Communication Services," David H. Ostroff, University of Florida.

"Corporate Social Responsibility," Pat Siccone.

"Selling Science to Society," Linn A. Weiss, Schering-Plough Corporation.

"Crime, Business Ethics, and Corporate Communication," Vaughana Macy Feary, Fairleigh Dickinson University.

"Get Tough on Crime: But Don't Lock 'em in My Back Yard," Diana Vance, Morristown, New Jersey.

"Supplying Your Own Banana Peels," Marion K. Pinsdorf, Fordham University.

"Toward Better Two-Way: Why Communications Process Improvement Represents the Right Response During Uncertain Times," Linda M. Dulye, PSE&G.

"Anytime, Anywhere: The Social Impact of Emerging Communication Technology," Valerie Perugini, AT&T.

"Efforts to Simplify Human-Computer Communication," Michael Cusack, AT&T.

"Europe and the European Union," Michael B. Goodman, Fairleigh Dickinson University.

Preface

During the last decade, companies expanded, restructured, downsized, right-sized, merged, and divested. In this complex and changing environment, the need for an organization to communicate its message efficiently, effectively, and coherently with its internal and external audiences remained. Some might argue, and I think rightly so, that the need to communicate in times of major change is critical to the very survival of an organization.

In making sweeping organizational change, many corporations consolidated traditional disciplines such as public relations, employee communications, advertising, training, and press relations under one management function called corporate communications. This effort to centralize communication seemed to contradict a trend toward decentralizing management functions.

However, having a central group be responsible for developing, projecting, and maintaining an organization's image and culture makes good management sense to many companies and organizations throughout the world. A corporate communications group consolidates numerous disciplines to meet the strategic goal of developing and perpetuating a corporate image and culture through consistent and coherent messages throughout various media, from print to television.

Communication has become more complex as businesses compete more and more in a global environment. The complexity brought on by an explosion in the number of tools for communication—computers, digital media, interactive corporate television, faxes, E-mail—has fueled the need for a corporation to consider its communications as being central to its strategic plans. Increased integration of advertising and public relations programs, as well as coordination with internal and marketing programs, is a trend underscored by the results of The Association of National Advertisers annual survey of corporate advertising practices.

Corporate Communications for Executives offers a close look at the growing professional practice of corporate communications. It provides a discussion of critical functions and collects commentary and case studies under nine categories arranged as chapters in this book:

Chapter 1 An Overview of Corporate Communication

Chapter 2 Corporate Communication Practice

Chapter 3 Corporate Communication and Corporate Culture

Chapter 4 Corporate Identity

Chapter 5 Corporate Citizenship and Social Responsibility

Chapter 6 Corporate Communication and Meeting the Press

Chapter 7 Corporate Communication and Crisis

Chapter 8 Corporate Communication and Technology

Chapter 9 Corporate Communication in Global Markets

Each category or chapter begins with an overview by the author, and is followed by commentary and case studies. Many of the essays began as papers that were presented at the annual Conference on Corporate Communication at Fairleigh Dickinson University and printed in the refereed *Proceedings*. The commentary and case studies provide numerous perspectives on topics such as ethics, science and society, employee motivation, corporate social responsibility, internal communication, global corporate communications, and communicating corporate culture. The commentary is also meant to stimulate thought, provoke discussion, and encourage additional research into these topics. At the end of the book is the Further Reading section—a list of books, articles, and other sources for further study. Its nine sections follow the chapters of the book.

As an executive function, corporate communication is a strategic tool to lead, motivate, persuade, and inform numerous audiences inside and outside the organization. This book, and its companion, *Corporate Communication: Theory and Practice*, also by the State University of New York Press (1994), further explores corporate communication as an executive and a managerial practice.

I would like to thank my colleagues at Fairleigh Dickinson University for their active support and participation in our annual Conference on Corporate Communication: Dr. Martin Green; Drs. Mary Cross and Walter Cummins, who have served as editors of the conference *Proceedings* every year since its inception in 1988; Professors Harry Keyishian, Walter Savage (emeritus), Don Jugenheimer, and Jack Colldeweih; Dr. Kenneth Greene; Dr. Richard Ottaway, Department of Management; Dr. Robert Chell, Psychology Department chair; Dr.

Harvey Flaxman, Visual and Performing Arts Department chair; Dr. Geoffrey Weinman, vice president for academic affairs; and Francis Mertz, university president.

Also, thanks to the members of our board of corporate advisors for our graduate program in Corporate and Organizational Communication: Linn Weiss of Schering-Plough; David Powell and Dennis Signorovitch of Allied Signal; Gus Merkel of AT&T Company; Robert Muilenberg (retired) of Jersey Central Power & Light; Hank Sandbach of Nabisco Brands; Dr. Craig Burrell (retired) of Sandoz; Dick Keelty of Warner-Lambert Company; and R. Charles Black (retired) of GPU Services.

Thanks to our Schering-Plough Distinguished Professors: Tom Garbett, corporate consultant and former executive at Doyle Dane Bernbach; Professor John Ryans of Kent State University; and Sandy Sulcer and Cleve Langton of DDB Needham Worldwide.

I am grateful to the hundreds of professionals and academics who have presented papers at our annual conference and published their work in the *Proceedings*. It is the active support of these people and those professionals and academics who attended the conferences that encouraged me to write this book and include in it commentary from the conference.

Credit also goes to my fine graduate research assistants at Fairleigh Dickinson University: Gwenn Noel, A. J. Rathbun, Mara Lipacis, Devon Brady, Phyllis Doyle, Victoria Rodriguez, Laura Hagen, Jill Reed, Karen Glover, Jane Schlesser, Adam Yates, Priyanka Kapoor, and Natalie Vuksan; and to department secretary Chris Napolitano. A special thanks to Pat Siccone for her additional effort, drafts, comments, and research on the corporate citizenship issues in this book; and to Mara Lipacis, who worked on the manuscript revisions and editing of this book.

Thanks to all of the executives and managers I have worked with over the years. I am particularly grateful to Andy Kaufmann, who taught me about life in a corporate environment and integrity. He was a special human being, and I miss his advice and counsel.

A special thanks to the graduate students I have had the pleasure to teach and learn from in my graduate corporate communication seminars.

I would also like to thank Dr. Don Cushman of the University at Albany, State University of New York, and SUNY Press.

And, finally, thanks to my wife Karen Goodman, my best critic, editor, and friend; and to my sons David Goodman and Craig Cook.

Michael B. Goodman
New York City, 1997

1

An Overview of Corporate Communication

Communication was an activity that seemed to be an afterthought for many organizations not so long ago. Executives and managers planned and implemented mergers, corporate restructuring, quality improvement programs, and new product development with little or no preparation for how best to present these plans. Employees, vendors, stockholders, community leaders, and labor representatives often found out about their company's actions from the six o'clock news or the morning newspaper. Communication was a response to the business environment—reactive.

Business has become too complex, and all of the stakeholders in an organization's operations are too interdependent for an executive to make plans without considering the strategic value of communications in day-to-day activity and in the long-term vision of the corporation.

In an information-driven economy, communication is now more than ever a cornerstone in strategic planning. A clear understanding of corporate communication can provide the vision a company needs to move in the often murky atmosphere of contemporary business. Communication is a strategic element of an organization's success, a proactive effort.

Corporate communication is the term used to describe a wide variety of management functions related to an organization's internal and external communications. Depending on the organization, corporate communications can include such traditional disciplines as public relations, investor relations, employee relations, community relations, advertising, media relations, labor relations, government relations, technical communications, training and employee development, marketing communications, and management communications.

Many organizations also include philanthropic activity, crisis and emergency communications, and advertising as part of their corporate communication functions.

Emerging technologies such as the Internet and the World Wide Web are becoming new multimedia manifestations for corporate

1

communication. These new technologies underscore the global character of communication.

In practice, corporate communication is a strategic tool for the contemporary corporate executive to gain a competitive advantage over competitors. Executives use it to lead, motivate, persuade, and inform employees and the public as well.

Corporate communication is more art than science. Its intellectual foundations and body of knowledge began with the Greeks and Romans—with rhetoric. Its foundations are interdisciplinary, drawing on the methods and findings of

- anthropology
- communications
- language and linguistics
- management and marketing
- sociology
- psychology

The people who perform these functions may have a variety of technical and professional backgrounds. But most have a firm grasp of the communication process, both written and oral, in a variety of contexts, from press releases to videotaped instructions; from a speech at a professional conference to a meeting of the local PTA; from a letter to a disgruntled customer to a letter to the editor of the *Wall Street Journal*.

The messages and actions put into motion by these professionals, like any in a successful business, are part of the company's strategic plan and are intended to achieve clear goals and objectives for the corporation.

CORPORATE COMMUNICATION AND ITS STRATEGIC IMPORTANCE

Communication has become vital to the health and growth of almost every business since our economy has firmly established itself as being information based, rather than manufacturing based. Customers, employees, investors, suppliers, and the general public now expect a high level of communication and candor from the companies that make and sell their products and services in the community.

In an environment that extols the virtues of decentralization to meet customers' needs quickly, many corporations consolidate their communications. A central group is responsible for developing, projecting, and maintaining the corporation's image and culture. The value of a central management structure for communication makes sense for many organizations, particularly ones with global operations.

A communication group within an organization can set policy and guidelines for written and oral communication. It can also develop training for the entire organization so its decentralized operating and functional elements can create a basic communication expertise for its own autonomous activities and still maintain the larger corporate image. Corporations centralize communications to meet the strategic goal of developing and perpetuating a corporate image and culture through consistent and coherent messages through various media, from face-to-face contact to print to video.

Executives can also use a corporate communication structure to manage the considerable complexity in the tools and the media for communications within the corporation itself through

- computer networks
- digital media (multimedia)
- corporate TV
- fax
- E-mail

Corporations also require a central corporate communication capability to communicate with the media on a routine basis, as well as in emergency and crisis situations.

Communication with various publics, both local and global, is more consistent and effective when the corporation delivers it with one clear voice. A central capability is useful for that and is essential for global operation. The need to translate a corporate message into another language and culture brings communication into the strategy for any transnational activity, no matter how small.

Corporate mission statements and company philosophies are, in ideal situations, the products of executives who recognize the strategic value of a clear statement of what the corporation stands for, its goals and its practices. Clear understanding and articulation of the company mission is the cornerstone for building an image in the mind of employees as well as the general public.

The clear statement of the company mission builds the organizational culture among employees. Since the early 1980s, much has been written about corporate culture and its influence on the behavior of employees. How often do we hear of a company described in cultural terms, its shared values and beliefs? These same beliefs are often the center of advertising campaigns and motivational programs for employees.

A strong corporate culture also creates a recognizable and positive perception of the company among its suppliers, vendors, and customers.

The "equity" a company image and culture amasses is then part of its value as a brand-name product, stimulating customer loyalty.

A strong organizational identity is the result of a strong culture, and the other way around. It has become commonplace in the minds of company employees and members of the community that the perception of strength, and its reality, are one and the same.

A strong image and culture cannot be imposed on a group of people, but it can be nurtured. Numerous corporations, from American Airlines to Microsoft, demonstrate this strength every day and communicate it through their newsletters and press releases, annual and quarterly reports, advertisements, videos, speeches, and interpersonal contacts with internal and external customers.

DEVELOPING A CORPORATE COMMUNICATION PHILOSOPHY

Speaking of business and philosophy often evokes jokes about other such oxymorons: *business ethics, military intelligence, political integrity.* Nevertheless, large and small organizations that have a strong commitment to communications with employees and the community have a definite philosophy of communication. Though many companies would not call it a philosophy, they may refer to it as their communication policy, or mission statement.

In both cases, the philosophy may be articulated with statements of commitment to employees, customers, and other stakeholders, such as the following statement from Levi Strauss & Co. about its aspirations:

> We all want a company that our people are proud of and committed to, where all employees have an opportunity to contribute, learn, grow and advance on merit, not politics or background. We want our people to feel respected, treated fairly, listened to, and involved. Above all, we want satisfaction from accomplishments and friendships, balanced personal and professional lives, and to have fun in our endeavors.

> When we describe the kind of Levi Strauss & Co. we want in the future, what we are talking about is building on the foundation we have inherited: affirming the best of our company's traditions, closing gaps that may exist between principles and practices, and updating some of our values to reflect contemporary circumstances.

> What type of leadership is necessary to make our Aspirations a Reality?
> . . .

Communications: Leadership that is clear about company, unit, and individual goals and performance. People must know what is expected of them and receive timely, honest feedback on their performance and career aspirations.

Empowerment: Leadership that increases the authority and responsibility of those closest to our products and customers. By actively pushing responsibility, trust, and recognition into the organization, we can harness and release the capabilities of all our people.

(Quoted in *Harvard Business Review*, September–October 1990, 135)

The communications philosophy may also be implied in a company pledge, usually found in an annual report. The following appeared in the 1990 Annual Report of Bristol-Myers Squibb Company after the two pharmaceutical giants merged:

To those who use our products . . .
We affirm Bristol-Myers Squibb's commitment to the highest standards of excellence, safety and reliability in everything we make. We pledge to offer products of the highest quality and to work to keep improving them.

To our employees and those who may join us . . .
We pledge personal respect, fair compensation and equal treatment. We acknowledge our obligation to provide able and humane leadership throughout the organization, within a clean and safe working environment. To all who qualify for advancement, we will make every effort to provide opportunity.

To our suppliers and customers . . .
We pledge an open door, courteous, efficient and ethical dealing, and appreciation of their right to a fair profit.

To our shareholders . . .
We pledge a companywide dedication to continued profitable growth, sustained by strong finances, a high level of research and development, and facilities second to none.

To the communities where we have plants and offices . . .
We pledge conscientious citizenship, a helping hand for worthwhile causes, and constructive action in support of civic and environmental progress.

To the countries where we do business . . .
We pledge ourselves to be a good citizen and to show full consideration for the rights of others while reserving the right to stand up for our own.

> Above all, to the world we live in . . .
> We pledge Bristol-Myers Squibb to policies and practices which fully embody the responsibility, integrity and decency required of free enterprise if it is to merit and maintain the confidence of our society.
>
> (Annual Report, Bristol-Myers Squibb Company, ii)

The written statement of corporate commitment to goals and values such as the statements of aspirations and pledges, is often the external manifestation of the communication philosophy. It is not necessary for the written statement to exist to have a philosophy, but if it does not represent some corporate behavior and belief and value system, its hollowness will be grossly apparent to everyone inside and outside of the organization.

Also, companies are now operating on a global scale, and a strong corporate communications philosophy can offer the foundation for a code of ethics that applies throughout the world. Working internationally places one under both United States and foreign laws and regulations. Most corporations have an ethics code with a section on international business ethics. *The Westinghouse Code of Ethics & Conduct* (1994) offers a fine model:

> Employees conducting business internationally are required to comply with all applicable U.S. and foreign laws and regulations. Compliance with such laws, as well as company standards (including this Ethics Code), is required even if they seem inconsistent with local practice in foreign countries, or would place the company at a competitive disadvantage. The penalties for noncompliance can be severe, both for the company and for involved individual employees.

KEYS TO COMPLIANCE:

Don't Make or Offer Unlawful Payments or Bribes	The *Foreign Corrupt Practices Act* bars the payment or offering of anything of value to officials or politicians of foreign governments, and others, to obtain or retain business. It also requires proper accounting for transactions. The company has a specific policy concerning retention of overseas sales agents.
Abide by Import/Export Controls	A number of U.S. government controls restrict, to varying degrees, the import and export of goods, services, and technical information to various countries, as well as the re-export of U.S. products from other countries. Foreign

	countries may have similar laws that apply to U.S. products. Employees must comply with these laws applied to their businesses and products, and specifically by obtaining the necessary general or validated import/export licenses.
Adhere To U.S. Economic Boycott Laws	U.S. laws restrict trading with certain foreign countries, and prohibit U.S. companies from complying with certain boycotts imposed by other countries. These laws cover U.S. persons and can also apply to Westinghouse subsidiaries located outside the U.S. Anti-boycott regulations also require notification to the U.S. government of any boycott request received from a foreign government or official. Boycott laws, including the countries affected, often change and must be closely monitored.
Refer International Trade Law Questions to the Law Department	The application of U.S. and foreign laws can be very complex. Sometimes, U.S. laws conflict with the laws of other countries. When such conflicts appear in the conduct of your business, contact the Law Department.

In the 1980s and 1990s, quality improvement and reengineering programs swept organizations in this country—from government to defense, from pharmaceuticals to computers, almost every organization of any size has some form of reengineering program. Such efforts are change agents intended to make the organization more efficient and productive and, as a result, more profitable. Such programs emphasize teamwork and empowerment and strive to create and perpetuate a humane environment in the workplace.

Communication is at the center of a successful quality or reengineering program. Newsletters, pamphlets, magazines, in-house television networks, videotapes, and questionnaires are some of the ways companies communicate their values and beliefs. In addition to these "one-way" communications, organizations are now training their employees in methods of communication, problem solving, interpersonal and small group participation, and management skills that support the company culture.

In practice we see the philosophy at work in how an organization communicates with its employees, external audiences, the press, and foreign customers. We see how the corporation presents itself to the world at large. Some signs—the company buildings, company vehicles, employee appearance—are easy nonverbal communications to observe. Others are harder to recognize at a glance—attitudes such as an innovative spirit, a commitment to community, and an understanding of the coexistence of fair play and competition. But these forces are shaping the corporation and are manifested in the organization's communications.

Corporate communication, from the perspective of an anthropologist, encodes the corporate culture. Corporations that do not value communication highly are doomed to wither. George Bush lost the 1992 presidential election, according to Peggy Noonan, Ronald Reagan's speechwriter, because the Bush administration failed to see the connection between words and deeds. ("Why Bush Failed," *New York Times*, November 5, 1992: A35 and "As Bush's Loss Sinks In, Finger Pointing Begins," *New York Times*, November 5, 1992: B5.)

Elements of corporate communication guide the development of

- a strong corporate culture

- a coherent corporate identity

- a reasonable corporate philosophy

- a genuine sense of corporate citizenship

- an appropriate and professional relationship with the press

- a quick and responsible way of communicating in a crisis or emergency situation

- an understanding of communication tools and technologies

- a sophisticated approach to global communications

Each of these is treated in the chapters that follow.

2

Corporate Communication Practice

Corporate communication, put simply, is the total of a corporation's efforts to communicate effectively and profitably. It is a strategic action practiced by professionals within an organization, or on behalf of a client. It is the creation and maintenance of strong internal and external relationships. Obviously the actions any particular corporation takes to achieve that goal depends in large part on the character of the organization and its relationship with its suppliers, its community, its employees, and its customers.

The enormous changes in the workplace have influenced the communication practices of corporations and organizations. A terse "No comment" to an intrepid young newspaper or TV reporter no longer suffices as an adequate communication policy or even as effective corporate communication.

A policy of developing strong channels of communication both internally and externally has become a standard for most organizations.

Not only has the nature of corporate communication changed over the last few decades, the type of people who create the company messages has changed as well. The typical corporate communication professional is college educated with a degree in the humanities. A major in journalism, English, marketing, public relations, communications, or psychology is common. Generally the practitioners are loyal company people with a long history in the organization. This reflects the importance of the strategic nature of the organization's communications.

Often the professional minored in economics or business or, depending on the company's core business, has had experience in some related technical discipline such as engineering or computer science. This may be in stark contrast to a previous generation of business professionals with a background in law or accounting who have handled the company communications.

Using a communication professional underscored another shift in the corporate communication emphasis from a total focus on the investment community or shareholders—any owner of the company's

9

shares or stock—to a broader interpretation of community that now includes all "stakeholders." A stakeholder is anyone who has a stake in the organization's success—vendors, customers, employees, executives, the local barber, and the kid on the paper route.

The explosion in the number and type of media available for communication has also had an impact on the communication professional. In the past, mastery of the written word was more than enough. Writing is still the core skill on which all others are built. But a mastery of the essentials of broadcast media is now essential to the creation of corporate messages for TV, radio, E-mail, cable news programs devoted to business topics, multimedia and digital communications on computer networks, and public speeches.

SKILLS AND TALENTS FOR INDIVIDUALS

Many organizations use personality profile instruments in human resource management, such as Meyers Briggs, to find the right person for the job. A corporate communicator should have

- written and oral communication talent;

- an understanding of and expertise in the communication process;

- face-to-face and telephone interpersonal skills;

- media savvy;

- an understanding of customer, stakeholder, and community needs;

- curiosity;

- active listening skills;

- an understanding of advocacy communication.

In addition, corporate communication demands an ability to solve problems in groups, to understand media and communications technology, to work ethically, and to feel comfortable in an international, a transnational or a global business environment.

The elements of communication continue to exert substantial influence in all transactions, from simple customer questions of front-line sales and retail personnel to the pressure negotiations involved in a multinational merger or restructuring. And since corporations communicate through people, the following forces must be considered by the organization as a whole and by its individual representatives:

- language and linguistics
- technology and the environment
- social organization
- contexting and face–saving
- concepts of authority
- body language and nonverbal communication
- concepts of time and space

These forces make up the core of communications skills for business on a national and an international basis.

Corporate communication has evolved into a complex profession, yet writing remains the central talent to create any communication in a corporate context. No matter what the medium of the final message, the ideas more often than not begin in writing. Even though we have experienced great changes in the number of ways we can now communicate with one another, we are still human. Understanding the writing process (see Figure 2–1) is fundamental to all types of communication and all types of media applications.

The writing process, which can also serve as a model for the communication process, emphasizes the following three main areas of analysis:

1. audience
2. environment or context
3. content or message

Corporations routinely target a message for a particular audience, meeting their needs while achieving the company's goals. All successful communication, corporate or otherwise, must make human interaction its center. Successful communication in a collaborative corporate environment seeks to win both for the organization and for its customers.

The type of person who has the skill and talent to collaborate is someone who can see an issue from several perspectives and create a message based on the analysis rather than on a personal bias. In a global environment, the sensitivity to issues from several perspectives is critical, since the culture, language, customs, and traditions of others have a tremendous impact on the development of an appropriate communication strategy. As discussed in chapter 9, using the direct approach, a common practice in the low-context culture of the United States, used in a high-context culture such as Japan or the United Kingdom, can be disastrous, or at least rude or "cheeky."

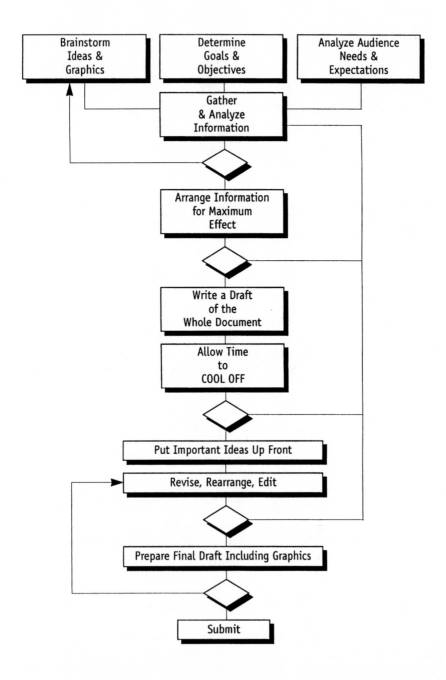

Figure 2–1.
The Writing Process Is Dynamic, Incorporating Opportunities
to Improve Text and Graphics

The ability to see a message as a graphic image, or series of images, is also essential. No American can deny the impact of our visual media, such as TV, regarding how we gather and process information.

America is an extremely media-literate society. Several media critics have observed that our media literacy has turned us into an oral rather than a print society. That is certainly true for mass communications. The proliferation of TV networks and stations and the decline in the number of daily newspapers underscores the changes in how most Americans receive their information.

Appropriate use of media internally and externally can generate interest in the message and influence the stakeholders involved. In a corporate environment filled with numerous messages, the art of corporate communication can be used to meet goals. Ford, for example, has used an integrated communication strategy in its advertising and internal communication to create and strengthen its image as a quality automobile manufacturer. Its "Quality Is Job 1" ads ran all over the country, but the emphasis of the ads in the cities where Ford had manufacturing and assembly plants was not just on attracting customers; it had an internal message for its employees to make a quality automobile, a self-fulfilling effort at building the pride and self-esteem its workforce needed to compete globally.

Curiosity is also a valuable personal attribute for professional communicators. The communicator must first have an interest in what is happening in the company and in its people and customers to be able to communicate that interest to others. Without interest, the writer's message is at best flat and bland, at worst phony and hollow.

Part of the ability to communicate effectively is the ability to listen carefully and actively. Communicators understand the need for this fundamental business practice: listen to your customers and employees. Active listening builds a relationship of trust. Consideration of the ideas of others places value on them and on one's relationship with them.

A fundamental understanding of the nature of advocacy communications is also essential to corporate communicators. A company spokesperson may be called upon to put aside personal opinion in favor of a company position. Because of this fact of corporate life, the ideal corporate communicator is a person who has been with the organization for a long time.

Integrity is extremely valuable for any organization, and any corporate spokesperson should instill trust in the audience. Without trust, the message is not likely to have the desired impact or much positive impact at all for that matter. Integrity and trust is built over time through attention to detail, consistency in message, and follow–through on promises. It is reinforced in face-to-face contact with customers and employees through body language and eye contact, as well as through words. Integrity and trust are built with every act and every message of an organization.

SMALL AND LARGE GROUP REQUIREMENTS

Corporations and organizations function through groups and as collections of groups. Notice the language used to describe a company: management team, quality circle, quality action team, management committee, board of directors, product management group, crisis committee; and even some older terms influenced by the military— management task force, strategic planning committee, tactical mission task force.

Whether an organization emphasizes old-style hierarchical leadership techniques, which have been called Theory X and Theory Y styles, or more contemporary consensus management styles, or Theory Z, the ability to work effectively in and with groups is an essential element in a broader definition of corporate communication.

The reengineering and quality revolutions that have swept the world in the last decade are built upon a foundation of shared commitment to corporate goals. Communication is a fundamental element in successful change initiatives. Most communication at work occurs in small groups. The gatherings can be formal or informal, in twos and threes or more. Most of us learned the etiquette of small group behavior in a business setting. Each corporation has its own way of handling such group encounters.

PRESENTATIONS: MEETINGS AND SPEECHES

Professionals give few formal speeches, but they often make many presentations related to company actions and projects. Companies and industries each have their own particular way of doing presentations. For example, in engineering or high-tech firms, the presentation or briefing is straightforward and factual. Engineers prefer an analytical presentation of the facts. Any visuals used tend to be overhead projections, or slides for a formal presentation.

Management presentations, on the other hand, are also brief and direct, with the use of slides and video. More effort, however, is spent on the glitz of the presentation than it would be for an audience of technical experts, as a presentation of the options, alternatives, and solutions, rather than an analysis alone, is expected. The results of an analysis must be seen in the presentation. Decision makers, then, expect a polished presentation, not a slick one.

Corporate communication professionals generally are involved in company-wide meetings and are called upon to write the speeches for the corporate executives. Meetings now are generally face-to-face. Increasingly, future meetings will be accomplished through interactive video networks, computer networks, and E-mail.

If Nicholas Negroponte, in his book *Being Digital* is correct in his prediction of the future, such new technologies will change both the nature and the style of business meetings. People will depend more and more on technology to send information. His vision calls for a shift in the way people think about ideas and actions, a "Paradigm Shift." Meetings and face-to-face communication can occur through computers, changing the way we make eye contact and the way we use facial expressions and body language. It will, like the telephone did a century ago, call for a whole new etiquette of human interaction. As these customs and rules develop, the corporate communicators will be in the vanguard of the change.

SELECTING MEDIA

The practice of corporate communications demands the professional to be able to determine the best media for both the message and the audience. High technology E-mail and digital multimedia to low technology posters in the company lobby; a new company logo to a "dress-down" Friday for employees are possible media for corporate messages.

Selecting the appropriate medium for the message plays a central role in the success of the communication (see Table 2–1). It also can result in a cost-effective effort.

The corporate communication professional selects media with the message, the desired effect upon the audience, and the corporate environment in mind. Cost is also a factor, since corporate resources—time, talent, and money—are limited and budgeted.

BECOMING A MULTIMEDIA PROFESSIONAL

Before 1993, corporate communicators did not have to be concerned with the ins and outs of computer networks because the emerging multimedia technologies were expensive and were being explored by broadcast media giants as the logical evolutionary step for mass communication.

The creation of the World Wide Web by the Conseil Európen pour Reclierches Nucléaires (CERN) in Switzerland changed all of that. Created as a way for scientists to use the Internet more effectively to communicate globally over computer networks, this breakthrough has

TABLE 2-1. Selecting Appropriate Media

MEDIUM	APPLICATION	IMPACT (High, Moderate, Low)	COST (High, Moderate, Low)
TV Network Video	Company annual meetings; motivational messages; news conferences; announcements; training	High	High
Radio	Company annual meetings; motivational messages; announcements; training	Moderate	Moderate
Film	Company annual meetings; motivational messages; company history; training	Moderate	High
Print	Company annual reports; newsletters; magazines; announcements; policies; reference documents	Low	Low
Computer network; E-mail; electronic bulletin boards & home pages	Time-critical messages; proprietary technical information; routine memos and action items; reference material; policies	Moderate	High
Displays; posters; bulletin boards	Motivational messages; seasonal announcements; safety and quality messages	Low	Low

captured the imagination of communicators. It has also created another communications tool and medium for corporations to use in reaching their customers, vendors, and employees.

The Internet is rapidly evolving from a communications tool for scientists and university professors to a tool for the next century. It is the concept upon which the "Information Superhighway" is being built. As an agent for change, it has been embraced by business, education, and government. Its use in corporate communications opens a new field for designers of Web pages, graphics, and interactive communications. For the Web to work effectively, its use demands active participation on the part of the audience, something not possible with most other media. Used effectively, the medium draws its audience into a discussion of ideas and facts.

Multimedia expertise has quickly become another skill needed for corporate communications.

Selected Commentary

The commentary selected for this chapter is adopted from a presentation at the annual Conference on Corporate Communication at Fairleigh Dickinson University. The author focuses on a part of communications practice in the context of some technological or cultural change in the organization and business environment.

Edmond Weiss explores the negative effects of the corporate desire to put information in the most positive light. His discussion underscores the need for corporate communicators to possess talent, skill, and judgment, as well as a well-defined sense of integrity.

The Odor of Mendacity
Root Causes of Poor Corporate Communication

Edmond H. Weiss

Much poor corporate writing and speaking stems from the desire to package and present information in a more favorable light than it deserves, nowadays often called "spin." This inclination is learned from our earliest days at school and reinforced on the job. While only the very unsophisticated student or business professional will tell an outright lie, nearly all learn the techniques of mendacity: recondite vocabulary; euphemism; overblown sentences; passive, oblique sentence forms; gratuitous "filler phrases," and constructions that swell empty passages. . . . Today's communicators must be taught that any deliberate wording of a statement so as to mislead the audience—even though such a statement is "technically correct" or even "legally acceptable,"—should be construed as a lie. And, more important, even though we make allowances for managers and sales professionals in their pursuit of business goals, no professional writers should lend their skills to the suppression of truth for the sake of "effectiveness."

THE ODOR OF MENDACITY

At the base of much bad writing is the intention to deceive. From the time we first begin to write our little school reports, what we are mainly

This commentary by Dr. Weiss, of Fordham University, first appeared in the *Proceedings of the Seventh Conference on Corporate Communication*, May 1994. An updated version appears here with his permission.

trying to do is make ourselves look good, that is, *to look better than we are*. A principal objective of nearly everything we write—from grade-school essays through the 40 years of correspondence, reports, and studies that comprise a career—is to create the impression that we worked harder and better than we actually did.

Young people who are good with words learn quickly the rewards of their gift. Not only do the various tests of intelligence favor those with the best vocabularies, even teachers who should know better can be taken in by a child who says *myriad* instead of *many*. The facile student, unprepared for an exam, hopes for an "essay test."

The idea takes hold in us at an early age that facility, the ability to cover pages with little effort, is almost a magic ring of invisibility that allows one to escape punishment for chapters unread and research not finished.

Most of the bad writing I see every day, I now believe, derives from a deliberate or a habitual attempt to impress, to ameliorate the unpleasant facts of a situation, or to lead us to unwarranted conclusions. In short, to deceive.

The people who try to mislead us like this are nearly always acting in a manner considered professional or businesslike. They have been *taught* to communicate this way, typically by people they admire, often by their professors. Moreover, most attempts to disabuse them of these habits count for nothing when compared to the apparent awards offered by their superiors for more of the same. In fact, many students of business "communication" wish they could be *more facile at impressing and misleading, not less*.

Consequently, there is a vague aroma about much corporate writing, a sickly sweet smell noticeable only when one reads or listens closely. I call it the "odor of mendacity," borrowing Big Daddy's phrase from *Cat on a Hot Tin Roof*. "Didn't you notice," he asks his son in Act III, "a powerful and obnoxious odor of mendacity in this room?" In part he is reacting to outright lies being told him about his failing health; the lies are meant to comfort, but they are still lies. But he is also talking about the unceasing chorus of praise and affection he hears, much of it aimed at influencing his will. (His son, Brick, like Lear's daughter Cordelia, will not tell him the flattering lies; unlike Cordelia, though, Brick is rewarded.)

And I call the "context of mendacity" that set of impulses and objectives that Big Daddy's family (and Lear's older daughters) pursue which such ardor that it affects every phrase: self-promotion, self-indemnification, unearned reward, amelioration of embarrassing or unpleasant truth.

THE TECHNIQUES OF MENDACITY

Bad writing is normal but unnatural. We learn it from our first days at school, and, more important, we are usually rewarded for mastering it.

A powerful motivator is the pervasiveness of vocabulary tests as measures of general intelligence. The influence of this construct, "verbal aptitude," can only be appreciated when we realize that, in America at least, IQ is actually an index of middle classness. Someone who understands that *mordant:dulcet* as *bitter:sweet* will not only score well on ITBSs and CATs and SATs, he or she will have access to better education, which, where we live, usually means access to the professions.

This is not to object to the teaching of vocabulary. Even I cannot help feeling indignant when I meet adults with advanced degrees who cannot define words like *incontinent* (in either sense) or distinguish *perversion* from *perversity*. (This last confusion is so widespread that Hollywood was forced to rename the film version of David Mamet's *Sexual Perversity in Chicago*.) Quite the contrary. Few things are more pleasing than a robust vocabulary in the command of a writer or speaker who makes intelligent choices and uses just the right words.

The problem is with "official" vocabulary, the notion that people who say *prioritize* are smarter than people who say *rank*, or that people who write *utilize* have better minds than people who write *use*. Although it is surely innocent enough to encourage students to use the words they have just learned in writing and speaking as soon and as often as possible, it is only a small step to convincing these students that good writers use *implement* in place of *begin* . . . all the time.

The best students—usually those young people best at deducing what their teachers expect and delivering it to them—learn a myriad of words, use them profligately, and are rewarded with praise and good grades. In fact, they have learned one of the deadliest habits of all: writing to impress. At every point they will choose words and construct sentences in a way that makes them seem pompous, evasive, inauthentic, distant, and dull. Even though what they have written would have scored well at school.

Then, beginning in high school, gaining momentum in what Sidney Hook calls the "tertiary" schools, is a second main force for bad writing: the premium on length.

From about puberty onward, the first requirement in nearly every written assignment we receive is minimum length, expressed in number of words or number of pages. Whatever other virtue a paper may have, if it is too short it fails. The understandable equation of length with substance or hard work affects students through to graduate school, where, except for certain hard sciences, no one receives a Ph.D. without delivering a dissertation with heft. (And the "softer" the science, the more paper is expected: social psychologists must write more than chemists; doctors of education must write more than even economists.)

Schools teach, reward, and inculcate the habit of writing long . . . at every level and in nearly every discipline. In contrast, few students are ever punished or scolded for *prolixity*. So that the good students (remember the earlier definition) learn quickly to write *make a selection with respect to* instead of *select* or *should it prove to be the case that* in place of that most marvelous word, *if*. Unconsciously, our students learn a short list of rules that double or triple the lengths of sentences, without affecting their substance. This new skill, applied to the habit of impressive vocabulary, creates the style of writing that is usually called "professional" or "official." Eventually, it will be harnessed to the goals of business and government. Before that though, it can be used to undermine all of undergraduate education.

For most university students, even including the best ones, the goal is to finish, to get on with whatever benefits accrue to the matriculated. The hard way to finish is to read, study, remember, assimilate, evaluate, and report. The easier way is to develop a certain facility in writing and use that as a substitute for honest work in any course that will allow it. The temptation is nearly irresistible.

Interestingly, the professors who teach reluctant students to write these days are frequently from separate and independent Department of Communications. What is best about this arrangement is that today, far more often than in my youth, the person teaching Basic Composition is genuinely interested in the topic and may even know something about it. This contrasts with the harried, somewhat disaffected graduate students of literature who were forced to teach it in my youth.

But what is worst is that this discipline called Communications is not an entirely trustworthy one. Unlike its ancestor, Journalism, Communications appeals not only to those who wish to learn the craft of truthful, understandable speech, but also to those mountebanks and casuists that Plato warned us about in the *Gorgias* dialogue, those who consider truthfulness and integrity relatively unimportant in the pursuit of advantage and rhetorical "efffectiveness"—winning, prevailing, looking good.

CORPORATE MENDACITY

At first, mendacity is deliberate, a learned technique for presenting one's self and one's company favorably. We master it on the job by imitating the speech of our bosses; we acquire flamboyant methods of deception from the advertising department, subtler ones from our attorneys, who teach us the craft of "avoiding exposure." In time, we internalize these techniques and language; they become second nature.

> This culture is built on three, questionably moral, propositions:
> First, short of outright lies, one should always put the most favorable
>   interpretation on one's self and one's employer. (*The Precept of Spin*)
> Second, it is always more cost-effective to reduce one's liabilities
>   through the use of expensive lawyers than through the practice of
>   more honorable actions. (*The Precept of Exposure*)
> Third, it is better to win an argument than to learn the truth. (*The
>   Precept of Campaign*)

The Precept of Spin teaches us that it is always possible to put things in a better light without actually lying. And for many, the main goal of business communication is to make themselves (and often their superiors) look as good as possible—typically, better than they are. The underlying argument is that errors can be turned into innocent mistakes, false promises into misunderstandings, sloppy performances into tolerably good work, larcenous charges into standard fees . . . all by writing about them effectively.

"Spin Doctors," the people Plato most dreaded, are people who think they can turn bad news into good news. For example, recently, a major American communications company announced that it will lay off 15,000 employees, but that these layoffs will include generous severance packages and other compensations. In the broadcast words of a company representative: "We decided with our heads but we're implementing with our hearts." This sentence is a pure example of professional spin: it is the clear work of professional "communicators" who toiled for hours or days to find the right bromide. What is astonishing is that its authors expect that the widespread agony and desperation brought on by their profit-motivated action will somehow be ameliorated with this bit of greeting-card sentimentality.

Most of the spin in corporate writing is not so slick or smarmy as this example. Indeed, most of it is artless and inconspicuous. "Unfortunately, the plan was rejected . . ." or "Because of budgetary constraints . . ." or "Hopefully, there will be a minimal impact . . ." or "there is insufficient knowledge with respect to this option . . ."

Much of it is an elaborate vocabulary for saying the unpleasant things that are inevitable in government and business.

- We don't want you or your plan.

- We don't know how or when.

- We performed incompetently. (We were late.)
- We broke our promise. (We never meant it, anyway.)
- We were mistaken.
- We forgot.
- We changed our mind.

The Precept of Spin encourages us to think that with a few passive verbs (to obscure agency), a sprinkling of *hopefullys* and *regretablys*—even the use of *we* or *The Company* in place of the more accurate *I*—the lapses and larcenies will go away.

The Precept of Exposure teaches us that it is just as good to be "not guilty" as to be "innocent." That is, "deniability" is at least as worthwhile as never having done something wrong.

This attitude is a product of lawyerism: NOT law, which has always prized truth and justice, but lawyers, who, even from Biblical times, have earned their largest fees from defeating both. It is not just legal jargon that is at issue; new students of writing often think mistakenly that replacing technical vocabulary with familiar vocabulary will make matters clear. On the contrary, effective lawyers, far from being the chronically bad writers that the public thinks them, know how to be clear or unclear at will. And their usual tactic is to be as unclear as they can be in defining their clients' obligations.

The lawyer's way of reviewing a business document is to "soften," that is, obscure the commitments of the client while sharpening the promises of the other party. Ironically, lawyers are the only large group in North America who understands the distinction between *shall* and *will* (at least in the third person) and attorneys use this knowledge to differentiate the elements in a contract into commandments (theirs) and remarks about the future (ours).

Responsible, well-paid lawyers want to keep their clients safe. "Reducing exposure" is the term-of-art. But this term-of-art is a euphemism for protecting people from the proper consequences of their misdeeds. Corporate attorneys try to do it before-the-fact, hedging all their clients' promises, building in smokescreens to obscure future problems that are already known. And they earn even bigger fees after-the-fact, putting absurd "interpretations" on their clients' nonfeasance, misfeasance, and malfeasance.

And this strategy is so often effective that executives and managers try to imitate it in their ordinary business and even technical communications. The chronic abuse of hopefully is not just a problem of usage; the term usually means nothing more than "don't hold me to this, but . . ." Such ideas as the "flexible specification" and the "guideline" are little more than a habitual, mendacious way of appearing to state predictions and requirements in a way that is not binding!

Too many business professionals believe that it is generally cheaper and easier to write one's way out of trouble than to do things right the first time. Ironically, one of the incentives for this deceitful vagueness is a fear of being wrong or missing a target. One cannot appreciate fully the business professionals' distrust of clear, simple assertions and predictions unless one realizes how terrified they are of ever admitting a mistake. During the 1990 Presidential debates, Clinton chided Bush not for raising taxes but for having been so reckless as to make the famous "read my lips" pledge in the first place.

Unlike scientists and scholars, business and government people believe that consistency and persistence are greater virtues than truthfulness and humility. Ours is a society in which candidates for leadership must NEVER admit to having been wrong and certainly never to having changed their mind. We are even hard on people who complain that they were deceived, implying that folks of good character are never mislead about anything.

The Precept of Campaign holds that anything can be proved through an aggressive program of assertion and promotion, and, more important, that the ability to wage such a winning campaign is far more useful than the ability to establish what is true. The corporate professional's attitude is put nicely by Michael Gilbert in *How to Win An Argument* (McGraw-Hill, 1979), who says that the first rule of arguing is "Never admit defeat unless you are absolutely convinced, and even then keep your mouth shut and wait till Monday." Viewed calmly, this is good advice; too often, in the heat of debate, we feel overwhelmed by an argument that is not as good as it seems at first. But viewed more cynically, it is one of the core causes of corporate mendacity.

Often, the purpose of corporate discourse is to determine controversial matters of fact or assign praise and blame. When the driving force is to have one's way, the whole range of tainted language, specious arguments, and material fallacies parade themselves as analysis and research. The typical feasibility study, for example, is a politically motivated proof that a *forgone* conclusion was reached *after* objective evaluation of risks and benefits. Indeed, most of the "scientific" documents produced during the life (or "life cycle") of a new plan or system are after-the-fact rationalizations of decisions reached through suspect means.

In recent years, the most mendacious form of campaigning has been the endless prattle about "quality" from executives and managers who have read nothing more substantial on the subject than an article in an in-flight magazine. They would be surprised to learn that W. Edwards Deming, the expert whose name they intone with such reverence, disavows the use of all targets and production goals and considers employee appraisals counterproductive! But this would not deter them from claiming to have a "total quality" program; If they say it often enough, they expect, people will think it is true.

AIRLINES, FOR EXAMPLE

The closest most corporate speakers and writers come to outright lies are their schedules, deadlines, and promised delivery dates. Because so much depends on low costs and quick schedules, people whose work entails budgeting and scheduling are quickly drawn into patterns of "acceptable" deceit. This deceitfulness eventually affects nearly everyone whose job is to meet tight deadlines or keep fixed schedules. It is an attitude that eventually corrupts those who must promise more than they can deliver or who must compete in arenas where they are unqualified.

And because it is nearly impossible to make airplanes take off and land exactly when we want them to, the writing and speech of airlines tends be the most noxious with mendacity.

Experienced air travelers have learned to dread messages from the airlines. When travelers peer up at the departure monitors, what they want to see is a lack of information: no curious discrepancies between the scheduled and estimated times; no untoward words like *Delayed* or, God help us, *See Agent*. They also like silence in the waiting area. The first time they want to hear the ambient hiss that signals the opening of a microphone is when the children and handicapped are invited aboard.

Airport announcements are nearly always bad news: big delays or cancellations. "Due to late arriving equipment . . ." the agent begins. Our bowels constrict in anticipation of missed connections, forfeited income, bootless nights in airport hotels . . .

Moreover, when things are going wrong, airline personnel are elevated to new heights of surrealistic mendacity. During open-ended delays, travelers are told to "remain comfortably seated," as though saying it would cause comfortable seating to appear in airports. When travelers ask for a revised departure time, they hear something like "I'm showing a 10:30 departure." The Rules of Spin, Exposure, and Campaign conspire to make it impossible for anyone to say: I don't know.

(Travelers also suspect that much of the evasiveness and mendacity of airline speakers has the effect of preventing them from switching airlines while there is still time.)

Airline speakers have been taught to talk in this irritating way. The remarks are from a library of spoken routines that include such utterances as "This plane is equipped for a water landing." Nearly every official sentence spoken by representatives of airlines or printed on an airline placard, in the airport or on the plane, is from this library, even though some speakers interpolate a bit of regional slang. And, moreover, nearly every such sentence is badly written.

To a student of language or teacher of writing, a sentence that begins with "due to late arriving equipment" is unbearably repugnant. First there is that incessant but misguided substitution of "due to" for "because of." (Yes, the world is still full of half-educated people who believe, unaccountably, that there is a rule against starting sentences with "because.") Then, there is the muddled syntax of "late arriving equipment"; in writing, a hyphen somewhere would help. And, finally, the painfully pseudotechnical use of the word "equipment" for "airplane." All this and we have not yet even reached the independent clause.

To a somewhat older student of language, though, the problem in this clause seems less syntactical than ethical. To understand why intelligent people would write or talk this way, we need only contrast the alternatives.

- Due to late arriving equipment . . .

- Because our plane is late . . .

Put simply, the peculiar grammar and usage of the airlines is the direct result of their continuing embarrassment. And of the belief—held throughout government and industry—that a certain tone of voice or style of speech can ameliorate the problem, even when the problem is an Act of God.

But, if this practice is widespread, why pick on the airlines? Simply because they are an instructive example of an industry whose main goal is to provide the impossible: errorless, frictionless, troublefree service to millions of people—under conditions that make this impossible. And, moreover, because the airlines, more than any other organizations in the private sector, believe that a resilient smile and the right string of sentences can distract us from what actually happens when we do business with them.

In 1988, for example, several organizations began to publish accounts of how often various airlines reached their destinations "on time." (That is, within 15 minutes of the scheduled arrival, not counting delays caused by bad weather.) Inevitably, the airlines that fared best in these comparisons began publishing the results in huge newspaper ads.

How did the airline I use most frequently respond to its chronically poor showing? *By lengthening the estimated time for all its flights.* Now, a 55-minute flight is scheduled as an 85-minute flight, and the company's "on-time performance" has improved dramatically.

(A representative of that particular airline told me that I should applaud their new policy of more honest estimates!)

A company that would embrace such a policy cares little for what the term *ontime* really means. Indeed, they care little for the meaning of most terms. They distort and coin words (*deplane!*) to suit themselves, but, unlike Humpty Dumpty, they do it not for power but for profit. Or so they believe.

Why would any decent-thinking person say "We have lost our connection capability" when he or she could just as easily say "We cannot make our connection."? Why "Due to a crew unavailability situation . . ." instead of "Because we lack a crew . . ."?

AN AGENDA FOR THE TRUTHFUL

Writing clearly and directly is relatively easy. It is easier than solving a partial integral equation; easier than removing a spleen; much easier than landing an airplane on an aircraft carrier. How is it, then, that people who can do these quite difficult things cannot write a readable letter of transmittal or announce a delay in departure? Those of us who teach writing to people in the learned professions are forever mystified by this paradox?

But perhaps I am naive. Perhaps most learned people *could be clearer*, but chose not to be. These writers want to be impressive; they want, more than anything else, to cover their inadequacies and obscure their shortcomings. And their style of writing—difficult, oblique, puffed-up, smarmy, hackneyed, saccharine—was the product of choice, not just ineptness.

Good writing, unfortunately, is moral writing. Just as good writers understand that one style of writing is better than another when it reduces the burden on the readers, so good writers should also understand that nothing worthwhile can come of deception, even when the deception has been sanctioned by the legal department.

Of course, everyone knows there are a thousand shades of gray; and of course there are no self-sacrificing Socrates-types in the boardroom.

Moreover, nowadays there are clever apologists for all this self-serving deceit. In 1993 David Nyberg published a sustained attack on the virtue of truth-telling (*The Varnished Truth*, The University of Chicago Press, 1993). This witty and provocative work argues that clever lying is an advanced technique of biological adaptation:

. . . a healthy, liveable human lifetime of relationships with others is to me inconceivable without deception; furthermore, I hold the prescription that life should be lived without aid of self-deception to be a distinctly unfriendly idea. I think deception is in our nature, and it is there for some reason: the mind does not evolve in ways harmful to itself. (2)

It's the artfulness we have evolved for avoiding both truth telling and lying at the same time that interests me most—the varnishing, the adding and subtracting, the partial display and concealment of what one person takes to be the truth while communicating with another. As a communicative strategy, deception is so often rewarded that it would seem to have become unavoidable and indispensable. It may actually serve to promote and preserve emotional equilibrium on a personal level, and a civilized climate for communicating with each other and living our lives together on a social level. (53)

But I still believe that most people know when they are mendacious; they know when they've omitted a fact, inverted a verb, stuffed a phrase, or otherwise decorated their mistakes and embarrassment with words meant to reduce their exposure. In a recent interview, for example, the actor Michael Moriarity spoke of NBC executives this way: "They don't lie, but they don't tell the truth."

And I also believe that, Nyberg's arguments notwithstanding, any conscious communication act meant to mislead the reader or hearer is best called a lie. In particular, I believe it is especially pernicious when persons trained to write and speak well lend their skills to such an enterprise. Why? Because it is unreasonable to exepect most business professionals—people who are driven to succeed, to sell, to win, to prevail, to manage, to control—to be overtly concerned with the truth. In contrast, who else but the professional communicator, someone who recognizes all the subtle techniques of deception and sophistry, is in a better position to expose and refute their mendacity.

Rather than trying to correct the problem through some ambitious program of indoctrination for business people, this is my only solution: that communication professionals should consciously resist all forms of deceit, and that they should either educate or expose the guilty.

Otherwise, we are all forced to live with the sentiment expressed by Big Daddy's son, Brick:

"Mendacity is a system that we live in. Liquor is one way out an' death's the other."

3

Corporate Communication and Corporate Culture

Forces within organizations and corporations shape and influence the behavior of individuals in subtle, yet powerful, ways. These forces, like the wind and the tides in natural environments, are often unseen and unnoticed themselves, but their effects can easily be observed. These forces combine to create the culture of a corporation.

Corporate culture has become a concept that, used appropriately, offers the intellectual tools for an insightful analysis of an organization's beliefs and behavior. Used improperly, it devolves into jargon and faddism.

In an anthropologist's terms, all human groups by their nature have a culture—the system of values and beliefs shaped by the experiences of life, historical tradition, social or class position, political events, ethnicity, and religious forces. In this context, a corporation's culture can be described, understood, nurtured, and coaxed in new directions, but rarely created, planned, or managed in the same way a company creates a product or service.

Nevertheless, an organization's culture plays a powerful role in its success and failure. For this reason, the discussion of a corporation's culture offers a foundation for understanding the group's behavior and suggests ways to either perpetuate or change the cultures.

DEFINING A CORPORATION'S CULTURE

Terrence Deal and Allen Kennedy popularized the term *corporate culture* in 1982 with the publication of their book *Corporate Cultures: The Rites and Rituals of Corporate Life*. In the book, however, they only approach a definition of this concept with: "Values are the bedrock of any corporate culture." Equally circuitous is J. Steven Ott's definition of organizational culture as "... the culture that exists in an organization." However, Ott redeems himself with this additional explanation: "... and consists of such things as shared values, beliefs, assumptions, perceptions, norms, artifacts, and patterns of behavior."

In analyzing a corporation's culture, we can divide Ott's list into the following three levels:

1. artifacts and patterns of behavior that can be observed, but whose meaning is not readily apparent;

2. values and beliefs that require an even greater level of awareness;

3. basic assumptions about human activity, human nature, and human relationships, as well as assumptions about time, space, and reality.

The last group is often intuitive, invisible, or just below the level of awareness.

Examples of *artifacts and patterns of behaviors*, the first level, abound: corporate logos, the company's headquarters, annual reports, company awards dinners, the annual golf outing, the business attire at the main office. The artifacts and behaviors can be observed. Often these are outward manifestations of what the corporation believes and values, no matter what it says its values and beliefs are.

Examples of the next level, the *values and beliefs*, may be articulated in a slogan or an ad campaign, such as Ford's decades old, "Quality is Job 1," or GE's "We bring good things to life." These are simple, yet effective, ways to put into words what may often be very complex and difficult to articulate. Both examples present a sort of complex pledge from the company to its customers to create products that improve their lives. Companies that actually write a values statement find the task difficult because the written presentation too often sounds like the values statement of almost any company. Clichés and platitudes can make the most honest presentation seem hollow.

Basic assumptions, the third level, is even more difficult to articulate because it requires the analysis of both what the company says and an observation of what it does, then a synthesis to determine conflicting areas. One example of a fatal conflict between the projected basic assumption and what lay beneath the surface was the demise of investment houses E. F. Hutton and Drexel Burnham in the 1980s. Both companies quickly lost clients' trust when scandals surfaced that undermined the integrity clients are supposed to feel is the central character trait of their investment bank.

Other aspects of corporate culture fall into the first category, but are often illustrations of company values and basic assumptions—company heroes, stories, legends, and myths. All of these reinforce the corporate culture, in the same way that religious stories present patterns of behavior and beliefs and values to members of the congregation. For instance, a high-technology organization that submits complex proposals to the U.S. government often presents a story to its proposal teams about a hapless fellow from a competing company who delivered a proposal a half hour late, thinking the submittal was due at the close of business rather than the stated 3:00 P.M. His dawdling cost the company a shot at the contract and cost him his job. The lesson of the story for the corporate audience is crystal clear: the proposal effort is very serious business to our personal and corporate survival.

How can I identify cultures? Deal and Kennedy described four groups of corporate cultures as a way to identify and understand the various types of corporations. They called them "corporate tribes".

- tough guy/macho culture

- work hard/play hard culture

- bet-your-company culture

- the process culture

Table 3–1 provides descriptive information about each of the four corporate tribes—examples, risk, feedback from the environment, rewards, people, organizational structure, and behavior.

Each of these tribes reveals itself through a careful analysis of

- the physical setting of the company

- what it says about itself

- how members of the company greet strangers

- how people spend their time in the organization

- the career paths

- the length of time people stay in jobs at the organization

- the stories, anecdotes, and jokes people tell

- what people write about or discuss

SIGNS OF A CULTURE IN TROUBLE

How can I identify a problem with corporate culture? Weak cultures have no clear values or beliefs. Members often ask for an articulation or

TABLE 3-1
The Characteristics of Four Corporate Tribes

CULTURE	Tough Guy/Macho	Work Hard/Play Hard	Bet-Your-Company Culture	The Process Culture
Examples	Advertising, construction, entertainment, publishing, venture capital	Consumer sales; retail stores	Oil, aerospace, cCapital goods, mining, investment banking, computer design, architectural firms; actuarial insurance	Banks, insurance, financial services, government, utilities, heavily regulated industries (pharmaceuticals)
Risk	High	Low	High	Low Risk—Low Stakes
Feedback from Environment	Quick	Fast (You get the order or you don't.)	Slow (years with constant pressure)	Very Slow to None
Rewards	Short-term focus; speed, not endurance	Short-term focus; endurance, not speed	High stakes; constant pressure; Long-term focus	Focus on how work is done; real world remote
People	"Cowboys"; individuals; rule breakers	Super salespeople are the heroes	Company over individual; heroes land the big one; young managers seek a "rabbi"	Achieving rank; V.P.'s are heroes (or survivors)
Structure of Organization	Flat for fast decision making	Flat for fast decisions; forgiving of poor decisions	Hierarchical; slow decision making	Hierarchical (many layers of management); slow decision making from the top down
Behavior	Informal; temperamental behavior tolerated; stars	Team players; informal atmosphere; friendly, optimistic, humor encouraged; no prima donnas	Formal, polite; team players; no prima donnas	Protect the system; "cover your ass" mentality; emphasis on procedures, predictability, punctuality, orderliness

a written statement of the mission of the group. When a mission statement is available, people in the organization routinely ridicule it as a fantasy having little to do with what the company really does.

Weak cultures also exhibit many beliefs. While that may seem to be a display of tolerance, no agreement on which ones are most important plants seeds of confusion and undermines motivated employees. Some beliefs may develop into an ingrown and exclusive subculture, and the subculture values then preempt the company's.

Destructive and disruptive heroes are apparent in cultures in trouble. In direct conflict with the organization's stated beliefs and values, an executive's abusive, harassing, or uncivilized behavior may be overlooked because he or she looks great on the bottom line.

Other signs include disorganized rituals of day-to-day life resulting in a pervasive sense of fragmentation and inconsistency. People in the organization do not know what to expect from one day to the next. As a result, the organization develops an inward, short-term focus. Signs of such deterioration can be observed in low morale, emotional outbursts, and subculture clashes.

CORPORATE CULTURE CHANGES

Reengineering, Total Quality Management, and other change programs have become a major preoccupation with the business community in the United States, particularly those involved with technical goods or services. In present practice in the United States and throughout the world, the quality process derives from W. Edwards Deming whose theories of statistical quality control took root in post–World War II Japan, not in his native America. United States corporations embraced the quality process as the tool to use to combat the Japanese challenge for world industrial supremacy.

In 1987, the Malcolm Baldridge National Quality Improvement Act made the trend official. The act also established the Malcolm Baldridge Quality Award, similar to the Deming Award for quality, given in Japan since the early 1950s. The European Community is now at work on similar quality initiatives called ISO 9000.

To underscore the power of such programs in the United States, such giants as Xerox, IBM, and Cadillac have pursued and won the Baldridge Award.

In American corporations, change programs have an impact on the corporate culture and on the relationships among all members of the corporation. The process emphasizes a rethinking or reengineering in management practices from hierarchical, authoritarian relations between managers and employees to a consensus approach to management. The new focus is on teams empowered to identify and solve problems and implement solutions.

Communications and a new customer orientation are the cornerstones of the culture change in both company attitudes and practices. These new attitudes and practices required corporations to make massive changes in the way the people in the corporation communicated with one another and with those outside of the company.

The workforce in America is becoming more diverse in ethnicity, race, gender, and age. Numerous government publications such as *Workforce 2000* underscore the fundamental changes in the makeup of Americans at work.

The need for individuals to work in groups or teams at work has increased as a result of greater technological complexity in the nature of work itself. Even before the building of the pyramids of Egypt or the Roman roads, large projects demanded group efforts. Technological effort in the 1990s and into the next century implies that individuals from a wide variety of backgrounds work together in groups. The quality process itself depends on groups of professionals and technicians at all levels working together to achieve the common goals of the group.

Interpersonal communication skill which begins with understanding and respect for each of the people in the group is the key to successful group performance. In a corporate culture of decision making by consensus, the efficient and effective interaction of members of a group is essential for communication.

Prejudice and bigotry have no place in corporate America.

PERPETUATING CORPORATE CULTURE

If corporate culture can be understood through analysis and observation, and if it can be modified through change programs, then corporate training can be used to nurture and perpetuate a culture that is desirable.

Several methods on how a culture tends to perpetuate itself afford an opportunity for training.

- preselection and hiring of new employees
- socialization of members
- removal of members who do not fit in
- presentation of behavior appropriate to the culture
- justification of behavior that is beyond the norm
- communication of cultural values and beliefs

Many corporations have a clear idea about the kind of people they wish to hire, and that profile provides them with a guide for recruiting. The analogy is a sports team that drafts players with certain talents and skills, but also drafts players who have the ability to fit in with the other players. A corporation does the same thing.

Once a person is recruited and hired, the corporation requires the socialization of its new member through a formal orientation program, followed by less formal socialization in the first few weeks and months on the job. Some organizations go further by instituting a mentoring program to reinforce the corporate culture.

Sometimes the match does not work out, so the member who does not fit in must be removed. For new employees, this is usually done within some initial probationary period. For employees and managers this can be done with careful record keeping and a pattern of performance that demonstrates the employee. The performance appraisal has come to be the instrument for perpetuating the corporate culture.

The behavior appropriate to the corporate culture is generally written in a formal employee handbook, a guide to ethical behavior, and a company code of conduct. These documents generally function as the formal presentation of the company culture. The informal code is in day-to-day activity, tradition, and company custom.

When a member of the company breaks the customs, the corporation must justify this apparent deviation from acceptable behavior. If the top salesperson looks a bit unkempt, with collar unbuttoned and tie loosened, or wears a sweater instead of a suit to the office, the company must justify the violation by clearly saying that the sales force must often dress to fit the client, rather than to fit in with the corporate culture.

Communicating the culture happens every day in small and large ways. Giving awards at the annual recognition ceremony, publishing news of employees who have had personal accomplishments, posting signs in corridors and lobbies, inviting discussions at meetings, and a hundred more actions communicate what is of value to the company and what is not.

Perpetuating the culture is also vital to the survival of the corporation if the culture is compatible with the business and economic environment. Of the hundreds of automobile makers in America just seventy years ago, only three major ones are left. Since chance and luck can happen to anyone, the survivors must have developed a culture that evolved with the changes in the market and technology. For any corporation to survive, its culture must continue to evolve to meet the rapid changes in the global marketplace.

Selected Commentary and Case Study

The two commentaries and the case study selected for this chapter are from presentations at the annual Conference on Corporate Communication at Fairleigh Dickinson University. Each of the authors focuses on a part of corporate communications theory and practice related to corporate culture.

Michael Goodman, Karen Willis, and Virginia Holihan examine strategies to meet the communication challenge of change brought about through planned transitions, by the stress of a crisis or as a result of the social transformation in work and the nature of work. They explore the cycles of change to create a foundation for understanding the communication of change to individual people in an organization. They examine the impact of reengineering as a change vehicle, the role of trust in reengineering, and some reasons reengineering appears to have shortcomings for individuals coping with change. A reengineering case study also is presented. Successful communication of change demonstrates an understanding of the cycle of change, the importance of trust in the communication process, the essential personal nature of change, the necessity for continuous face-to-face communication, and a recognition that current global changes are symptoms of a shift in the human condition.

Paul Baard introduces the concept of psychological fusion to explain the dysfunctional behavior of some employees as a source of stress in the organization. He offers ways to resolve the problem and reduce the stress. His discussion offers a way to understand cultures in trouble and how to help the individuals in them to change.

Elliott Hebert's case study describes the corporate culture at Warner-Lambert. He explores the impact on the culture of a major restructuring in the late 1980s that set the corporation on a new course.

Communication and Change
Effective Change Communication is Personal, Global, and Continuous

Michael B. Goodman
Karen E. Willis
Virginia C. Holihan

"Thoughtful, consistent with simple messages; constant feedback" *Response of the Human Resource Director of a major first class department store to the question, How would you describe the way professionals in your organization communicate change?*

("Change and the Corporation," interviews, 1996)

"Small group meetings [because] people are more likely to talk back in a small group." *Response of Organizational Effectiveness Manager of a division of a pharmaceutical manufacturer to the question, Which communication vehicle works best for your organization?*

("Change and the Corporation," interviews, 1996)

"E-mail [because it is] ubiquitous to the entire group." *Response of the Human Resource Manager of a business unit of a Fortune 50 telecommunications company to the question, Which communication vehicle works best for your organization?*

"Change and the Corporation," interviews, 1996)

Dr. Goodman's article began as the keynote address at the West Coast Conference on Corporate Communication, January 1994. It appeared in different form in Cushman's *Communicating Organizational Change* (SUNY Press, 1995) and in *The Journal of Communication Management* 2 (London). The article presented appears here with his permission. Ms. Willis is a consultant, and Ms. Holihan is with the Schering-Plough Research Institute.

To inherit the future, corporations have to survive today. No matter how good a company's vision is; no matter how excellent the company is; no matter how much quality they put into their products; no matter how much team effort they direct toward their customers; no matter how much they reengineer their processes; no matter how they continuously improve their products and services—many companies may not survive into the next century, NO MATTER WHAT THEY DO.

What does a corporation need to survive? Sometimes nothing more than what John D. Rockefeller said of his wealth, that he just happened to be close by as an enormous door to opportunity opened, and he was lucky. CHANCE AND TIMING. The present and the future are dynamic, constantly changing, adapting, and moving forward. Yes, it helps to be at the right place at the right time, and to be smart enough to recognize the opportunity that changes bring. It certainly worked for Rockefeller.

However, the nature of work and the processes of work have changed dramatically in the last decade, and indeed since 1900 (Brimelow 1996; Passell 1996). Peter Drucker (1995) has called this social revolution the century of social transition in which the emerging society is based on knowledge and the knowledge worker.

> It is the first society in which ordinary people, common people—and that means most people—do not earn their daily bread by the sweat of their brow. It is the first society in which "honest work" does not mean a callused hand. It is also the first society in which everybody does not do the same work, as was the case when the huge majority were farmers or were, or seemed likely only forty or thirty years ago, going to be machine operators.
>
> This is far more than a social change. It is a change in the *human condition*. What it means—what the values are of this society, what its commitments are, what its problems are—we do not know. But we do know that they will be different. We do know that the twenty-first century will be different—as regards politics and society, but above all, as regards humans. (Drucker 1995, 232–33) (See boxed text that follows.)

Groups of stakeholders exert an influence over the corporation in an effort to attract the scarce resources available at any particular time. Owners, investors, and stockholders present the most powerful force. Managers and administrators throughout much of this century exercised considerable influence over the behavior of organizations. Unions also exerted collective power to change the way organizations operated, particularly during the industrial revolution. The society as a whole grants any business a formal or informal license to operate. In this context, the contemporary corporation must be mindful that the community it is in is now global. (See *RSA Inquiry: Tomorrow's Company*, 1994, 1995.)

THE CYCLE OF CHANGE AND ITS IMPACT

For some time now corporations have been undergoing an uncomfortable, often painful period of global change brought on by enormous political, financial, social, and technological forces. One can look at the process of change as linear, or historical; events happening in a unique sequence. Or one can see the events as cyclical, happening with predictable repetition, as the seasons of the year. A third view puts the two together in a state of uneasy compatibility—seasons come and go, but no season is exactly the same as the last.

Often external forces can help an organization achieve its vision, or speed its demise. Such power must be understood to either work with it, or to determine if it can, like a force of nature, be harnessed and at what cost.

VISION IS THE FUTURE WE WANT TO HAPPEN. And according to William Bridges (*Transitions*, 1980), vision is the third and last phase of change. (See boxed text that follows.) It follows: 1) the beginning phase—the *end* of the old; 2) the neutral—neither old or new—a rite of passage like the "Vision Quest" of the Plains Indians, or *"ma,"* Japanese for full of nothingness.

Understanding the Three Phases of The Cycle of Change to Manage Organizational Transitions

- The "Ending Phase"—Letting Go (Beginnings = Endings)
  - Disengagement—Leave the known; Grieving
  - Disidentification—Loss of emotional investment
  - Disenchantment—Loss of emotional closure

- The "Neutral Zone" Phase (Neutral Zone = Hanging in mid-air)
  - Disorientation: ("ma"—full of nothingness); Struggle to gain control
  - Disintegration: "You are lost enough to find yourself now" Frost, *Directive*
  - Disconnected from the past
  - Not certain about the future
  - Discovery: "Vision Quest" of the Plains Indians

- The "Vision" or New Beginning Phase (Endings = Beginnings)
  - Plunge into the new and uncharted experiences
  - Built on the oblivion of the old

Understanding the cycle of change is essential, as well as realizing that change is nothing new. What is new is the accelerating rate of change. And restructuring, according to one analyst, "is not big news, unless you are one of those being fired." (Johnston 1996) But even that is relative to the individual and the individual's experience and capacity to absorb the dissonance brought on by change (Conner 1992).

IMPACT OF CHANGE ON THE NATURE OF WORK		
from MASS MARKET	*to*	CUSTOMER FOCUS
from MASS PRODUCTION	*to*	"MINI MILLS"
from SEGMENTATION	*to*	INTEGRATION
from ISOLATING	*to*	INCORPORATING
from MECHANICAL	*to*	NATURAL
from MIND NUMBING	*to*	CHALLENGING
from HAZARDOUS	*to*	SAFE
from REPETITIOUS	*to*	CREATIVE and VITAL
from STRESSFUL	*to*	FUN

Dealing with the effects of change is different for each person depending on personality, experience, desire, and intellect. An individual's attitude to change strengthens the natural adaptability to the environment and stress. Change also has an impact on work itself and how people perform at work (See the boxed text on the Impact of Change on the Nature of Work and on the Process of Work.)

IMPACT OF CHANGE ON THE PROCESS OF WORK		
from CENTRALIZED	*to*	DECENTRALIZED
from FUNCTIONAL GROUPS	*to*	PROJECT TEAMS
from ASSEMBLY LINE	*to*	EMPOWERED GROUP
from COMPARTMENTALIZED	*to*	MULTIDISCIPLINARY
from FRAGMENTED (task oriented)	*to*	RESULTS DRIVEN
from STRESSFUL (physical & mental)	*to*	FULFILLING
from DICTATORSHIP	*to*	DEMOCRACY
from PROTECTIVE	*to*	CREATIVE

Organizations resist change. And when they do change, they often look to the past for the keys to the future (Martin 1993). The essential disruptive quality of change implies a movement from stability through chaos and instability to be able to reach the desired goals. "For employees, . . . including middle managers, change is neither sought after nor welcomed. It is disruptive and intrusive. It upsets the balance." (Strebel 1996, 86) The nature of organizations is stability, and for organizations to resist change is merely the social animal being true to its nature. (See the boxed text on Negative Reactions to Change.)

COMMON NEGATIVE REACTIONS TO CHANGE

* Refusal to deal with change

* Defensiveness in response to change

* Quick fix actions often lead to *low* morale & *low* productivity

* Emotional outbursts—anger, threats

* Reliance on past performance as a substitute for change

TRUST IS CRITICAL DURING THE CYCLES OF CHANGE

The negative reactions of employees to change (see boxed text) can be, in part, the result of the message corporations send. "In effect, then, managers are sending their employers conflicting messages, on the one hand, they are encouraging them to go for the top of Maslow's Pyramid, to realize their greatest aspirations. On the other hand, managers are telling their employees that their most basic needs for safety and security are not guaranteed. No wonder, in such a climate, that trust becomes a critical issue. Trust in a time of change is based on two things: predictability and capability." (Duck 1993, 114)

Trust means you can rely or depend on something with confidence. The rapid rate of change in corporations means employees and managers can no longer depend on the same things as they had in the past. Transformational change initiatives such as reengineering question the fundamental business process by asking, Why do we do this at all? So considering the disruptive nature of radical change, a high level of trust is essential for success. It is an unusual person indeed who can be objective about the personal impact of change.

Change is a personal issue—not an intellectual issue.

We conducted a survey of corporate employees to determine the importance of trust during change. The questionnaire we developed and used contained a set of twelve statements and a Likert scale (1 strongly disagree, 2 disagree, 3 undecided, 4 agree, 5 strongly agree) to gauge the level of trust employees have in an organization. The statements and the six categories they fell into were as follows (Willis 1996):

ON VISION
- Management has a clear vision about the future direction of the organization.
- The organizational vision is one all employees can support.

ON VALUES
- Management models organizational values through their behavior.
- Employees can clearly identify the organizational values.

ON COMMUNICATION
- At work, people freely pass on information that might be helpful to others.
- Management listens attentively to the needs of employees.

ON COMPENSATION
- All employees share in the financial success of the organization.
- Merit pay is based on clearly defined objective data.

ON ENVIRONMENT
- Management creates an environment free of harassment.
- Personal information is kept confidential.

ON PERSONNEL DECISIONS
- Employees are aware of the career paths available to them.
- Hiring, firing, promotions and transfers are clearly linked to organizational objectives.

Each category and the corresponding statements were selected because they are categories that directly reflect the level of trust an employee has in the organization. Strong agreement on these twelve statements can be interpreted as a high level of trust in the organization. In addition to the statements and demographic information, three *yes or no* questions determined (1) if people were involved in a reengineering effort, (2) if positions had been eliminated because of reengineering, and (3) if individuals were looking for a job with another organization.

The results indicated, contrary to what might be expected, people in reengineered corporations reported a higher percentage of medium and high trust, and a lower percentage of low trust than did those in non-reengineered corporations. People in reengineered corporations, then, more often agreed that their corporations succeeded in adhering to the twelve statements.

Since this outcome was unexpected, we looked for some explanation. In the survey we had asked the size of the company the person worked for. They could check a box: under 50,000; over 50,000. The size of the company was a factor in the results. More large companies, those over 50,000 employees, reengineered, and they also had higher trust levels. So a correlation between the size of the company and high level of trust existed—the size of the company influences higher levels of trust. Companies with over 50,000 employees showed higher levels of trust. Larger companies, it can also be implied, are better equipped to adhere to the twelve statements because they have and use management and communication structures and processes.

They may have a stronger Human Resource function which is in a better position to make the necessary changes in the compensation or evaluation system to support the reengineering effort. These larger companies may also have more tools to communicate to employees.

Another explanation could be that because these systems were in place before the reengineering effort began, these employees are still registering high trust based on the previous structure and the effects of reengineering have not yet influenced their responses. However, United Parcel Service (UPS), a very large company undergoing reengineering, recently conducted an employee satisfaction survey. Employee satisfaction rated higher than it has in the previous two years. UPS believes the positive outcome is the result of effective communication with employees who know clearly how reengineering will effect them. The UPS experience can be very good news for corporations undertaking a major change initiative.

Loss of jobs related to the reengineering effort is also a factor. If jobs are eliminated during reengineering, then there will be less trust in the organization: lower trust increases, high decreases, medium remains the same. This means that once positions are eliminated, some people no longer agreed the corporation adhered to the statements. People with high trust lost that trust. Organizations undergoing change need to pay attention to the needs of their strongest supporters when going through a change effort. Change efforts such as reengineering have been misused and mislabeled.

Organizations that adhere to the twelve statements can expect improved employee trust, and trust is critical to success in any task involving collaboration among people.

OCCASIONS FOR COMMUNICATION

The occasions for communication within an organization are all related to change. Effective organizations communicate when:

- introducing something new
- changing something familiar
- terminating anything

Such a suggestion seems so simple and so intuitively correct, yet it is often overlooked in the cycles of change. Ineffective programs for change also assign their average performers to lead the change, apply measurements only to the plan, settle for the status quo, and overlook communication. "They tend to use only one method of communication, like memos, speeches, or PR videos." (Hall et al. 1993, 129) But successful communication requires more than professional use of the medium, it must also demonstrate an understanding of the complex relationship of message and medium with the audience.

To cope with change effectively

- share information honestly
- involve employees in decisions
- first communicate face-to-face
- allow for autonomy and flexibility
- show appreciation for people's efforts
- consider the meaning and purpose of work

Use of clear, continuous, personal communication on a face-to-face or small group basis is one of the primary characteristics of effective change programs during each of the three phases of change.

THE THREE PHASES OF THE CYCLE OF CHANGE

COMMUNICATING DURING THE CYCLE OF CHANGE:
Coordinate Messages with Phases of Change

- The "Ending" Phase—Letting Go
  - Hear and respond to rumors
  - Provide information to fill the "vacuum"
  - Anticipate questions and misinformation
  - Announce the change quickly and positively

- The "Neutral Zone" Phase—Hanging in Mid-air
  - Kick off the transition with ceremony
  - Provide metaphors, symbols, language
  - Create the new environment for everyone
  - Justify new rules and procedures concisely

- The "Vision" Phase—The New Beginning
- Signal the results through events
- Articulate the meaning of the change
- Admit errors and ways to correct them

Phase I

The people in an organization must be ready for change. A workforce ready for change reflects the beliefs, attitudes, and intentions regarding the necessity for change and the capability to make the changes successfully. These people must have the "cognitive precursors" to change, for example, support for change replaces the resistance to change. And consistent with the image of proactive managers, change agents work as coaches rather than monitors. Then the organization can successfully approach and complete Phase I of the Cycle of Change.

A case in point is the utility company GPU, based in Parsippany, New Jersey, with facilities throughout the United States and recent acquisitions in the United Kingdom and abroad. It responded positively to the revolutionary changes and deregulation that are turning the process cultures of utilities into global organizations. Its corporate identity and logo changes were directed to all their stakeholders: customers, investors, local communities, employees, vendors. The physical changes—signs, trucks, letterhead—were accomplished over a weekend, underscoring consistency and a coordinated effort (Black 1996).

Phase II

The next phase of the Cycle of Change can be thought of as climbing stairs, a sort of controlled fall. As you start you are stable on two feet, then lifting one foot and falling forward to plant that foot on the next step demands balance and confidence. Such instability in the process of change demands constant, personal, and supportive communication. The uncertainty and disorientation of this phase must be experienced and transcended to achieve the third phase, vision. Trust is a major factor during this phase, as we have mentioned.

This is the Phase that Lucent Technologies finds itself in six months after it became that company. Previous to February 1996, the company had been AT&T Bell Laboratories, known throughout the world for its technological innovation, and Nobel Prize–winning research. With the trivestiture of AT&T beginning in September of 1995, plans included the formation of a new corporation. Employees proud of the Bell Labs reputation of excellence and innovation were in the neutral zone beginning with the kickoff meeting for all employees presented just before the public news release. The meeting and corporate video gave the employees the rationale for the change, and the language for the new company introduced to the world in February of 1996.

Another example of an organization in the second phase or neutral zone is Birmingham Airport (U.K). After it received status as an international gateway, the employees, managers, and vendors changed from being part of a regional airport to a global one. Efforts to communicate change were instituted throughout the organization in spring 1996. Its efforts to communicate change are the result of a benchmarking effort of major international airports owned and operated by local municipalities. Its communication program is managed through the computer network and follows the best international practices of the industry. Communication at the airport is now customer-driven, which means the airport actively communicated with air carriers, passengers, and vendors. As a note, security is high and officers armed with automatic weapons are plainly in sight. In the U.K. the sight of any armed police officer sends a strong message.

Phase III

One way to create the future—the vision or third phase—has been through the eyes of visionaries—artists, prophets, seers, yes, even madmen. So it is not without surprise that corporations occupy a special place in artistic concepts of the future. Future corporate and municipal concepts tend to be utopian—no dirt, no disease, no dissent. Of course, every realist knows that such *static states* are undesirable at least, and destructive at best. *Stasis* is by definition an absence of movement, in short, intellectual and physical death.

An example of this last phase is AT&T prior to its September 1995 announcement that it would become three companies. The corporation was widely regarded as excellent. It was time for the cycles of change to end the vision with a new beginning. Had it chosen not to change, it would have stagnated as a vibrant enterprise and eventually been unable to meet the multiple challenges of technology and its competition in the industry.

VISIONS OF THE CORPORATE FUTURE

Movies supply some popular VISIONS of the Corporate Future: the Martian mining village in the science fiction movie *Outland* with Sean Connery (*High Noon* set on Mars); or the black, dark urbanscapes of the futuristic *Blade Runner* with Harrison Ford; and the same overpowering dark images in both *Batman* movies; the intellectual hell of Bradbury's *Fahrenheit 451* and Orwell's *1984* are clearly evident in the movie versions of these books; even the technological hell of *2001: A Space Odyssey* remains powerful for those who have a long attention span.

These images of the corporate future, however, seem out of focus; not a useful map to get from *here and now*, to *there and tomorrow*. An anti-technology subtext informs them—a longing for the good old days, which never were. Memory miraculously washes away the grime of the past; and prediction can numb the labor pains for the future.

In addition to being the future we want to happen, VISION implies a dream; and that in itself is enough to fuel the drive for the future. In a similar time of turbulence (born in 1865 the end of the Civil War and died in 1939 the year Hitler invaded Poland) Irish Senator Statesman, poet, essayist, playwright, Nobel–prize winner William Butler Yeats wrote a complex and mystical book called *A Vision*, in which he attempted to explain the progress of history, as well as the creative spirit. Part mysticism, part meditation, part mumbo-jumbo, Yeats *did* articulate a concept that serves as a map of ideas and events, or at the very least he attempted to conceptualize the apparent chaos of events. In *A Vision* Yeats describes his notion of the progress of events as a conical helix. He saw the movement of events as a dynamic "Gyre" or conical helix, rather than linear movement which prevailed at the time (see the figure below).

His concept shows the progress of time as a line following the surface of a cone. It appears linear up close, but from afar it moves in cycles, a curve. Without getting into conflicting theories of physics, Yeats was on to something. Of course, Albert Einstein's relativity concepts ($E = mc^2$ & time slows as matter approaches the speed of light) were more successful and caught on. Nevertheless, Yeats gave us a metaphor to explain the progress of change, and the apparent acceleration of change.

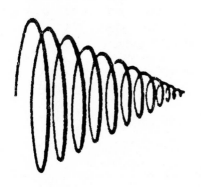

Figure 1. Yeats saw the movement of events as a dynamic "gyre" or conical helix, rather than as linear movement which prevailed at the time.

Like following the line on the cone, the participants in events are so close to the present that they cannot see that what appears to be a line, is actually a curve. It is as if we are all 15th century Europeans before Columbus sailed West, to go East. To move involves risk and probable loss, as well as opportunity and possible gain; not to move at all is to whither and die. We must give up the "old" world for the "new." Organizations throughout the world are moving, changing, reengineering.

THE METAPHORS OF CHANGE

Often the underlying, usually unarticulated understandings about a situation are shaped and revealed metaphorically. For example, how often do we hear people in organizations say this in response to the news that the organization is contemplating a change: "If it ain't broke, don't fix it!" These understandings are critical to how people assess the need for change—and indeed, their conception of change itself. Our lack of metaphors may blind us to forces in the organization that are very strong; forces like gravity or the tide, which often go unnoticed. Paying attention to managing the metaphors of change becomes a critical competency for leaders and change agents. Each of the four types of organizational change: (1) MAINTENANCE; (2) DEVELOPMENTAL; (3) TRANSITIONAL; (4) TRANSFORMATIONAL—can be identified by the language people use to discuss it, the metaphors which encode change. (See the boxed text that follows.)

In the 1992 Presidential election, H. Ross Perot used a metaphor to describe the change he envisioned for a revitalized America. In his Texas home-spun twang he said the economy was like a car and all you had to do was open the hood and get underneath and fix it. He had used a "maintenance" metaphor to describe a radical "transformational change." People who heard his message had an intuitive feeling that his words and the deeds he wished to come true had parted company.

METAPHORS ENCODE THE TYPES OF ORGANIZATIONAL CHANGE

MAINTENANCE
- Change is equated to something being poorly maintained or broken
- EXAMPLE: Change means something is wrong and needs to be fixed
- IMAGE: Fix and Maintain; "A Repair, An Adjustment"
- AGENT: "Repairperson," Maintenance Worker, Mechanic

> ### DEVELOPMENTAL CHANGE
> - Builds on the past and leads to better performance over time
> - EXAMPLE: Better Teamwork
> - IMAGE: Build and Develop; "An Improvement"
> - AGENT: Trainer, Coach, Developer
>
> ### TRANSITIONAL CHANGE
> - Involves a move from one state or condition to another
> - EXAMPLE: Manual to Automated Operations
> - IMAGE: Move and Relocate; "A Journey; an Expedition"
> - AGENT: Planner, Guide, Explorer
>
> ### TRANSFORMATIONAL CHANGE
> - Implies the transfiguration from one state of being to a fundamentally different state of being
> - EXAMPLE: Regulated monopoly to market-driven competitive business
> - IMAGE: Liberate and Recreate; "A Revolution"
> - AGENT: Liberator, Visionary, Creator

Here are some suggestions for managing the metaphors of change.

- Note the words and images used to describe change.

- Say what you mean; make the metaphor coincide with literal meaning.

- Describe the change using the four metaphor types to gain insight.

- Align the language with people's behavior.

- Use metaphors, symbols, and images to shape the way people think about change.

- Change the metaphors and images as a way to get "out of the box" and stimulate new ways of thinking.

In addition to the metaphors of change, the literature of change offers analogies for corporate structures. For example, ARCHITECTURE in Tomasko's *Rethinking the Corporation* uses the dome as a much better analogy for a corporate structure than a pyramid since it is strong, economical and adaptable. To understand the cultural forces in organizations ANTHROPOLOGY is the analogy in Deal and Kennedy's *Corporate Cultures* and in Ott's *The Organizational Culture Perspective*. They provide us with process cultures like utilities and governments; work hard–play hard cultures like sales driven stores and businesses; macho tough guy cultures like ad agencies and construction companies; bet-the-company cultures like aerospace and pharmaceuticals. SCIENCE is used in Tompkins' *Organizational Communication Imperatives: Lessons of the Space Program* to explain why The Challenger space shuttle disaster happened. And ENGINEERING is the central image in Hammer and Champy's *Reengineering the Corporation* to explain the need for many organizations to start over from a clean sheet of paper. Such analogies offer powerful frames of reference for us to discuss the new in terms of the known and familiar.

REENGINEERING AS A VEHICLE OF CHANGE

Whether the business environment is in a state of evolution or revolution, the flood of books and articles that try to make sense of the upheaval all use some verb with a RE- prefix: *re*-invent, *re*-engineer, *re*-think, *re*-structure (Goss 1993; Hammer and Champy 1993; Larkin and Larkin 1996; Oram and Wellins 1995; Tomasco 1993; Strebel 1996; Quirke 1995). (See the boxed text that follows for a primer on reengineering.)

These verbs imply that something can be done to re-verse a downward trend; or to keep those organizations that are not on a destructive course from drifting into one. Indeed, people and their organizations and technologies can have substantial impact on the world. As a metaphor for change, reengineering is TRANSFORMATIONAL.

And reengineering sounds extremely tempting: "The fundamental rethinking and radical redesign of business processes to achieve dramatic improvements in critical, contemporary measures of performance such as cost, quality, service, and speed." (Hammer and Champy, 32) Reengineering taps into the power of starting over, a particularly inviting solution for American business that has a tradition of innovation and change. But often powerful, yet subtle forces have an enormity that must be understood in order to use them productively, or to be overwhelmed by them. These forces can stop change and threaten the survival of the corporation. These forces may explain why "leading practitioners of radical corporate reengineering report that success rates in Fortune 1000 companies are well below 50%, some say they are as low as 20%" (Strebel, 86).

REENGINEERING—A PRIMER

THEMES: process orientation; ambition; rule-breaking; creative use of information and technology

REENGINEERING IS NOT:
- another name for downsizing or restructuring
- the same as automation
- software reengineering
- the same as reorganizing, delayering, or flattening an organization technology
- the same as quality improvement or TQM

REENGINEERING IS:
- starting over
- beginning again with a clean sheet of paper
- rejecting the conventional wisdom and received assumptions of the past
- inventing new approaches to process structure

REENGINEERING—FUNDAMENTALLY
- is about reversing the industrial revolution
- rejects Adam Smith's industrial paradigm:
  - the division of labor
  - economies of scale
  - hierarchical control
- searches for new models of organizing work

IMPACT OF REENGINEERING PROCESSES
- people make choices and decisions instead of taking orders
- assembly line work disappears
- functional departments lose their reason for being
- managers behave more like coaches than supervisors
- workers focus more on customers' needs; less on bosses'
- attitudes and values change in response to new incentives

CASE STUDY
DRUG SAFETY SURVEILLANCE DEPARTMENT OF SCHERING-PLOUGH RESEARCH INSTITUTE

This case study (Holihan 1996) suggests that certain organizational factors seem to be prerequisites for successful business process reengineering.

- strong, committed leadership
- ability to manage effectively the organizational culture's resistance to change
- the speed of implementation

Contributing, but not essential, factors are senior management support; internal facilitators; and the use of consultants. Managers considering radical change such as reengineering should understand these factors, then analyze the organization to be sure they are present, and the resources to support them.

The Drug Safety Surveillance Department of Schering-Plough Research Institute, a division of Schering Plough Corporation, develops and markets prescription drugs and biologics, over-the-counter drugs, veterinary products, and toiletries. During the drug development process and throughout the drug's marketed life, the Drug Safety Surveillance Department collects, analyzes, disseminates, and reports safety information to governmental health authorities. The department maintains the central database for worldwide safety information and generates single case reports and cumulative analyses for submission to regulatory health agencies throughout the world.

The radical transformation process began with a crisis. In October 1993, an internal audit showed that the department of pharmacists, nurses, and clerical staff would shortly be unable to meet the new health authority regulations that were to be enacted in the United States and in Europe. The new regulations called for changes in both adverse event reports and cumulative safety reports by the U.S. FDA, the European CPMP, the European EMEA, the International Conference on Harmonization, as well as increased emphasis on pharmacovigilance and signaling of trends in a drug's safety profile.

For the company to be in worldwide compliance, senior management's evaluation of the situation dictated radical changes in work flow and in technology. The over-the-counter drugs were spun off to a separate company; the department kept prescription products. The Senior Director and Director were replaced, and a physician was brought in from another area to head up the group and keep it in compliance. Senior management then mandated that an entire reorganization of work and the organization be completed in less than one year.

An outside consulting firm was hired for quick analysis, process redesign, and implementation. Work began in January 1994. Six months later, after a successful pilot program, the department began implementation of the project. One year later the group celebrated victory, having achieved a remarkable turnaround in performance.

- one hundred percent compliance; one hundred percent of the time

- customer satisfaction

- proactive, responsive organization

- outstanding productivity

- surveillance expertise

Strong leadership for the effort came from the new physician, who was trusted by the department. He was able to elicit the trust of the group through his sense of purpose and control. Weekly staff meetings were held to communicate the progress, as well as the problems encountered by the design team. He also made it clear that every effort would be made to ensure that people's jobs would be safe. He also was able to drive the program to keep pace with the deadlines. He did not shy away from risk-taking, and thoroughly enjoyed thinking "outside the box." Yet he was also very patient in discussing the changes with all the employees.

When the new process was introduced and the consultants moved in, many employees countered with strong resistance at almost every step. Even though everyone in the department knew that the old system was badly flawed, most people refused to accept the idea that radical changes were necessary. Middle managers, especially, wanted to "fix it" rather than change it. Suggested changes by consultants were seen as threats.

One of the most effective methods used in the model to counter resistance was to involve as many people as possible in the redesign phase of the project. Whether change is perceived as positive or negative depends on the degree of influence people think they can exert on the situation (Conner, 70). Allowing the employees to contribute to the redesign gave them a sense of control over what was happening to the department and helped them to accept change more willingly. An especially critical factor here was enlisting the participation of the middle managers. Although this was a gamble, by doing so, they became part of the solution, when in reality they were a major part of the problem. Internal team facilitators contributed to the project's success.

Finally, frequent communication among the teams about their progress greatly enhanced the acceptance of the changes by the rest of the staff. These communications helped the others to understand what was being done and the reasons behind the changes. This also kept the vision of the new department alive in everyone's mind, and greatly helped to obtain buy-in from the others.

All too frequently companies simply buy a consultant's prepackaged model in hopes of a successful organizational transformation. Instead, it is essential for everyone in a company to take ownership of the reengineering effort and tailor the change process to its own culture. A reengineering effort that succeeds for one group may fail miserably for another.

Speed is also a critical factor for successful change. Dragging out changes does no good to anyone involved, and may in fact derail the project for a number of reasons.

- loss of enthusiasm

- loss of resources to competing projects

- team member exhaustion

Eighteen months was the consensus for the optimal time for the implementation of changes, and in the case study project this was initiated by the sixth month. Since the launch of the changes, the processes continue to be re-evaluated and fine-tuned on a continual basis.

OTHER FORCES DRIVING CHANGE
ORGANIZATIONAL INERTIA AND MOMENTUM

Organizational Inertia and *Corporate Culture Momentum* are powerful organizational forces. In corporations we can observe the effects of these forces either propelling the organization into the VISION of the future it desires, or derailing it into oblivion. These two terms borrowed from Physics might help to provide a metaphor or an analogy to help describe the motion to the future. *Inertia* is the tendency of a body to resist acceleration; or it is the tendency of a body in motion to stay in motion in a straight line unless disturbed by an external force. That's physics, but it is also the resistance to motion, action, or change. And *organizations have inertia.*

Momentum is the force of motion; impetus; or impetus in human affairs; an impelling force; an impulse; something that incites, a stimulus; loosely a force or energy associated with a moving body. Because it is associated with a body already moving, the implication is that the force of inertia has been overcome. *It is a positive force* that like the tide or the wind, we sense the subtle power. In a big sporting event we sense which team has MOMENTUM, and which does not. We cannot measure it or see it, but we know it is there nevertheless.

These two forces of an organization can be thought of as part of the culture of the organization. In an environment of change, understanding how these forces work can determine actions and outcomes of change programs.

In that spirit this discussion treats momentum as a positive force in the perpetuation of a corporate culture, thus Corporate Culture Momentum. Ott's concept of the organizational culture perspective deals with change as the force to perpetuate the organization. (Ott 1989)

In attempting to understand the organizational behavior of corporations in transition or under stress, the tools of cultural anthropology can prove powerful in illuminating the forces at work in these situations. The forces of culture at work drive one company, such as Johnson & Johnson did in the *Tylenol* poisonings, to react quickly and responsibly; and another to be slow and unresponsive. The management communication problems of NASA that contributed to the Challenger disaster can be attributed in part to organizational inertia (Bell 1987; Esch 1986; Goodman 1995; Lenorovitz 1993; NASA 1993; Presidential Commission Report 1986; Shuttle 51–L Loss 1986; Space Shuttle 1992).

The examination of change in organizations has been large and has focused on the understanding the nature of change (Watzalawick 1978; Miller and Friesen 1984; Hinings and Greenwood 1988), the need for change (Child and Kieser 1981; Meyer 1982; Bartunek 1984; Dutton and Duncan 1987; Milliken 1990), the process of change (Kanter 1983), the use of change as a strategic tool (Quinn 1980).

Inertia appears in the literature of change as part of the understanding of change. Hannan and Freeman (1984) developed a structural inertia theory in which organizational reliability and accountability give formal organizations an advantage over loose collectives. Reliable performance means timeliness and quality to customers. Accountability is of value to customers of products and services that have some risk, such as medical care or air travel. To provide reliability and accountability an organization must be stable over time and capable of reproducing itself. Such organizations use institutionalization and standardized practices to achieve these goals. The ability for the organization to change is sacrificed to stability. The irony for many organizations is that the very processes that created success, often eventually lead to failure. (Hammer and Champy 1993).

Change represents a threat to such organizations. Inertia exists in an organization when its core features are changing less rapidly than the changes taking place in the environment the organization is in. Organizational Inertia then for many organizations, particularly older and larger ones, increases the chances of failure. AT&T has been struggling with just these issues since divestiture in the early 1980s, and particularly in its latest trivestiture efforts to divide itself into three companies to meet the market challenges of the next century. Bob Allen, AT&T CEO, expressed the dilemma well.

> Trouble is, the benefits of competitiveness are often long term. And people do not live in the long term. They live in the here and now where mortgages have to be met, and tuition paid. And too many people are living with economic anxiety. After almost 39 years with AT&T, it saddens me that our company has become a symbol of this

anxiety. I firmly believe business has a responsibility to help people cope with the personal impact of competitive change; I certainly don't have all the answers, but I think three key areas hold promise.

Lifelong Learning: I'm convinced this is far and away the best way to help people take advantage of the new jobs being created. It has to begin with our public schools, making sure they graduate young people with competitive skills. Then business has to invest in people so they can update skills throughout their working lives. At AT&T, we spend $1 billion a year on employee education. Nobody can guarantee lifetime employment, but updating skills can guarantee lifetime employability.

Industry-Wide Job Banks . . .

Bridging the Gap: When people have to leave AT&T, I can look them in the eye knowing that they're getting a good financial severance package plus a year's free health insurance coverage for themselves and their families. We also provide departing managers up to $10,000 for relocation and retraining . . . The time has come to seriously explore ways to make transition from one employer to another more seamless. I've talked to hundreds of people affected by downsizing, and one of their biggest fears is losing benefits. We need to find a way for people who lose a job to keep the benefits they've built up . . .

We can't turn back the clock . . . But corporations can see that more people are prepared to share the benefits of the changes shaping our future. (Allen 1996)

As an organization that has used communication to overcome organizational inertia, AT&T has been a model in treating change as a personal communication issue.

Momentum in organizational change is relatively undiscussed, much less studied. Kelly and Amburgey (1991) have discussed the concept. In their study of change in the U.S. certified air carrier industry 1962–1985, they mention the concept of momentum.

We definitely saw momentum in organizational change processes. These organizations were significantly more likely to repeat changes that they had experienced in the past. We suggest that the concept of momentum is complementary to inertia theory and that a useful way to think about inertia is that it is high when organizations continue to extrapolate past trends in the face of environmental change. (Kelly and Amburgey, 608–9)

They go on to suggest that the issue is important and needs further investigation since it is related to internal characteristics such as culture, power, decision making, communication, and leadership.

Instead of conceiving momentum as "complementary" to the negative connotations in inertia, the meaning of momentum is positive and implies that inertia has been overcome to produce or change movement. Its use in the discussion of change in organizations should be positive as well.

MEETING THE CHALLENGE OF CHANGE

As corporations begin to reengineer, reinvent, rethink, restructure, or start their "journey" of change, considering the culture of the organization is a critical step in becoming ready for change. If an organization prepares inadequately for change, resistance emerges, organizational inertia thrives, and the efforts to change fail. The vision of the future flickers as forces slow, deflect, and eventually stop its progress.

As we have noted, successful communication of change demonstrates an understanding of the cycle of change, the importance of trust in the communication process, the essential personal nature of change, the necessity for continuous face-to-face communication, and a recognition that current global changes are symptoms of a shift in the human condition. Also, any organization that uses its cultural momentum to overcome the forces of inertia moves toward its vision. It has a much stronger chance to attain the reality of its vision, and to survive into the next century.

REFERENCES

ACAS Publications: "Employee Communications and Consultation," "Redundancy Handling," "Self-regulating Work Groups: An Aspect of Organisational Change," "Time for a Change: Forging Labour-Management Partnerships," "A Change of Culture," "Management of Change" (London: Advisory, Conciliation and Arbitration Service).

Allen, Robert E. "The Anxiety Epidemic: Downsizing is A Necessary Evil. But Business Needs to Do More to Ease the Pain" a "My Turn" Newsweek column (April 9, 1996) in *Forum News* (an AT&T electronic newsletter) April 1, 1996.

Barber, Brenden. Trades union council executive. Conversation at Wroxton College (Wroxton, U.K.), June 4, 1996.

Barton, Laurence. *Crisis in Organizations: Managing and Communicating in the Heat of Chaos*. Cincinnati, Ohio: South-Western, 1993.

Bartunek, J. M. "Changing Interpretive Schemes and Organizational Restructuring," *Administrative Science Quarterly*, 29 (1984): 355–72.

Beauchamp, Tom. *Case Studies in Business, Society, and Ethics*, 2nd ed. Englewood Cliffs, N.J.: Prentice Hall, 1989: 40–47.

Bell, Trudy E., and Karl Esch. "The Fatal Flaw in Flight 51-L," *IEEE Spectrum* (February 1987): 36–51.

Birmingham Airport: Case Study. Site presentations for Wroxton College. June 1995 and June 1996.

Black, R. Charles. GPU communication executive. Interview August 2, 1996.

Bridges, William. *Transitions: Making Sense of Life's Changes*. Addison-Wesley, 1980.

Brimelow, Peter. "What Happened to All Those Blacksmiths?" *Forbes* (May 6, 1996): 46–47.

"Change and the Corporation." Interviews of corporate managers and executives held in conjunction with a seminar on Corporate Communication and Change at Fairleigh Dickinson University, Spring 1994, January 1995, January 1996.

Child, J., and J. Kieser. "Development of Organizations Over Time," In *Handbook of Organizational Design*. Oxford: Oxford University Press, 1981, pp. 28–64.

Civilian Downsizing: Unit Readiness Not Adversely Affected, But Future Reductions a Concern. Washington, D.C.: United States General Accounting Office (GAO/NSIAD-96-143BR), April 22, 1996.

Conner, Daryl R. *Managing at the Speed of Change*. New York: Villard Books, 1992.

Deal, Terrence, and Allan Kennedy. *Corporate Cultures: The Rites and Rituals of Corporate Life*. Reading, Mass.: Addison-Wesley, 1982.

Drucker, Peter. *Managing in a Time of Great Change*. New York: Truman Talley Books/ Dutton, 1995.

Duck, Jeanie Daniel. "Managing Change," *Harvard Business Review* (November–December 1993): 109–18.

Dutton, J., and R. B. Duncan. "The Creation of Momentum for Change through the Process of Strategic Issue Diagnosis," *Strategic Management Journal*, 8 (1987): 279–95.

Esch, Karl. "How NASA Prepared to Cope with Disaster," *IEEE Spectrum* (March 1986): 32–36.

"Executive Pay," *The Wall Street Journal* (April 11, 1996): R1–R18.

Fallows, James. "The Americans in Space," *The New York Review of Books* (December 18, 1986): 34–48.

Farkas, Charles M., and Suzy Wetlaufer. "The Ways Chief Executive Officers Lead," *Harvard Business Review* (May–June 1996): 110–22.

Feynman, Richard P. *"What Do You Care What Other People Think?"—Further Adventures of a Curious Character.* New York: Norton, 1988.

Gates, Bill. *The Road Ahead.* New York: Viking, 1995.

Goodman, Michael B. *Corporate Communication: Theory and Practice.* Albany: State University of New York Press, 1994.

———. "Organizational Inertia or Corporate Culture Momentum." In *Communicating Organizational Change,* Eds. Cushman and King. Albany: State University of New York Press, 1995, pp. 95–112.

Goss, Tracy, Richard Pascale, and Anthony Athos. "The Reinvention Rollercoaster: Risking the Present for a Powerful Future," *Harvard Business Review* (November–December 1993): 97–108.

Gottlieb, Marvin, and Lori Conkling. *Managing the Workplace Survivors.* Westport, Conn.: Quorum Books, 1995.

Hall, Gene, Jim Rosenthal, and Judy Wade. "How to Make Reengineering Really Work," *Harvard Business Review* (November–December 1993): 119–34.

Hammer, Michael, and James Champy. *Reengineering the Corporation.* New York: HarperBusiness, 1993.

Hannan, M. T., and J. Freeman. "Inertial and Organizational Change," *American Sociological Review,* 49 (1984): 149–64.

Hinings, C. R., and R. Greenwood. *The Dynamics of Strategic Change.* Oxford, U.K.: Blackwell, 1988.

Holihan, Virginia C. "Creating a Model for Successful Business Process Reengineering." Masters thesis, Fairleigh Dickinson University, May 1996.

Hurst, David K. *Crisis & Renewal: Meeting the Challenge of Organizational Change.* Boston: Harvard Business School Press, 1995.

Johnston, David. "Nabisco to Eliminate 4,200 Jobs and Trim Product Line by 14%," *The New York Times* (June 25, 1996): C1, C17.

Kanter, Rosabeth Moss. *The Change Masters.* New York: Simon & Schuster, 1983.

Kelly, Dawn, and Terry Amburgey. "Organizational Inertia and Momentum: A Dynamic Model of Strategic Change," *Academy of Management Journal,* 34:3 (1991): 591–612.

Larkin, T. J., and Sandar Larkin. "Reaching and Changing Frontline Employees," *Harvard Business Review* (May–June 1996): 95–104.

Lenorovitz, Jeffrey. "Station Foul-ups Spur Calls for Radical Change at NASA," *Aviation Week and Space Technology* (March 8, 1993): 58–59.

Management Reform: Status of Agency Reinvention Lab Efforts. Washington, D.C.: United States General Accounting Office (GAO/GGD-96-69), March 1996.

Marshak, Robert. "Managing the Metaphors of Change," *Organizational Dynamics* (summer 1993): 44–56.

Martin, Roger. "Changing the Mind of the Corporation," *Harvard Business Review* (November–December 1993): 81–94.

Meyer, A. D. "Adapting to Environmental Jolts," *Administrative Science Quarterly* 27 (1982): 515–37.

Miller, D., and P. H. Friesen. *Organizations: A Quantum View*. Englewood Cliffs, N.J.: Prentice-Hall, 1984.

Milliken, F. J. "Perceiving and Interpreting Environmental Change," *Academy of Management Journal*, 33 (1990): 42–63.

NASA: Major Challenges for Management: Testimony Before the Legislation and National Security Subcommittee, Committee on Government Operations, House of Representatives. Washington, D.C.: United States General Accounting Office (GAO/T-NSIAD-94-18), October 6, 1993.

National Aeronautics and Space Administration. *Report to the President: Actions to Implement the Recommendations of the Presidential Commission on the Space Shuttle Challenger Accident—Executive Summary*. Washington, D.C.: NASA, July 14, 1986.

New York Times, Special Series on Downsizing. Articles by Rick Bragg, Kirk Johnson, N. R. Kleinfeld, Elizabeth Kolbert, Adam Clymer, Sara Rimer, Louis Uchitelle. March 3–8, 1996. Articles begin on page A1.

Nolan, Richard L., and David C. Croson. *Creative Destruction: A Six-Stage Process for Transforming the Organization*. Boston: Harvard Business School Press, 1995.

Ott, J. Steven. *The Organizational Culture Perspective*. Pacific Grove, Calif.: Brooks/Coles, 1989.

Oram, Mike, and Richard Wellins. *Re-engineering's Missing Ingredient: The Human Factor*. London: Institute of Personnel and Development, 1995.

Passell, Peter. "Why the Best Doesn't Always Win," *The New York Times Magazine* (May 6, 1996): 60–61.

Presidential Commission on the Space Shuttle Challenger Accident [The Rogers Commission]. *Report to the President: Report at a Glance*. Washington, D.C.: United States Government Printing Office: 1986 O-157-336.

Quinn, J. B. *Strategies for Change: Logical Incrementalism*. Homewood, Ill.: Irwin, 1980.

Quirke, Bill. *Communicating Corporate Change.* London: McGraw-Hill, 1996.

"Reengineering: A Light That Failed?" [An interview with James Champy], *Across the Board* (March 1995): 27–31.

RSA Inquiry: Tomorrow's Company: The Role of Business in a Changing World— Interim Report. London: Royal Society for the Encouragement of Arts, Manufactures and Commerce, 1994.

RSA Inquiry: Tomorrow's Company: The Role of Business in a Changing World. London: Royal Society for the Encouragement of Arts, Manufactures and Commerce. 1995.

Shuttle 51-L Loss [Special Section with numerous articles], *Aviation Week and Space Technology* (February 3, 1986): 16–29.

Shuttle 51-L Loss [Special Section with numerous articles], *Aviation Week and Space Technology* (February 10, 1986): 18–24, 53–65.

Shuttle 51-L Loss [Special Section with numerous articles], *Aviation Week and Space Technology* (February 17, 1986): 18–27; 100–7.

Shuttle 51-L Loss [Special Section with numerous articles], *Aviation Week and Space Technology* (February 24, 1986): 22–30.

Space Shuttle: Status of Advanced Solid Rocket Motor Program: Report to the Chair, Subcommittee on Government Activities and Transportation, Committee on Government Operations, House of Representatives. Washington, D.C.: United States General Accounting Office (GAO/NSIAD-93-26), November 1992.

Steinberg, Jacques. "Connecticut Store Owner Sentenced in Tax Fraud," *New York Times* (October 21, 1993): B1 and B6.

Steinberg, Jacques. "Papers Show Greed, Calculation and Betrayal in Stew Leonard Case," *New York Times* (October 22, 1993): B5.

Strebel, Paul. "Why Do Employees Resist Change?" *Harvard Business Review* (May–June 1996): 86–92.

Tomasko, Robert. *Rethinking the Corporation: The Architecture of Change.* New York: AMACOM, 1993.

Tompkins, Phillip. *Organizational Communication Imperatives: Lessons of the Space Program.* Los Angeles, Calif.: Roxbury, 1993.

Watzalawick, P. *The Language of Change.* New York: Basic Books, 1978.

Willis, Karen E. "Reengineering and Trust." Masters thesis, Fairleigh Dickinson University, May 1996.

Yeats, W. B. *A Vision.* New York: Collier Books, 1937/1966.

Interpersonal Stress in the Organization
The Role of Psychological Fusion

Paul P. Baard

An emotionally charged reaction to the words of another is a common-place occurrence in corporate America, particularly in times of heightened stress such as following layoffs. The dreading and avoidance of year end evaluation sessions—by managers and subordinates alike—is evidence of anxiety attached to receiving input from others. Similarly, much corporate time and energy is wasted as subordinates wonder what a manager meant a look or nonresponse to suggest. In addition, many CEOs continue to be surrounded by "yes-persons" who attempt to say the politically correct thing rather than offer their genuine opinions. And many a meeting lacks needed vitality and creativity as colleagues fail to act as teammates and aggressive talk leads to outrage or silence.

All of these dysfunctional behaviors have an insidious phenomenon as a root cause. Psychological fusion describes the process by which a person fails to realize where he or she ends and another person begins. It accounts for why another is able to "make us" feel bad (or good). Fusion, as the term is used in physics, pertains to the merging together of diverse elements into a unified whole, often resulting in an explosion such as with a hydrogen bomb. Psychological fusion, in effect the joining together of two minds, also has explosive consequences,

---

This commentary by Dr. Baard, of Fordham University, appeared in the *Proceedings of the Sixth Conference on Corporate Communication*, May 1993, and in different form in the *IEEE Transactions on Professional Communication* 37:1 (March 1994): 14–17. An updated version appears here with his permission.

although there are times when an implosion occurs. The results of fusion between two people can be readily observed when arguing is soon followed by distance, whether overt ("I won't sit in a meeting with him!") or covert, where one or both parties sit in silence, not contributing to the discussion.

Recently, a leading management journal published a case study wherein one member of a committee of peers was able, through his aggressive attacks on others' ideas, to render the group entirely useless (Wetlaufer 1994). The other members allowed this antagonist, who had no legitimate authority over anyone on the team, to "make them" feel hurt and angry. The legitimate leader of the group feared criticizing the aberrant since the CEO had indicated that this individual was key to the organization's success—even though, in reality, he was precluding it. The group head, and its members including the aggressive one, were all suffering from the effects of psychological fusion.

PSYCHOLOGICAL FUSION DEFINED AND ILLUSTRATED

The phenomenon called psychological fusion is well understood by psychotherapists trained in family systems theory (e.g., Kerr and Bowen 1988; Bowen 1976; Satir 1983), yet the concept has had limited exposure beyond practitioners trained in this school of thought and the families with whom they have worked.

The failure of an individual to differentiate herself or himself from the perceived attitudes of others creates stress in organizations. It leads to a preoccupation with approval. The discipline of family systems psychology identifies a dysfunctional process rampant in today's stressed work environments: psychological fusion (Baard 1994; Kerr and Bowen 1988; Bowen 1976). This pattern of interaction stems from insufficient self-definition by an individual, resulting in a dependence upon others to meet a desire to feel approved and accepted. Any criticism, real or imagined, is perceived as threatening to one's "self." Critical feedback, necessary for growth, is therefore resisted as intimidating to psychological survival.

Fusion is perhaps best explained by description and illustration. Any two people are, by definition, separate personalities, distinct from all others. One cannot, therefore, be made happy or sad or angry by another unless one becomes "fused" or psychologically joined with that other person. Similarly, a person cannot know the thoughts and motivations of others unless told of them by their authors. Yet many of the arguments, upsets, and frustrations commonly experienced occur because people act as if others had such direct control over their emotions that "they" can actually "make" another feel a certain way.

Likewise, some engage in a version of mind-reading wherein they so anticipate the (probable) reaction of another to an initiative they are considering undertaking that they fail to introduce the idea or proposal "knowing" the other would not approve it anyway. These non-initiators then go on to experience anger at the other for his or her "response."

The literal definition of fusion pertains to two things coming together to form one larger whole, such as the fusion of two adjacent vertebrae when a spinal disk becomes herniated, and then removed. Psychological fusion occurs when two minds, in effect, occupy one head, as when one attempts to climb into another's head to try to understand what the other is thinking and meaning by, for example, a look or comment. Some relationships are characterized by such exchanges. Since a person already has his or her own ideas, the intruder is expelled, often by way of an explosion.

Another way of defining the concept is through contrast. Differentiation, or separateness, is the opposite of fusion. When an observer sees the thoughts, opinions, and actions of another as being the property of that other, that observer will be less vulnerable to being affected by hearing criticisms or compliments. While not a call for adopting an uncaring manner, it is a recognition that another's behavior is the property of that other person. Psychological fusion is a way of relating to others characterized by the failure to see oneself as separate from those others. It is generally attributable to an uncertainty in self-definition, either at a global level (i.e., of one's entire self) or of a particular dimension of self (e.g., how one is at administrative tasks). Fusion is a way of dealing with the outside world. If someone does not feel particularly good about him-/herself, the individual becomes vulnerable to fusing with anyone in his or her pursuit of feeling "OK."

Psychological fusion is an attitude, a stance toward the outside world, differing from the concept of co-dependency in that the latter is typically focused on a particular individual. Fusion exists when others can get inside one's head and make one feel.

THE ORIGINS OF PSYCHOLOGICAL FUSION

At one time in every life a person is actually and purposefully fused. In the womb, a child is physically fused to the mother, needing her, quite obviously, for life itself. If she had too much coffee, the infant's heart would race. If she lost a loved one, the unborn's heart rate would slow down.

After birth, the child becomes psychologically fused to its family. They were needed to determine if he or she was "OK." The parents' approval or disapproval could emotionally make or break that new person. Tears could be brought to the emotionally driven child by even a frown indicating disapproval by a parent. If they said, "You're a terrific little kid," that young being felt terrific, and walked around feeling confident. But if Mom and Dad said, "You sure aren't quick like your brother," the child was made to feel dull-witted. If told he or she was clumsy, the son or daughter felt clumsy. All started out emotionally fused, and whatever Mom or Dad said "made us feel."

As a child grows, however, it becomes the job of a family to start the process of separation or differentiation. For example, if a child comes home from social studies class and offers, "I think socialism is a better way to run a country than capitalism," a family might respond in either of two ways. In what is described as an open systems family, one might hear, "That's interesting. Your mother and I don't feel that way. We probably wouldn't have this lovely house if our country was run by socialism. Still, your thoughts are interesting so let's talk about the topic over dinner." With this reaction, the parents are saying "You are different from us. You have a different idea, and that's OK." Difference isn't threatening; they treat the child as a personality separate from their own.

In what is referred to as a closed system family, however, the response might be more like, "We're capitalists here, and that's the end of the discussion." The parents are not open to new and different views, and the child is implicitly admonished to conform in order to "be a full part of" that family. Openness, in this context, is not a call for excessive permissiveness. It is, rather, the identification of the need to acknowledge a child as a separate entity. Although mother and father once delighted in saying such things as "You've got your Mom's eyes and your Dad's sense of humor," the job of parents becomes that of recognizing this distinct individual with his or her own thoughts and desires. This process of differentiation results in either an individuated human being or a fused or nondifferentiated one, still feeling his or her worth is dependent upon that conditional approval of others.

THE CONSEQUENCES OF PSYCHOLOGICAL FUSION

Characteristic of fusion is a *need* orientation. If a person needs the approval of a boss, and does not get it, that individual will feel as if a part of his or her personhood is under threat. This is often articulated in words such as, "He gets me so angry when he doesn't listen!" The fact of the matter is (or just may be) the other person did not listen; the getting angry is what the complaining party decided to do with the other's non-listening. This subsequent reaction is probably attributable to the pain/frustration of not getting him to appreciate or value what was being said: the speaker feels devalued by the listener. For some, this then becomes "You don't care about me," and an explosion—or inhibited implosion—ensues.

Similarly, if the esteem of friends and colleagues is terribly important, not getting it will seem almost as if an element of self is missing from the fused person. For example, if someone worked for a prestigious company and was fused to the idea of having the esteem of colleagues, that individual might be very uncomfortable with the thought of working for a "lesser" employer since the admiration and approval of others might not be as forthcoming. This could leave that employee fused with the employer, feeling a need of it for (psychological) life itself.

The consequence of fusion is distance. A person caught up in fusion will often implode; while raging inside, he or she appears cool on the surface, yet is no longer willing to engage in social intercourse with the other. Or the conflicted individual might explode—venting anger in a conspicuous manner, and then visibly distancing from the "threatening" source. In either event, the fused individual is rendered unable to be in close emotional proximity to the other, precluding meaningful interaction. This dynamic is illustrated in the upper portion of Figure 1.

When a manager avoids, delays, or minimizes an evaluation meeting with a subordinate because of fears of that individual's anticipated negative response or overreaction to criticism, that supervisor has "fused" with her/his direct report, inappropriately taking responsibility for the other. "Will I hurt her (his) feelings by providing critical feedback?" The thinking reflects the notion that the manager could somehow "make" the employee think or respond in a particular way. Certainly the supervisor can be empathic, choosing appropriate assertive language and providing negative feedback in the richer context of a largely positive assessment (if accurate). But the fusion occurs when the manager believes he or she can actually cause a subordinate's reaction. Fusion also explains why managers themselves fear being hurt by the employee: What if she/he challenges the rating I assign, or protests to my boss?

A recent case study in a business journal addressed such interpersonal conflict (Wetlaufer 1994). It offered a vignette describing how one team member, acting only in his role as peer to other department heads, succeeded in decimating the work of the group by his aggressive verbal actions toward colleagues. The team leader struggled with the issue of providing critical feedback to the offender. The concept of psychological fusion was used to explain how grown adults could end up being "driven" from the room by the aberrant's verbal behavior, and what might be done to ameliorate this problem.

	Potential threat to self-esteem—such as critical feedback received	
FUSED RESPONSE Defense or counter attack		UNFUSED RESPONSE Reality-check
IMPLODE—intrapersonal conflict		IF AGREE—modify behavior or accept as a deficiency
EXPLODE - interpersonal conflict		IF DISAGREE—challenge or ignore
Distance required		Proximity permitted

Figure 1. The process of psychologically fused and non-fused responding to the stimulus critical feedback.

One cannot provide a motivational environment in which workers are free to take chances, grow, and cooperate if fusion is a significant issue at the individual or group level. While an organization chart may suggest a top administrator has six high-level nurse executives from which to draw counsel, if that leader has encouraged a fused environment where the greatest concern is to appease the boss, that manager has effectively reduced sources of advice to none or few.

CONTAINING PSYCHOLOGICAL FUSION

It is because of an excessive level of psychological fusion that a supervisor or subordinate fears being hurt in the feedback encounter. If the evaluatee makes an honest self-assessment before the review, he or she will be less vulnerable to an emotional reaction to critical input since the information would already be known and accepted. If one has accepted the totality of oneself, that is, having strong points as well as weaknesses, then confirmation or discovery of either of these becomes less threatening.

Managers can best ameliorate the effects of psychological fusion by recognizing it in themselves and in others. Having done so, they are then able to proceed unilaterally in providing the feedback expected of them. When they observe this phenomenon occurring in others, they are able to guide the afflicted individuals through a more non-fused way of responding to critical feedback (see lower portion of Figure 1).

Often, just becoming aware of the phenomenon—being able to recognize fused responding in oneself and in others—begins the process of getting it under control. Having responses emanate from thought rather than emotion also keeps inappropriate reactions to a minimum.

Where psychological fusion seems more acute in an individual, as with those rendered virtually dysfunctional due to hypersensitivity to criticism—real or imagined, it may be appropriate to identify outside resources available for counsel.

When individuals become the sole source of their self-esteem, they become less vulnerable to being brought high by compliments and low by criticisms. This is what the concept of autonomy is all about, and it is found to be at the heart of the experience of intrinsic motivation (Deci and Ryan 1985) and worker empowerment. One technique found effective in enhancing self-esteem is to have an individual take inventory of his or her attributes. By the time a person reaches the age of twenty or so, choices have already been made about what matters to that individual. Some will pride themselves in academic accomplishments, others in being a reliable person, presenting themselves in a professional manner, having developed a particular talent, etc. The point is all have chosen, consciously or not, to become a unique individual, characterized by selected attributes. Some psychotherapists find it helpful to have an interested person list, with operational definitions, his or her desirable traits, and to occasionally reflect upon them. This compilation can help an individual draw self-esteem from having objective reality staring him or her in the face, a more contemporary and potent reality than the vague recollections of a parent who long ago might have implied that person had little worth. For some, the damage done is too severe to be corrected by this simple exercise, of course, and a more extended therapeutic treatment may be appropriate.

Managers, often cast in the role of coach and mentor, are in a unique position to detect when a subordinate is acting out of a fused condition, and to help guide that person to help.

CONCLUSION

Managers and subordinates must become free to act unilaterally—to offer ideas in an atmosphere wherein it is safe to go at risk, to be genuine. Deming (1990) and other contemporary management experts call for greater opportunities for workers to experience intrinsic motivation, found to lead to greater worker involvement and enjoyment. Deci and Ryan (1985) identified the conditions under which an individual experiences intrinsic motivation, that which is characterized by excitement in a task, a feeling of being optimally challenged and having some sense of control over being engaged in the activity. This latter variable, drawn from the earlier work of deCharms (1976), was found to be the primary determinant in whether a person was operating in an intrinsic mode or was pulled into an extrinsic, or controlled, one. The introduction, for example, of an external reward to an activity that had been intrinsically rewarding was found to undermine that initial motivation for the task and shift the focus of the person to the extrinsic variable (i.e., the reward), causing the sensation of being under another's control.

By its very nature, fusion carries with it the feeling of being under another person's emotional control, impairing the sense of acting in a self-determining fashion. This ultimately precludes the experience of intrinsic motivation. How can a manager really be free to lead people, take risks, provide support and autonomy, promote confidence, encourage people, challenge them, do all these things considered essential for leadership if he or she uses subordinates to meet his or her self-esteem needs? How can any employee be free to devote his or her energies to the work at hand if every word or look from another is perceived to be a potential threat, often producing a need to "get even?" For these afflicted souls, a proposal put forth in a conference room becomes an extension of that person and must be defended to death rather than viewed as one idea of many that she or he has to offer.

Human resource professionals and inspired top managers recognize the need to have their organizations equipped to detect such psychological phenomena as substance abuse, sexual harassment, and stress. The better companies do something about these matters by providing training and qualified counsel. Psychological fusion belongs on that short list.

REFERENCES

Bowen, M. "Theory in the Practice of Psychotherapy." In P. J. Guerin (ed.), *Family Therapy*. New York: Gardner Press, 1976.

deCharms, R. *Enhancing Motivation: Change in the Classroom.* New York: Irvington, 1976.

Deci, E. L. and R. M. Ryan. *Intrinsic Motivation and Self-determination in Human Behavior.* New York: Plenum Press, 1985.

Deming, W. E. Interview with editor of *Workplace: Managing Change. The Wall Street Journal* (June 4, 1990): B38, B41.

Kerr, M. E., and M. Bowen. *Family Evaluation.* New York: W. W. Norton, 1988.

Satir, V. *Conjoint Family Therapy* (3d ed.). Palo Alto, Calif.: Science and Behavior Books, 1983.

Wetlaufer, S. "The Team that Wasn't," *Harvard Business Review* (November–December 1994): 22–38.

Corporate Culture
Add 99 Years of Seasoning

Elliott Hebert

Warner-Lambert is an unusual company in terms of identity and image. It can be called an "old–new" company. Old because its corporate history can be traced back to the 1850s when a Philadelphia pharmacist named William R. Warner began experimenting with a new tablet coating process to encase harsh-tasting medicines in a sugar shell.

Warner-Lambert also can be called a "new" company because it has evolved into a widely diversified company reflecting the many acquisitions and mergers along its corporate path.

It is interesting to note that, at least for part of its corporate life, Warner-Lambert and its executives intentionally downplayed the company's historical development in favor of establishing an entirely new identity in the modern business world. However, when the company began serious self-analysis in the early 1980s, it recognized that, indeed, it was the fruit of its heritage. In fact, the conglomeration of different companies from which it grew eventually provided the core identity and principles which the company espouses today.

There were five men—all strong, entrepreneurial types—who played a role in establishing Warner-Lambert's composite identity over a period of almost 50 years. The first was William R. Warner. The others were Jordan Wheat Lambert, Thomas Adams, Harvey C. Parke, and Colonel Jacob Schick.

This case study by Elliott Hebert, director (retired) of corporate communications at Warner-Lambert Company, appeared in the *Proceedings of the First Conference on Corporate Communication*, May 1988. It appears here, with some changes, with his permission.

William Warner founded a very successful drug manufacturing company, propelled by his unique coating process to make pills more palatable.

Jordan Wheat Lambert, a St. Louis pharmacist, helped develop the original formula for Listerine antiseptic in 1879. He founded his company on what has become one of the most successful proprietary products in American marketing history.

Thomas Adams, a New York inventor, launched the chewing gum industry in the late 1860s when he was trying to find a way to use a large supply of rubbery fluid known as chicle, taken from the sapodilla trees of southern Mexico.

Harvey C. Parke, a Detroit businessman, was one of the founders of the pharmaceutical firm of Parke Davis & Company, manufacturing chemists, which in 1903 was awarded Biological License No. 1 by the U.S. Treasury Department "for the manufacture, barter and sale of vaccine viruses, serums and toxins."

Col. Jacob Schick reached his fame in New Jersey in the 1920s when he put his knowledge of the repeating rifle to work by inventing the Magazine Repeating Razor, which became the Schick Injector razor, and the foundation for a successful wet-shave business in razors and blades.

Each one of these business giants eventually became entwined in the evolution of Warner-Lambert, a company that today has annual sales of $3.5 billion—sales that include drugs, and Listerine, and Schick razors, and chewing gum. Each of the entrepreneurial founders contributed to important cornerstones of the new Warner-Lambert Creed, which espouses creativity, innovation, and a "restless discontent" in the pursuit of "better products, better service, and better ways to run our business." Their contributions are recognized in a new Warner-Lambert booklet titled "Heritage," and their names have been invoked as corporate pioneers in numerous executive speeches. In short, they have become an integral part of Warner-Lambert's corporate culture.

DID IT START WITH PERICLES?

The concept of "corporate culture" has been enjoying a renaissance in the late 1980s, presumably the result of American industry trying to find its way back up the ladder of worldwide competition. That is as good a reason as any, and it certainly applies in the case history of Warner-Lambert. Most students of corporate culture agree, however, that every business organization has a culture, whether it wants one or not. The term is used more today to refer to a culture pattern within the corporation that has been carefully crafted and is studiously managed and communicated.

John Clemens, a professor of management at Hartwick College writing in *Fortune* (October 13, 1986), traced the birth of corporate culture to a speech made by Pericles at a funeral of Athenian soldiers in 431 B.C. The father of Athen's Golden Age, as Clemens puts it, was attempting "to coalesce his people into a unified team" in their conflict with Sparta. Pericles, according to Clemens, thereby delineated the two most important guidelines in establishing a corporate culture. First, determine what makes the organization different. Second, eloquently communicate those differences to the organization's members.

Pericles was more than eloquent in establishing the individual as part of the organization. "Here," he said, "each individual is interested not only in his own affairs but in the affairs of the state as well. Even those who are mostly occupied with their own businesses are extremely well informed on general politics. This is [a] peculiarity of ours. We do not say that a man who takes no interest in politics is a man who minds his own business; we say that he has no business here at all."

On a more modern note, Ford Motor Company revitalized itself in the 1980s by creating a corporate culture deeply rooted in quality of product. The company also challenged years of executive autocracy by mandating participative management: "Everyone with legitimate input to your decision should have the chance to be heard."

General Motors' culture objective was to create a more dynamic, risk-oriented environment characterized by a "do-it-yourself" management. All GM management people carry "culture cards" in their pockets. They read, "The fundamental purpose of General Motors is to provide products and service of such quality that our customers will receive superior value, our employees and business partners will share in our success, and our stockholders will receive a sustained, superior return on their investment."

Probably the most talked-about corporate creed in recent years is that of Johnson & Johnson, dating back to the early 1940s. The company said, and the nation believed, that Tylenol was pulled from the shelves in 1982–83, voluntarily, at tremendous cost, because the J&J creed said so, as follows: "We believe our first responsibility is to the doctors, nurses and patients, to mothers and all others who use our products and services. In meeting their needs, everything we do must be high quality."

THE ENVIRONMENT FOR THE BIRTH OF A CREED
(*THE WARNER-LAMBERT STORY*)

In 1979, Warner-Lambert began what it termed "a period of decisive transition." The next few years certainly turned out to be that, and more. The company sold 40 businesses that were responsible for $1.3

billion in sales, but which were producing little or no profit. More than 30 manufacturing facilities worldwide were either closed or divested. Employment was cut from 61,000 to a low of 32,000, with the help of divestitures and a liberal voluntary early retirement program. In the words of a top executive, "We had a number of businesses that didn't fit into our scheme of things. . . . The vision was to have a company oriented to health care and consumer products—a company that would be highly profitable, with a good growth rate, and recognized as one of the leaders in our industry."

There is little doubt that the Warner-Lambert restructuring process was a success, by its own standards as well as those of the financial community. The company was praised in the business press and in reports by financial analysts for having improved earnings, profit margins, stockholders equity, employee productivity and every financial yardstick applied to such evaluations.

At the same time, however, there were interesting developments on the human front, not all planned, but certainly encouraged by the company and recognized as significant and opportune. It became obvious to Warner-Lambert's executive management in the early 1980s that as the company progressed through its difficult restructuring period, the reduced complement of employees would need to be orientated to the task and in agreement with its logic. In addition it would be crucial to the long-term success of the company that the remaining employees be unified in purpose as well as convinced that they were working for a progressive company marked by fairness and maturity in dealing with its employees.

In that regard, Joseph D. Williams, newly named Chairman of the Board in addition to his role as Chief Executive Officer, delivered a speech in October 1985 directed to all employees: "Unless company objectives are in harmony with your objectives, unless our corporate way of life is compatible with the way you want to work and what you want to achieve, there's no way we can succeed, no chance to excel. But how do we make sure the goals of the corporation are consistent with the goals of our employees? How can we get everybody working together to push this company out front? The answer is simple. Start talking. Define the rules by which we shall play the game. Start talking about our philosophy. Write it down, criticize it, change it if it needs changing. Then let it stand out there so we can be measured and challenged to make it even better."

The promise of measurement against goals has been actively underway at Warner-Lambert ever since that speech was delivered. The talking, and the definition of rules called for by Mr. Williams, had begun several years earlier.

A key management conference took place in the summer of 1984 when 30 top management personnel met to focus on "Barriers to Growth." Five were identified.

- the importance of risk-taking

- the quality and training of management

- white-collar productivity

- the need for better forecasting

- the utilization of leading-edge technology in all corporate functions

A Barriers to Growth Task Force was formed to attack each target. Some, by the nature of their challenge, dealt primarily with sharpening routine corporate skills. Others had to ply uncharted waters. Some were already underway. Concerns with the quality and training of management, as an example, were being addressed with a series of annual off-site conferences under the continuing title of Leadership training. Each session involved 20 to 30 upper management people, with a mix of disciplines as well as geography. The agenda for Leadership I ranged from lengthy discussions of Situational Leadership models to group analysis of Henry Fonda's psychological leadership in the film *Twelve Angry Men*.

Another management development technique which evolved during "Barriers" task force deliberation was the Management Continuity Program. Each year more than 300 high potential employees, including female and minority candidates, are identified and reviewed through formal procedures. As a result of the program, dozens of high potential employees have been reassigned to different operating groups, different responsibilities, and different countries to broaden their management exposure. Because of this program, almost all key management openings are filled from within the ranks of the company.

One of the most exciting task force efforts aimed at Barriers to Growth was the group analyzing the importance and status of risk-taking within Warner-Lambert. The conclusion of the task force was as follows: "While the actions of top management indicate a healthy risk profile (trough restructuring and acquisitions), attitudes toward risk may be less than optimal at middle and lower management levels."

There was little doubt that the task force felt existing attitudes were definitely "less than optimal" and required strong action. First, the task force submitted 17 action recommendations spelling out such directions as demonstrating "a strong bias for action," avoiding the punishment of subordinates who innovate and fail, creating a climate that does not kill ideas, and providing rewards and recognition for significant results. Then the task force boldly submitted its own "mission statement" titled, "Managing at Warner-Lambert."

Executive management adopted the statement without change and packaged it as a complement to the new Corporate Creed that was released at about the same time. The "Managing at Warner-Lambert" statement reads as follows:

> Among the managerial characteristics we prize most highly are personal innovativeness and the ability to stimulate and nurture innovation among subordinates. Through innovation, we seek to develop significant competitive advantages in each facet of our business. Thus, our managers foster innovation not simply in product development, but in every function and department within our company. We are committed to the belief that there is always a way to improve our operations.
>
> Truly innovative managers continually conceptualize and test a range of ways in which to better even the best elements of their functions. In pursuing this goal, it often takes many unsuccessful attempts before success is attained. We must exhibit a tolerance for failure and the fortitude to continue to pursue well-conceived, well-planned projects. And we particularly value innovation which leads to quantum change rather than incrementalism. While incremental improvements are encouraged, only quantum change offers the opportunity to truly outstrip our competitors.
>
> In this stage of global markets, rapid technological changes, information explosion, and an intense competitive environment, neither our managers nor our employees can afford to relax. We all must exhibit a "restless discontent" in our pursuit of better products, better service, better ways to run our business. Our Company's ability to remain a viable business entity depends on our ability to innovate, create and change as the world around us changes.

One of the more interesting developments resulting from the "Managing" statement was an almost instantaneous outcropping of entrepreneurial, or "intraprenurial," programs within the company's operating group . They are funded by operating budgets—one profit center allocates $200,000 a year—and are open to all employees in the group. Project proposals are submitted to a review committee and receive dollar grants upon approval. The entrepreneurs assemble their own teams to include the necessary disciplines to achieve their objectives. This usually involves marketing, manufacturing and research and development. The "entrepreneurs" dovetail their additional project into their normal work pattern. Periodic progress reports are submitted to the entrepreneur program committee, but there is no interference in project planning or implementation. The concept is based on the desire to free the entrepreneurs from corporate bureaucracy in order to shorten decision-making cycles and bring new products and services to fruition more quickly.

To date, entrepreneurial teams have been responsible for the marketing of a new hand cream and a nighttime sleep aid product. Others are under development. More notably, an entrepreneurial team within the American Chicle Group proposed and implemented a highly successful Nostalgia Gum marketing program in the fall of 1986. It was so successful on a national basis that is was repeated in 1987, doubling the sales of the previous year. The nostalgia team coordinated the introduction and promotion of chewing gum brands formerly marketed by American Chicle, but no longer on the market, including Beeman's Clove and Black Jack. The project was awarded $50,000 under the entrepreneurial program, primarily to adapt existing manufacturing equipment to handle the switch to the nostalgia gums. The large amount of attention given to the nostalgia products by the media completely overshadowed minimal paid advertising and was mostly responsible for the success of the project.

IN THE MIDST OF MOMENTUM, THE CREED APPEARS

The evolution of the Warner-Lambert Corporate Creed statement can be traced back to the management Leadership training conferences that began in 1981. Part of each conference was devoted to open-end and work-group sessions to develop ideas on how to improve the company, sharpen its objectives and, as stated, to remove barriers to growth. Analysis of the output of these sessions produced an unprompted but repeating pattern from dozens of different management groups: The corporation needed a credo, a mission statement, so that everyone could focus on exactly what the company thought it was, and wanted to be, and how it must change in order to meet its idealized image.

A creed committee of top managers was formed and began the task of outlining a document. It was discussed , circulated, and revised many times among more than one hundred top managers over a period of a year. The document was formerly introduced at a Leadership III meeting in early 1985 involving 80 senior members of the executive management team. Each was charged as a "Creed missionary" to return to their particular corner of the globe to discuss the Creed and its precepts with their peers and subordinates and develop action plans to insure the credibility and viability of the Creed statement. In all, 2,700 management people participated in those discussions and developed 273 action plans to support the Creed.

This "seeding" procedure set the stage for the unveiling of the Creed to all employees via the company-wide newspaper, the Warner-Lambert World, in March 1985. Chairman and CEO Williams was quoted as follows: "The corporate Creed that we are now adopting is both old and new. It is old because the Creed restates the principles under which the company has tried to operate for many years. But it is also new, because the Creed reflects the deep corporate analysis that I and the entire management staff have gone through with the strategic plan over the past four years."

Mr. Williams commented on what he perceived to be the most important aspect of the introduction of the new Creed: "All of us can admit that no one is perfect. But we have set our standards and we will do our best to live by them. We mean what we say."

Here is the Warner-Lambert Creed in its entirety, a total of 287 words:

Our mission is to achieve leadership in advancing the health and well-being of people throughout the world. We believe this mission can best be accomplished by recognizing and meeting our fundamental responsibilities to our customers, employees, shareholders, suppliers and society.

To Our Customers
We are committed to providing high-quality health care and consumer products of real value that meet customer needs. We are committed to continued investment in the discovery of safe and effective products to enhance people's lives.

To Our Employees
We are committed to attracting and retaining capable people, providing them with challenging work in an open and participatory environment, marked by equal opportunity for personal growth. Performance will be evaluated on the basis of fair and objective standards. Creativity and innovation will be encouraged. Employees will be treated with dignity and respect. They will be actively encouraged to make suggestions for improving the effectiveness of the enterprise and the quality of work life.

To Our Shareholders
We are committed to providing a fair and attractive economic return to our shareholders, and we are prepared to take prudent risks to achieve substainable long-term corporate growth.

To Our Suppliers
We are committed to dealing with our suppliers and all our business partners in a fair and equitable manner, recognizing our mutual interests.

To Society
We are committed to being good corporate citizens, actively initiating
and supporting efforts concerned with the health of society,
particularly the vitality of the worldwide communities in which we
operate. Above all, our dealings with these constituencies will be
conducted with the utmost integrity, adhering to the highest
standards of ethical and just conduct.

Shortly after the unveiling of the Creed, a support program was
activated to maintain the momentum of communications and employee
attention. A 17-page survey was distributed among 3,000 members of
middle and upper management to establish a corporate benchmark on
the perceived evaluation of the company in relation to the commitments
outlined in the Creed. The survey was assembled and analyzed by the
management consulting firm of Towers, Perrin, Forster & Crosby.
TPF&C organized the questionnaire based on 20 "shared value" statements identified in a series of interviews related to the Creed. These
included such qualities as capitalizing synergies, providing high quality
products to customers and high quality services to internal clients,
developing future leaders of the company from within, and creating a
lean organization by maximizing the utilization of the company's
workforce.

A critical aspect of the survey was to determine employee opinions
as to how important each of the values was to the corporation (what the
company "says") as compared to how much the company "does" to
reinforce each value. The paired questions, therefore, provided not only
a yardstick on the values themselves but also gap analysis between
commitments and action.

In the initial 1985 survey, three values were shown to be fully supported by company actions with no perceived gap: providing quality
products; conducting business ethically; and meeting goals. The others
needed attention.

The employee survey was repeated in the summer of 1987 among
7,000 exempt employees, reaching deeper into the organization than did
the first survey. The response rate was 72 percent. The second survey
was conducted by Science Research Associates (SRA), a Chicago-based
subsidiary of IBM. Warner-Lambert has stated its commitment to
employee surveys as a means to measure the development of corporate
culture and to evaluate conduct in keeping with the corporate Creed.
Surveys will be conducted every two years.

The results of the second survey, compared against the benchmark
study, indicated that considerable progress was made in the two
ensuing years toward entrenching and reinforcing the commitments

originally set out in the Creed statement. Among the 20 corporate values tested in both surveys, employee response showed that the company was perceived as being more active in 19 of the areas after two years, while reducing the gap between "say" and "do" in all 20 categories. Of particular importance to management, the second survey showed significant improvement in encouraging creativity and risk-taking, providing training opportunities, encouraging an open and participatory work environment, and demonstrating respect for the contribution of all employees.

One of the strongest commitments to employees that emerged from the Creed is strengthening of the Performance Management System (PMS) in dealing with evaluation of performance and career development. All employees are promised at least two structured discussions each year with their supervisors for review of performance, establishing agreed-upon goals and discussion of personal growth opportunities.

In addition to benchmark checks on the original 20 value statements, the second employee opinion survey accomplished three other significant objectives. First, using SRA database statistics, employee attitudes toward the company were compared against industry averages. (Warner-Lambert ranked between the 76th and the 95th percentiles in favorable responses.) Second, a special series of questions probed reactions to the company's employee benefit programs to provide guidelines for planning improvements in benefits and administration. Third, with the help of computer analysis, 127 sub-reports were developed to pinpoint employee opinions within operating groups, divisions and even departments, while maintaining anonymity of responses. Based on these subreports, each operating unit was required to submit to the Office of the Chairman a series of action plans to meet specific concern of its employees. These action plans are being monitored for implementation and effectiveness.

THE FIRST TWO YEARS OF CREED-DRIVEN ACTIVITIES

The first two years following the launch of the Warner-Lambert Creed was a period of heavy activity for Creed-related communications and programs. The most ambitious was a 30-minute video program, shown to all U.S. and many international employees, introducing the Creed and billed as an informal discussion with the Chairman of the Board. He was joined in the unscripted video chat by the vice presidents for Human Resources and Public Affairs. Each commitment outlined in the Creed was illustrated by cutaway video footage showing the Creed already in action within Warner-Lambert. Video examples included an employee-entrepreneur team, employees participating in focus groups and Quality Circle team, and a supplier who worked closely with the company to redesign his production procedures for bottles to better meet the "Just-in-Time" production needs of a Warner-Lambert plant in Pennsylvania.

Once the Creed began to become an official part of the company's infrastructure, it spawned new culture-oriented programs and provided impetus for the enlargement and improvement of other programs already in place. Management task forces were created to align with the five commitment areas of the Creed, namely, customers, employees, shareholders, suppliers, and society. The task forces developed new Creed program targets and tracked implementation in reports to management.

In the area of commitment to customers, action programs were directed internally as well as externally. The Parke-Davis Pharmaceutical Group initiated a customer relations program among physicians and pharmacists. Sample groups are invited to a company location for a day of dialogue to critique service and products and to develop suggestions for improvement and new ventures. Other task force recommendations include the creation of customer advisory boards and periodic visits by management to key customers.

The Creed also heightened the concept of serving internal customers. Employees are reminded frequently that everyone has customers, even if it is the next person down a production line who is depending on the previous work station to do its job in a quality and timely fashion. The importance of serving internal customers is especially relevant to the company's service divisions. As a result, a number of "customer surveys" have been conducted by the legal, travel, human resources, and technical operations divisions. Each has served as a base to identify problem areas and institute corrective action. Equally important, the surveys help create the feeling that "somebody cares."

In the area of commitment to suppliers, Warner-Lambert strongly advocates the development of long-term, mutually beneficial relationships with suppliers to help improve quality, delivery and cost-effectiveness. Price is no longer the major determining factor in the selection of vendors, resulting as it does in frequent turnover. To communicate this objective to suppliers, company facilities have developed new programs to allow suppliers to make presentations and discuss possibilities of new procedures, which would not be feasible under short-term, tenuous contracts. Some company facilities have established Supplier Recognition Programs and the centralized purchasing department recently conducted a survey among 58 major suppliers to measure their opinions of dealing with the company. The primary complaint was delay in processing invoices, and those procedures are under review.

In the area of commitment to society, Warner-Lambert increased its level of corporate charitable contributions by 9 percent in 1988 to $6 million, representing 2 percent of U.S. pre-tax sales. The company also refocused its giving toward health care organizations and civic programs where its dollars and management support could be more meaningful to corporate objectives. The Creed society task force has recommended that the company encourage employees to participate in voluntary civic work. Inducement plans are under study to officially recognize employee volunteer efforts and to provide financial support for organizations with which employees are involved.

An unusual Creed project took place in the company's U.K./Ireland region in 1987, crossing the lines of commitments to society, as well as to employees. It exemplifies the infiltration of Creed-thinking into all levels of daily corporate life. Three years ago, Warner-Lambert launched a non-commercial public health program in West Africa called Tropicare. It involves the preparation of audio/visual training programs for health care personnel on such subjects as tropical diseases, nutrition, and childhood maladies. Warner-Lambert medical sales representatives are required to spend one day each week conducting the training programs in isolated areas throughout West Africa.

Management in the U.K./Ireland region wondered if their employees fully understood the commitment being made by the company in sponsoring Tropicare. They hit upon the idea, germinated in a Creed discussion, to select three employees for a paid week-long trip to Africa to observe the program in action. The ambassadors were chosen from submitted essays. Upon their return, they were interviewed as part of a U.K. quarterly television report to employees.

The U.K. incident reflects the extent to which the launch of the Warner-Lambert Creed has been exported to company operations in other countries. The Creed has since been translated into 12 other languages and international affiliate companies have developed more than 300 action plans to reinforce the Creed and tailor its commitments to their own countries.

EMPLOYEES ARE MAIN FOCUS OF CREED-DRIVEN ACTIVITIES

Corporate culture, and the Creed that gives it direction, generally focus heavily on employees because they are the most integral part of that culture and can have the greatest impact in extending the culture to outside publics.

One of the key areas of need identified in Warner-Lambert surveys was to provide a means of recognizing employees for their contributions and achievements, separate and apart from merit pay increases and promotions. As a result, a broad range of recognition programs has sprung up, touching every working level within the company. First came the annual Manufacturing Excellence Awards given to 10 facilities around the world for excellence in such judged areas as productivity, human resources programming, innovation, quality and safety. Presentations of the awards are gala events. Scientific performance in research and development is recognized by an annual Chairman's Distinguished Scientific Achievement Award. Meritorious Scientific Achievement Awards are now presented annually by the Parke-Davis and Consumer Products research divisions. Additionally, the company's service and marketing divisions also have established annual awards with such criteria as innovative performance, concern for customers, and special achievements.

The task force studying the company's commitment to employees still felt that a broader recognition program was needed. The outcome was the Warner-Lambert Employee Recognition Policy, adopted in April 1987. It is open to all employees in the U.S. and Puerto Rico up to a job grade level that approximates middle management. The program is funded in annual operating budgets based on a formula dictated by the number of employees in each unit. Supervisors are encouraged to recommend their subordinates for an award based on creative ideas, accomplishments, team leadership and contributions beyond normal job assignments. Applications are reviewed by a Human Resources committee. Awards range from non-cash to minimal and modest cost. Non-cash awards include letters of commendation and bulletin board notices. Other awards, normally not exceeding $500, take the form of merchandise, overnight trips, dinner for two, theater tickets, and sporting events. They have become widely popular and highly treasured.

"TELL US MORE AND LISTEN TO US MORE OFTEN"

Another employee concern identified in both opinion surveys was a desire for increased communication of company business developments and activities and the need for upward communication so that employees could be heard. Significant improvements were achieved over a period of two years.

In early 1986, Warner-Lambert launched its first "State of the Company" presentation to employees. For the first two years it included visual presentations by the Chairman of the Board and the President to 600 managerial employees at the headquarters site. A full videotape of the events was then made available to all English-speaking company locations around the world.

In January 1988, the "State of the Company" presentation was broadened to a four-hour meeting including presentations by the

Chairman, the President, and six operating group presidents. The change in meeting format was dovetailed with the launch of a new Quarterly Video Report to employees. The first QVR of each year now incorporates selected footage from the "State of the Company" presentations along with other QVR features including Newsline, feature reports, and a "Postscript" message from a member of management.

The QVR concept was designed specifically to nurture employee feedback by designing the video reports as the cornerstone of employee meetings at the local level. The meeting formats include discussion of local matters of interest as well as Q&A and open discussion. Feedback reports are analyzed by management for further strategic planning.

The corporate communications department took a cue from the employee attitude surveys and launched editorial changes in the corporate newspaper to encourage "an open and participatory work environment," as mandated by the Creed. A new Opinion page in the publication is devoted to editorials, letters from employees, and op-ed messages from readers. The editorials, while company oriented, are accompanied by an editor's note which states that the opinions expressed "do not necessarily represent the official position of the company since no executive review was requested or conducted." The op-ed articles, under the banner of "Viewpoint" are submitted by employees on matters judged to be of interest to a large number of readers. While the program is still in its infancy, subjects have included the problems and advantages experienced by working mothers, the frustration of "lefties" working in a "right-handed" world, and the dangers of creating fragmented work attitudes if too much emphasis is placed on competition between company departments and functions.

Warner-Lambert management has expressed satisfaction with the Creed efforts to date, but openly admits that much has yet to be done and that the task will require years to firmly establish a new corporate culture. Creed task forces continue to meet and gauge results against objectives. The next major push forward will be the implementation of Creed action plans by divisions and departments tailored on specific employee comments in the 1987 opinion survey.

The ultimate test for a widely communicated Creed-culture program is decision making in highly critical situations which could have long range economic impact on the company. The J&J *Tylenol* decision serves as a good example. To date, the Warner-Lambert Creed, because of its infancy, has not been adequately tested in this regard. Members of management have stated their opinion that Creed precepts will ultimately apply in any such situations. One such early test supports that belief. When Warner-Lambert executive management decided in 1986 that a major manufacturing facility at the company's

New Jersey headquarters location would have to be closed in several years for economic reasons, the decision had to be made whether to tell employees immediately or delay the announcement until later to protect against any possible loss in productivity. In a Creed-driven decision, employees were told in June 1986 that the plant would be shut down in 1989. The outcome so far has proved the decision to be right. Employee consultation, retraining, and outplacement assistance have created a smooth and humane transition to shutdown in 1989 with no forced terminations despite a gradual phasedown in operations.

Some doubt could exist as to how many of Warner-Lambert's new programs and activities merely represent routine corporate momentum over time, with or without focus on Creed and culture. Any comparison of the diversity and range of the new programs, compared with previous years, would lay such criticism to rest. There is no doubt that Warner-Lambert has been Creed-driven, to a surprising extent, since the mission statement began to evolve three years ago.

A focus on corporate culture tends to homogenize the development of corporate programs and becomes self-sustaining. Once it has been set in motion and given substantial management endorsement, a corporate Creed takes on a life of its own. If for any reason it should lose vitality, or credibility, employees "first, your weak indulgence shall accuse."

4

Corporate Identity

Any company that confuses its image with its identity is in for trouble. The investment bank E. F. Hutton, in the 1980s, projected an image of substance and trust. It was a leader in its field. The TV ad line, "When E. F. Hutton talks, people listen," seemed to stand for its solid reputation. That was the image the company projected. When it was caught in a check-kiting scheme, the negative company identity surfaced and the illegal practices shattered the positive image, sending the company into a tailspin that ended in its demise and eventual takeover.

Corporate identity is a combination of more than the sum of these parts: mission statements and corporate philosophies; logos, letterhead, and annual reports; advertising; internal perception programs; and external communication and public perception of company image. People learn to recognize a company by everything it does, from the products and services it sells, to its buildings and employees.

The corporate culture (discussed in chapter 3) provides employees, managers, and investors with patterns of behavior, objects and symbols, and values and beliefs that make up the organization's identity. Just as an individual's identity is the personality characteristics thought of as a persistent entity; so, too, a corporation's identity is the whole of the characteristics by which it is known or recognized. Public perception of a company's image is part myth and part reality. Image and identity coincide when the character of the company projected to the public is also the character of its actions, values, and beliefs.

Vivid images of American business and business leaders are not hard to find in our literature and entertainment media. The contemporary business environment is full of images of business and corporate life projected to the public through movies, books, television, and magazines. For example, an American literature classic, Twain's *A Connecticut Yankee in King Arthur's Court* (1889), is a damnation of business technology and industrialism over the human spirit. Melville's Captain Ahab in *Moby Dick* (1851) is often seen as the megalomaniacal leader of the "American" ship of state. Whole industries were fair game in books like Upton Sinclair's *The Jungle* (1906), an exposé of Chicago meatpacking written during the period when journalists were called "Muckrakers"—the turn-of-the-century investigative reporters.

Award–winning plays such as Miller's *Death of a Salesman* (1949) and Mamet's *Glengarry Glen Ross* (1981) paint a bleak and predatory image of entrepreneurship and American business.

Movies and TV create the image of the unethical or often diabolical corporation and equally villainous corporate leader. A short list of image-making entertainment includes Gordon Gekko in *Wall Street* (1987), Henry Potter in *It's A Wonderful Life* (1946), *The Man in the Gray Flannel Suit* (1956), and the executives in *The China Syndrome* (1979).

The villains in recent science fiction movies are corporations, the mining company with its operations on Mars in *Outland* (1981), the space salvage company in *Alien* (1979), and the company that enforces law with *Robocop* (1987). *Network* (1976), *9 to 5* (1980), and *Working Girl* (1989) all use corporations or executives as villains.

Local and network news focus on financial and business misdeeds, small and monumental. Almost every station has a consumer advocate who gets to the bottom of scams, frauds, and cheats.

In a simpler time the Western was a staple for books, movies, and TV. The good guys wore white hats and the bad guys wore black. Whether or not one feels that corporations are rightly or wrongly portrayed in literature and the media, it remains a state of the contemporary environment, a sort of popular culture reality, that in telling a story of fiction, the villain in a business suit has come to be plausible.

How does any corporation fight such negative images of business in general?

One place to begin would be to build an image more compatible with the community's desire for companies to fulfill their role as a good neighbor and corporate citizen. Companies that enjoy a positive image in the minds of the public and their own employees are generally good companies. The identity and the image cannot be too far apart from one another.

A positive corporate identity and image can be created and perpetuated through coherent and thoughtful programs directed internally and to the public at large.

The mergers and acquisitions of the 1980s and the downsizing and restructuring that followed have treated corporate reputation and image rather roughly. From GM to IBM the face of business has changed dramatically. The need to build corporate identity has never been more important to a company's survival than it is leaving the twentieth century and entering the twenty-first.

MISSION STATEMENTS AND CORPORATE PHILOSOPHIES

The corporation's mission statement is the first formal act of the creation of an organization's identity. The written mission statement defines the corporation, its goals and operating principles, and its values and beliefs. The first of the three parts is relatively straightforward and brief. An example follows from Schering Research, part of the Schering-Plough Corporation:

> Schering Research is engaged in the discovery and development of unique pharmaceuticals that save, enhance, and prolong life. To achieve that mission, the scientists of Schering Research are extending the limits of medical knowledge in their search for pharmaceuticals that provide significant therapeutic advantages for a wide range of diseases. (*Schering Research*, Kenilworth, New Jersey, 1986, Inside Front Cover)

The presentation of goals and operating principles calls for more detail, and of course each company or organization's discussion will vary according to the products and services it creates and the communities and customers it serves. An example follows from the Confederation of British Industry (CBI):

> Most industrialised countries have a national spokesman for their business communities—Britain's is the Confederation of British Industry, the CBI. Founded in 1965, the CBI is an independent, non-party political organisation funded entirely by its members in industry and commerce.
> It exists primarily to voice the views of its members to ensure that governments of whatever political complexion—and society as a whole—understand both the needs of British business and the contribution it makes to the well-being of the nation.
> The CBI is acknowledged to be Britain's business voice and, as such, is widely consulted by government, the civil service and the media. But it is not solely concerned with major national issues—an important part of its task is to represent business interests at the local level, too. It is also directly involved in providing essential information and research services for its members.
> (CBI brochure, 1991)

The expression of a company's values and beliefs, which is also covered in a larger context in chapter 3, is the most difficult of all since it is an effort to express the corporate philosophy. It is difficult because we generally associate values and beliefs with philosophical or religious activities, not commercial ones. The clash between the world of commerce and the world of philosophy requires clear and articulate expression to maintain believability in the skeptical environment that was described at the beginning of this chapter.

Johnson & Johnson's "Credo" provides an excellent model.

We believe our first responsibility is to the doctors, nurses and patients, to mothers and all others who use our products and services. In meeting their needs everything we do must be of high quality. We must constantly strive to reduce our costs in order to maintain reasonable prices. Customers' orders must be serviced promptly and accurately. Our suppliers and distributors must have an opportunity to make a fair profit.

We are responsible to our employees, the men and women who work with us throughout the world. Everyone must be considered as an individual. We must respect their dignity and recognize their merit. They must have a sense of security in their jobs. Compensation must be fair and adequate, and working conditions clean, orderly, and safe. Employees must feel free to make suggestions and complaints. There must be equal opportunity for employment, development, and advancement for those qualified. We must provide competent management, and their actions must be just and ethical.

We are responsible to the communities in which we live and work and to the world community as well. We must be good citizens—support good works and charities and bear our fair share of taxes. We must encourage civic improvements and better health and education. We must maintain in good order the property we are privileged to use, protecting the environment and natural resources.

Our final responsibility is to our stockholders. Business must make a sound profit. We must experiment with new ideas. Research must be carried on, innovative programs developed, and mistakes paid for. New equipment must be purchased, new facilities provided, and new products launched. Reserves must be created to provide for adverse times. When we operate according to these principles, the stockholders should realize a fair return.

("Our Credo," Johnson & Johnson)

Johnson & Johnson's expression provides a benchmark for others to follow since it includes everything experts agree should make up a clear statement of corporate philosophy.

The expression of a corporation's philosophy is often aligned with the mission statement, and in practice it is difficult to draw a clear line marking the end of a mission statement and the beginning of a corporate philosophy. Generally, however, such statements cover a company's commitment to

- quality and excellence
- customer satisfaction
- stockholder return on investment
- profits and growth
- employee relations
- competition and competitiveness
- relations with vendors
- ethical behavior
- community relations and corporate citizenship

and recently

- diversity in the workplace
- preservation of the environment and resources

Often a complex corporate code of conduct, ethics policy guidelines, or handbook of business practice follows the company statement of philosophy. The written code acts as an implementation guide. Such codes, guidelines, or policies often include a section on

- applicability and purpose
- policy regarding general business conduct; disclosure; compliance and disciplinary action
- workings of the corporate business ethics committee
- compliance with laws

    securities—insider information; financial inquires

    disclosure of company information

    political contributions

    relations with government officials, domestic

    relations with government officials, foreign

    commercial bribery—kickbacks, gifts

    record keeping

    anti trust—Sherman Antitrust Act, Clayton Act

    mergers and acquisitions

    international operations
- bidding, negotiation, and performance of government contracts

- conflict of interest
- equal opportunity
- working conditions
- the environment

LOGOS, LETTERHEAD, AND ANNUAL REPORTS

The logos of companies such as AT&T, the United States Postal Sevice, Apple, and IBM are familiar by their design.

If the company name is not recognized instantly, the logo has done a poor job of graphic communication. Even if the logo is a graphic design of the letters of the company name, it is the artwork that captures attention time and time again, that reinforces positive reaction through the visual stimulus. The logo and company colors build corporate image by giving a nonverbal message that reinforces the company image in the mind of the viewer.

Shape, use, color, and placement are all tightly and centrally controlled to build and maintain a corporate identity. Even in an age of decentralized management practice, the central control of the corporate graphic images is an essential strategy in successfully building and keeping a corporate image.

The annual report, aside from its primary function as the marketing tool to persuade investors that the company is a sound place to put capital, promotes corporate image and identity. It is the one publication that is given freely to introduce the company to the outside world.

It is also the publication, the corporate report card, that provides information about the company's progress and accomplishments for the investment community, stockholders, employees, and the general public. An indirect but essential goal of the annual report, and one other way to justify its expensive production, is its role in the perpetuation of the image and identity of the organization. Copies of the report not only go to all registered stockholders, but also to Wall Street analysts, the business press, students, libraries, vendors, trade associations, and professional groups. The report is often a requirement in new business proposals to clients and the government, and it is frequently used for employee recruiting.

Given all of these uses, every element of the annual report, contained in the following list, is designed to contribute to the positive image of the company.

- the artful covers
- the letter from the CEO

- the list of officers

- the excellent photography and artwork

- the summary of the year's accomplishments

- the discussion of plans for the coming year

- the operation statement

- the balance sheet

- the ten-year comparison of financial highlights

- the statement from the auditors

- the footnotes to satisfy all Securities Exchange Commission (SEC) regulations and guidelines

ADVERTISING AND COMPANY PERCEPTION

Corporate advertising, different from product advertising, is designed to create a positive image of the corporation in the mind of a particular group, from investors to the general public. Corporate advertising presents a general image of the company or presents an issue the company wants to be associated with.

Corporate advertising can feature issue advocacy as well as the presentation of views on social issues such as the environment, recycling, conservation, acid rain, and world hunger. It could be found in special sections of the Sunday newspaper magazine section, market prep or issue ads on the Sunday morning news analysis shows, the Corporation for Public Broadcasting documentaries, sponsorships of special art and museum exhibitions, or sporting events and concerts.

Examples could include print and television commercials from AT&T, IBM, Mobil Oil, Boeing, and General Electric. According to the Association of National Advertisers annual survey, *Corporate Advertising Practices 1992* (17), the intended audiences for corporate advertising continue to be customers first. Then follows trade, employees, Wall Street, and Washington, which are all very close together, but over 30 percent behind customers. This is a significant change since 1990, when the gap was less than 20 percent.

INTERNAL PERCEPTION PROGRAMS

Internal communication programs are often motivational and developmental. One spin–off of these programs is the creation and definition of the company values and beliefs for the employees. The previous chapter provides more detail on corporate culture.

These internal programs generally begin with an orientation to the company itself, its history, policies and procedures, mission, and philosophies. In this direct manner the members of the company understand clearly what it means to be a member of that organization.

EXTERNAL COMMUNICATION AND PERCEPTION OF COMPANY IMAGE

Programs for the community create a perception of the organization in the minds of the people who are customers, but also neighbors. Macy's throws a traditional parade on Thanksgiving Day as a way to entertain the community, but also to emphasize its commitment to everyone in the family.

Many corporations sponsor literacy and reading programs to demonstrate their commitment to the society around them. In fact, many of the corporate citizenship efforts discussed in chapter 5 are attempts to project the company image as a good citizen and neighbor.

These external programs had been the public relations efforts for an organization. The stories generated by the media have been regarded as being more valuable than advertising, since such discussion of the company as news draws the reader into an objective view of the company. By contrast, most people approach advertising with at least some degree of skepticism.

RELATIONS WITH VARIOUS PUBLICS

Corporate identity can also be demonstrated through a traditional relationship with various publics. The corporation's role has been expanded to include philanthropic programs and policy (see chapter 5), outreach programs, and government relations—local, state, and federal regulators and agencies. For organizations with retail and consumer goods activities, customer relations can take on the visible role of corporate citizenship.

For corporations with research and development ties, the corporation often demonstrates its identity through the support of its employee membership and participation in professional, scientific, and scholarly societies and organizations. Such support includes attendance at conferences and the encouragement of leadership roles in organizations.

Traditionally, the public relations function in a corporation was concerned with the interaction of the company with the local, state, national, or international communities in which it was located or in which it conducted business.

To that end, public relations may have included a factory tour for the public, a sponsorship of various sporting events, and support of local causes. It may have included press releases that were distributed about company products, people, and activities of interest outside of the organization. It also may have included a company newsletter for its "internal public."

The practice of public relations began early in this century after the industrial revolution with people like Ivy Ledbetter Lee, one of the fathers of modern public relations. Lee counseled Standard Oil and the Rockefellers to cultivate the favor of the general public as a positive way of counteracting the ill will that often existed between owners and their workers and, by extension, the community in which the workers resided.

Public relations has come a long, enlightened way since its beginnings, when wealthy company owners handed out nickels to the crowds. It is now a strategic element in the business plans of most corporations. Public relations plans contain clearly articulated goals, methods, and measurements that coincide with larger corporate goals.

OUTREACH PROGRAMS

Corporate outreach programs in the 1990s are closely allied to the core business. For instance, the public utility company may sponsor and run a series of seminars at retirement homes and villages about coping with power outages due to a thunderstorm or hurricane. The same company may offer courses for home owners about how to handle and repair electrical appliances safely.

Restaurants such as the Union Square Cafe and American Express may participate in urban harvest-type programs that take surplus, day-old, and unused food from restaurants and distribute it to shelters for the homeless. Other companies may donate services like a telephone bank or computers to help with fund–raising. Merrill Lynch routinely opens its offices at Christmas so that ordinary citizens can call relatives and loved ones all over the world. Often a company will set aside a day to help the local community by building a community playground or renovating a park. And more and more organizations are sponsoring a section of a highway for litter control, their participation indicated by signs along the roadside.

Outreach programs also may include corporate education programs in communities, schools, and universities. Nabisco has supported literacy programs at the preschool and elementary school levels.

Sometimes outreach programs consist of adult courses in first aid, water safety, crime prevention, and recycling. Company representatives often speak at the local high school or college about a career in industry and about a specific career in their company. Blood drives for the local Red Cross as well as the United Way depend on corporate participation.

Companies also offer in-kind gifts such as used but useful office furniture and equipment to local charities and schools. During natural disasters, corporations are a valuable source of volunteers, as well as equipment, food, clothing, and medical supplies.

Such programs like corporate citizenship activities are often conducted with little or no fanfare, depending on the corporate attitude toward volunteerism.

GOVERNMENT RELATIONS: LOCAL, STATE, AND FEDERAL REGULATORS AND AGENCIES

Government relations, what some people refer to with a smirk or a sneer as "lobbying," involves meeting with local, state, federal, and in some cases international agencies to advocate for the corporation about matters in its interest. Some corporations will provide legislators and agency professionals with position papers and information designed to inform and persuade the agency. In the marketplace of ideas, such advocacy efforts often make the decision clear.

Individual corporations have in recent years avoided direct lobbying efforts in favor of joining an industry advocacy association or group that does the work for all companies in a given industry. A quick scan of the telephone directory in New York City or Washington, D.C., under "Association of . . ." will provide a snapshot of the tens of thousands of groups formed to represent a particular point of view about an issue or a particular industry.

Because of past abuses regarding attempts to influence the government decision-making process, this area of corporate communication demands the highest ethical standards. Each company develops its own Code of Business Conduct that often includes standards and procedures for ethical practices with fellow employees and subordinates, customers, vendors, the community, and the government. Professional organizations and societies, such as the Public Relations Society of America, also issue standards of ethical practice for their members and for the profession or industry as a whole.

The American consumer has become highly skeptical of business practices and intolerant of companies that operate unethically. No contemporary corporation seeks an investigative reporter's exposé or a spot on the *60 Minutes* hot seat. Maintaining the highest standards for propriety and ethical behavior is the best approach to developing a reputation for honesty and integrity.

CUSTOMER RELATIONS

Customer relations is often considered the front porch of a corporation. How a corporation routinely treats customers and vendors and how it handles an angry customer's telephone call about a product or service that does not live up to that customer's expectations form the foundation on which the corporation's image is built in the minds of individuals. That image may be inviting and cooperative, or cold and impersonal.

Successful companies make every effort to meet their customers' needs. The old cliché, "The customer is always right," is not a cliché for most companies. It is an informing philosophy. It also is a central principle in the quality movements that have infatuated American businesses through the 1980s and 1990s. Satisfied customers return; disgruntled customers do not, and they also tell at least ten others about their bad experience. Good customer relations depends on positive word-of-mouth communications.

The service industry has made customer relations not only central to a company's business strategy, but an art form. You might think of junk food and fast food as one, but when you visit an American fast food restaurant almost anywhere in the United States and around the world, you can count on quick, congenial service. Go into almost any retail store with a problem purchase, and the company will either repair or replace the item, no questions asked.

In a market–driven economy, companies that have established close relationships with their customers have a better chance of surviving difficult periods than companies that are not interested in listening to their customers' needs. Solid, positive relations with customers is a fundamental part of the quality revolution in America.

PUBLIC BROADCASTING SPONSORSHIPS AND CORPORATE IDENTITY

If you think public television in the United States is "upscale" in its programming, audiences, and operations; if you think it is above politics; if you think programming decisions are made nationally; and if you think it is similar to commercial television in its operation—you share the impressions of most marketing practitioners—and you are dead wrong (see Table 4–1).

Because of PBS programming on WNET, Channel 13, in New York City and on WGBH in Boston, there is a popular misconception that the public television audience is upscale. "Some people watch public television's more sophisticated shows and think, 'I am sophisticated. I am watching public television. Public television [audiences] must be

TABLE 4-1
The Reality of Public Television Is Very Different From What Most Americans Think

MISCONCEPTIONS ABOUT PUBLIC TELEVISION	THE REALITY OF PUBLIC TELEVISION
Elite, sophisticated, better-educated audience	About the same demographics as commercial TV
Funds for public TV are prime targets for budget cuts	Of all the lobbies or causes trying to get the attention of Congress, public television is one of the strongest.
PBS is a station; ad agencies are located in New York City, Chicago, Boston, and think all stations are like Channel 13 or WGBH.	PBS is a library
National audience	Audience is fragmented; two tiers—local and national
Commercial rating systems, which measure eyeballs, work with public television audiences	Much of public television is focused on whether a student learns a subject such as geometry, totally unrelated to current measurement systems; "We need all kinds of new ways to measure." (Chalmers Marquis)
Common programming	Stations carry what they want; they air programs when they want, any time of day or night; no penalty for not airing a program

sophisticated.' It just ain't so . . . [According to public TV comparisons of all people and their audiences,] the public TV audience is ever so slightly more educated, but it is darn close. Income is almost identical." One additional indication of the blurring of public TV and commercial TV programming is the introduction of *Think Twice*, a weekly prime-time quiz show meant to compete with CBS and Fox. (Rifkin 1994)

Channel 13's mission is national, and it produces a great deal of programming that is distributed widely. The local stations can create programming in theory, but they do not do so in practice. However, local interest programs such as high school football are carried. Stations fall roughly into national and local tiers.

Whether market–driven or image–driven, organizations increasingly participate in public television as part of their corporate identity actions. Why spend the money? What are the risks and rewards a corporation can expect from such relationships? Is a corporate sponsorship of public TV right for your company?

TABLE 4-2
Half the Sources for the $1.5 Billion for Public Television Are Private,
with Only 20 Percent from Federal Taxes

SOURCE OF PUBLIC TELEVISION INCOME	Percent of Total
Federal	23 (increasing)
State and Local	21 (steady)
Colleges and Universities	8 (states increasing; privates decreasing)
Individuals	23 (increasing)
Foundations and Business	17 (increasing)
All Taxed-based Sources Combined	50
All Private Sources	50
TOTAL:	Approximately $1.5 Billion

SOURCE: Corporation for Public Broadcasting & Chalmers Marquis

Chalmers Marquis, one of the founders of public television in this country, provides guidance. Local stations—315 of them in 250 organizations in all fifty states—are in charge of public broadcasting in the United States, as contrasted to broadcasting in the United Kingdom and in the countries of the European Union that began as a public enterprise controlled by the government. "They own and operate PBS; they decide exactly what they want to do," said Marquis. The missions of these stations vary widely.

For example, the New York area includes the New Jersey Network, with a budget of $2 million and a mission to support the elementary and secondary schools in New Jersey; New York's Channel 13 (which is licensed in Newark, New Jersey) at $240 million and has a very different mission; Long Island's WLIW; New York City's WNYC; and New York City Board of Education's WNYE.

How important is the concept of public television? According to Peter Downey, PBS's Senior Vice President for Business Affairs, public TV is the "last best hope for American TV."(*Public TV: A Public Debate*) The philosophy of producers and public TV station owners considers the viewer as a citizen, rather than as a market. Public TV viewers number approximately 100 million per week. Public TV is free to American citizens, unlike cable-based services, and costs roughly $1 per person per year in tax money (see Table 4–2).

The impact of public TV in this country has created an awareness in the audience that the marketplace is not always the answer. The focus of public TV is on quality programming, which is expensive. Public TV has produced extremely fine programming with limited resources considering the yearly outlay of the entire industry of public broadcasting (approximately $1.5 billion) is less than the Fox network paid to get NFL Football from CBS.

Also consider that, until recently, public TV has enjoyed broad bipartisan support, and it is also heavily involved in classroom learning and classroom activity at the local and national levels. (*Public TV: A Public Debate*)

The origins of American public television go back to 1953. The debate then was against the politicians to have one commercial-free channel. The basis of the argument was that the broadcast spectrum, just like public land, belonged to the public.

As America spread west, following its "Manifest Destiny" or "Territorial Imperative," the Morrill Land Grant College Act allowed a portion of the land to be used for educational purposes. Every county in the United States had reserved land. With the broadcast technologies of radio and TV, the principle of public land was extended to public "air." The principle now extends from 4 percent to 7 percent of the channels for the public.

MISCONCEPTION: PUBLIC TV AND CORPORATE ADVERTISING

For corporations and traditional advertising approaches, public television poses some daunting barriers. The public television audience 60 percent cume means an audience of 2 percent turns over thirty times. Justifying the expense of sponsorship based on such a small share of the eyes on the screen may be difficult, since programming is so decentralized.

However the blurring caused by the enormous changes in media and technology and the number of channels and other media sources available to people through the Internet make participation in a proven quality medium such as public television less risky.

But getting traditional answers to the audience makeup for public TV is difficult. One example demonstrates the challenge: children's programming is carried in day care centers where Nielsen does not have any measurement. In addition, programming for any PBS affiliate is still a *local* decision, even though most of the production is done on a national level. And for further complication, sometimes a public TV program airs on cable instead of the broadcast outlet because the station owner also owns the local cable outlet.

Table 4–3 offers some ways for corporations to participate in public TV.

TABLE 4-3
Benefits of Participation in Public TV

METHOD OF PARTICIPATION	BENEFIT TO THE CORPORATION
Receptions and Promotions	Influences Congress
Underwrite programming; books tied to the programming; promotion tied to the programming	Establishes positive public image; puts it on marketing materials and letterheads
Sponsor local programming	Builds equity in the community
Fund equipment in schools	Provides strong link with the community
Sponsor courses; training; teacher training; literacy; math	Associates company with the subject

TABLE 4-4

Contributions and Benefits from Public Television	Response
Yes, firm has contributed to public broadcasting in last three years	48%
No, has not contributed	53%
Base: Total answering	(80)
Yes, company has benefited from identification with public TV	56%
No, has not benefited	44%
Base: Total answering	(55)

Given all of the variables and barriers of public TV for business promotions, is it worth it? In terms of traditional advertising, the answer is not clear. But if the issue is seen as a form of corporate advertising—to build image and "image equity"—then the use of public TV and the support of its programming is valuable. The responses to our survey confirm the benefit of supporting public TV. (See Table 4-4.)

Sandy Sulcer, Cleve Langton, and I surveyed corporate executives regarding their attitudes toward and participation in public television. Their responses showed that half (48%) have contributed financially to public television in the past three years; and over half (56%) believe their firm has benefitted from such generosity.

PUBLIC TV AND THE CORPORATE MARKETPLACE

Aetna underwrote the *U.S. History Series: The American Experience,* which WGBH in Boston produced. The association was linked, according to Elizabeth Krupnick, Vice President for Corporate Affairs, to their community programs. To let audiences know about their involvement with PBS, it targeted insurance decision makers through ad placements in *Time, Newsweek, The New Yorker,* the *New York Times Magazine,* and the *Smithsonian.* To reach customers, it sent out millions of statement stuffers in policy material and provided a viewer's guide to its employees throughout the country.

McDonald's, in addition to its citizenship efforts (discussed in chapter 5), is a strong supporter of public TV. As one of the largest employers of young people in this country, its interest in the education of youth is clear. The company underwrote the *Behind the Scenes* series for kids, hosted by comedy magicians Penn & Teller and produced by WNET. Its aggressive promotional effort included "Happy Meals" filled with program-related products; ads on network and cable; tray liners; in-store displays; educational outreach kits for use by all public TV stations; an eight-page supplement in *Parents* magazine; and a six-page brochure mailed to all third- through sixth-grade teachers, with a request form for a 24-page teacher's guide.

The forces of competition and citizenship need not clash. Large, well-run, U.S. corporations achieve both corporate communication and public policy objectives through support of public TV. Their participation yields a public benefit as well as a grateful audience. Sponsorship of the *MacNeill Leher News Hour, Sesame Street, The Civil War, NOVA, Great Performances, Masterpiece Theater,* and *The American Experience* provides the public with quality viewing, but that is not enough. Corporations must link their corporate citizenship investments to their communication, advertisement, and identity strategies.

Case Study

The case study selected for this chapter is from a presentation at the annual Conference on Corporate Communication at Fairleigh Dickinson University. The authors focus on a part of communications practice in some aspect of creating, developing, or perpetuating corporate identity.

David Ostroff, Dawn Donnelly, and Alan Fried describe the impact of new communication technologies on the internal communications of Florida Power and Light. They also explore how demographic and business environment changes, as well as emerging technologies, will affect the company's employee communications.

The Business Environment, Demographics, and Technology
A Case Study of Florida Power and Light's Electronic Employee Communication Services

David H. Ostroff
Dawn Donnelly
Alan Fried

THE COMPANY

Florida Power and Light (FPL) has profited from and been affected by Florida's explosive population growth. Founded in 1925, FPL began as a montage of enterprises: small electric generating plants, ice plants, water, gas, cold storage and telephone facilities, even an ice cream factory and a sponge fishing boat. Florida was largely rural and informal. Meter readers often identified customer homes by such descriptions as "third from the railroad tracks," or "house with red shutters," and some customers received no bills for two years. In 1925, the company served 76,000 customers in 58 communities; it had 230 miles of transmission lines and 1,149 miles of distribution lines.

Today, FPL is the fourth largest investor-owned utility in the United States. The company is a subsidiary of FPL, Inc., a holding company with interests in management consulting, real estate, agriculture, cable

This case study by Dr. Ostroff, of the University of Florida, appeared in the *Proceedings of the Fourth Conference on Corporate Communication*, May 1991. An edited version appears here with his permission. Ms. Donnelly is with Florida Power & Light, and Mr. Fried is with the University of Florida.

television, and insurance. Recently the parent corporation has determined that its future will be best assured by devoting its greatest attention to its core utility business and is seeking to divest some or all of its other activities.

FPL has 15,000 employees spread among five geographic "divisions" and corporate and utility company headquarters. Facilities include 45 customer service offices, 13 operating plants, two of which are nuclear, and more than 400 substations. The average FPL employee is 37 years of age, and has been with the company only eleven years.

As with all public utilities, FPL is under close regulation by the state public utilities commission. However, the generation and sale of power has been greatly deregulated in recent years, increasing the competitive environment in which FPL must exist.

The company's long-time employers now find themselves joined by newcomers, including many highly educated specialists in finance, engineering, and nuclear power plant operation. Although the company traditionally found its top executives within its own power generation and electrical engineering ranks, many current corporate and utility company executives have largely been recruited by outside corporations. The change in the corporate environment has also seen a growing number of women, including in the technical and professional ranks. Customer service has become a watchword of the company, creating additional demands by employees for the information needed to serve those customers.

One important step in FPL's efforts to focus its efforts on customer services was implementation in the late 1980s of a "Quality Improvement Program." The program, which required an intensive reformulation of the corporate culture, created strains between management and workers, and also within those groups.

While the company's efforts were successful enough to receive recognition as the first U.S. recipient of Japan's Deming Prize for quality, FPL has now retreated from strict adherence to the more formal procedures of its programs. Both the implementation of the program and the later modification increased the communication traffic between all levels of the company, and created some strains and problems of trust.

FPL'S ELECTRONIC EMPLOYEE INFORMATION SERVICES

Unlike most businesses, virtually every FPL employee is in direct contact with customers: friends, neighbors, relatives may all rely on FPL for power. FPL has taken the position that its employees need information to accurately reflect the company to its customers, and to counteract what FPL sees as negative or unfair information about such topics as environmental protection, uses of nuclear power, utility rates, etc.

Recent meetings between top management and employees has uncovered a related effect: an employee's ability to understand and explain the company's actions to outsiders improves his or her morale. A survey of employees conducted by the Corporate Communications department in the summer of 1990 found more than 12% of open-ended responses indicated employees want the company to inform them of actions before they learned of it from the mass media.

Most of the communication is routine: reports about the company's financial activity, regulatory actions affecting FPL, important personnel changes, recognition for employees reaching anniversary milestones or retirement. Announcements pertaining to sanctioned activities such as blood drives or the United Way campaign are also communicated through employee information systems.

The ability to communicate rapidly becomes particularly important during crises. While a nuclear power plant "incident" would be a particularly dramatic potential crisis, other natural events may be more likely to occur.

The Employee Information section is part of FPL's Corporate Communications Department. Corporate Communication, under direction of a company vice president, has undergone some reorganization in recent years. In addition to Employee Information, Corporate Communication's functions currently include media relations, nuclear power information, creative services (advertising and information and marketing materials), audiovisual services, speakers bureau, issues management, speech writing, and gerontological and education relations services. The department is located in the utility company headquarters in Miami, on the same floor as the company's senior executives. FPL, Inc., the corporate parent, is headquartered in Juno Beach, Florida, about a two-hour drive north of utility company headquarters.

Employee information media includes both print and electronic. Electronic vehicles are primarily responsible for timely distribution to all or selected employees, while print materials provide in-depth follow-up information.

The ideas for exploiting FPL's electronic technologies have come from within the communications department, rather than from senior executives. However, organizational imperatives, such as the need for rapid crisis communication, have played a role in spurring development. Senior executives, however, do pay attention: compliments and criticisms of specific messages have been received from the highest levels of both the utility company and the parent corporation.

ELECTRONIC MEDIA SYSTEMS

Electronic media systems include the following:

1. *Insta-News Network.* An instantaneous and continuous 24-hour videotext network.

2. *FPL Television Network.* Riding FPL's fibre optic network to 18 sites, the three-year old full-motion video network provides a means for training and information transmissions.

3. *CIS News Pages.* The Customer Information Service is a computer on-line information system for customer service representatives throughout the company's service area.

4. *NewsFax.* Most of FPL's employees work at, or are assigned to, a site that can be reached quickly through a fax machine network.

5. *G.O. Cable Network.* FPL's general office is served by its own dedicated 6-channel video network.

6. *FPL Close-up.* This monthly video magazine is a 12-minute compilation of company news and feature stories, focusing especially on activities of company employees. The program is played continuously on the FPL network and the cable network.

7. *Media Monitoring.* While the media relations department takes primary responsibility for reviewing print coverage of the company, employee communication keeps track of broadcast and other electronic information.

Monitoring the wire service allows the media relations department to take a proactive stance, correcting facts, or providing "spin" to stories before they are reported in the print or broadcast media. It also enables management to monitor issues of interest to FPL, such as industry news, state and federal regulatory actions, as well as the distribution and accuracy of press releases.

Impact

In the summer of 1990, Corporate Communications commissioned a small survey designed to measure the reach of the various employee information media, and to assess the degree to which employees found themselves useful. About 1,200 questionnaires were returned (a 33% return rate) in the latter survey. While methodological differences between the surveys (one done in 1988 as well) do not allow for strict comparisons, the results suggest an overall improvement in employee opinions about the company's communication efforts. Seventy-five percent indicated they felt "somewhat" or "very" informed about the company.

Interestingly, the 1990 survey found employees reporting a greater preference for the mediated information sources. At the same time, the "most helpful" sources found the print and personal sources ranking higher than the electronic sources.

The other major factor to consider in evaluating the impact of the electronic systems is their limited use so far. First, a significant reason for their existence is for use in a major emergency. There have been "practice alerts" (required by the Nuclear Regulatory Commission to assess the practices in case of a problem at a nuclear plant); these have primarily assessed operations within the department.

Second, FPL has undergone significant changes in the executive ranks in recent years; for example, the CEO of utility took charge in August 1990, replacing the retiring president.

THE FUTURE

FPL has attempted to meet changes in its environment by adapting communications technologies to improve employee communication. While there seems to be some evidence of success, it is clear that the company is unable to remain static. In a recent statement to employees, James Broadhead, CEO of FPL's corporate parent, wrote, "New programs, new facilities, and new ways of serving customers are better preparing us for what lies ahead. This will become increasingly important as we move further into the 1990s, because every indication is that the pace of change in our industry is going to accelerate" (Broadhead 1991). A corporate strategic planning study has concluded, "The electric industry will become increasingly competitive . . . Customers will have more alternatives. The industry will, as a requirement, become more customer-driven in its approach. Electric utilities are confronted with a significant challenge. If they are to continue to prosper, they must become more customer-oriented, more cost-efficient, fast and flexible, and quality-driven. Those that fail to adapt, or adapt inadequately or too late, will serve their shareholders, customers and employees poorly" (How Our Industry, 3).

FLORIDA'S LABOR FORCE IN 2000

The Florida Department of Labor and Employment Security has produced a detailed set of historical statistics and projections which illustrate the population of the workforce trends in the state. More than half the population growth in the entire United States through the year

2000 will be in five states: Florida, California, Texas, Arizona, and Massachusetts. Florida's population more than doubled between 1940 and 1960 and doubled again between 1960 and 1980. From 1980 to 2000, population gains are expected to increase by 60%. Growth in Florida's population moved it from the twentieth most populous state in 1950, to the fourth in 1987, and possibly third after the turn of the century.

From 1972 to 1986, the number of Floridians who joined the labor force almost doubled from 2.9 million to 5.4 million. The state predicts the rate of growth will be slower from 1986 to 2000, but that it should reach 8.1 million by the turn of the century. Two factors affect this growth: a general slowing of the rate of growth measured against a larger base and a marked shift in the state's demographic trends.

Florida's Demographic Shift

Perhaps the best way to analyze trends is to compare shifts in the share of different age groups from 1986 to 2000. While nearly one quarter (24.0%) of Florida residents were under 18 in 1986, only one of five Floridians (20.0%) will be a child in 2000. The share of workers of entry-level age will also decline.

According to national forecasts, 80% of the net new growth in the labor force will come from three groups: women, minorities, and immigrants. Florida's demographic trends show a gain in the non-white population from 14.6% in 1986 to 17% in 2000. The state predicts that tight labor markets should foster employment of youth, minorities, women, the elderly, and the handicapped.

By the beginning of the next century, Florida's economy will generate nearly eight million jobs, an amount projected to be the third highest in the nation. The services industry division, which includes three of the four fastest growing subsectors in the state, will dominate the economy (2.52 million jobs). Wholesale and retail trade will employ 1.95 million workers, the second largest number. These industries will also be the fastest growing, 57% and 48%, respectively.

FLORIDA'S PUBLIC UTILITY SERVICE INDUSTRY

The state has estimated that Florida's electric, gas, and sanitary services industries registered employment of 35,900 jobs in 1987. They estimated that 48% of these jobs were in production, construction, maintenance, and other operations. Another 29% were in clerical and administrative support positions. Fifteen percent were in professional, paraprofessional, and technical occupations, and the rest were in managerial and administrative occupations. Projecting from these percentages and

growth in the requirement for these skills and abilities, the state projects
that this division will require 48,800 jobs in the year 2000.

Demographics and Communication

Two of the demographic trends noted above seem to have significant
implications for employee communications. First, the competition for
entry-level workers will become greater. Thus, organizations will have
to search for ways to attract these employees, and keep them happy
once they are on the job.

Second, the expected career "plateau" that many "baby boomers"
will face as their tenure in a company lengthens will require that steps
be taken to create a satisfactory work environment. The alternative, of
course, will be either disgruntled employees or, as the state of Florida
predicts, turnover in employees.

While there will have to be a number of creative steps taken to limit
the harm from these trends, it seems clear that insuring that employees
receive timely and appropriate information is related to job satisfaction
(Pincus and Rayfield 1989). The communications history of members of
both of these groups may also prove significant. Both have grown up
with video and other electronic systems as their preferred source of
information. The younger group, particularly, may expect information
be presented in a form comparable to the interactive systems they have
become used to through computers, video games, and similar
technologies. Thus, electronic information systems may become even
more important to a company like FPL.

COMMUNICATIONS TECHNOLOGY

The literature makes clear that certain communication technologies are
likely to become available as the decade progresses. To a great extent
many of these advances will have only an indirect or small impact on
the immediate communication needs of a company like FPL.

Most significantly, the company's growing infrastructure and
expertise in operating fibre optic distribution will allow the company to
take advantage of the merging of video and computer displays into
multimedia. While the company currently maintains its own dedicated
fibre optic network, this function may be taken over by the telephone
company, which many expect to have broadband ISDN service
available on a business-to-business basis by the end of the decade
("Technology 1999").

Multimedia will have some useful advantages for employee communication (Birkmaier 1991). The ability to combine text with video and

graphics should increase the capacity to make the messages more interesting and more informative. On the other hand, there will be demands on the technicians creating the messages to have the resources and expertise necessary to fully utilize the technologies. For example, a library of prerecorded "file" video may be helpful in many instances (a sequence showing a company executive, or an aerial view of a specific power plant), but there will clearly be limited use during sudden and unexpected announcements. Of course, this is a dilemma that television news organizations often face, and the ability of employee communication departments to begin archiving and storing useful footage will be important.

Of course, a second advantage of multimedia will be the ability of employees to store and recall messages at the discretion of the user. This has significant advantages for employee communication. For example, a lineman returning from a day in the field could simply access a menu of employee information stories, and access those of specific interest. Depending on one's home equipment, it would be possible to download information and review it at home.

As the telephone companies and the cable television industry move to complete the replacement of existing copper distribution systems with fibre, it will become increasingly possible to link the broadband technologies such as multimedia with home workstations. This may accelerate the "work at home" phenomenon, as information-based employees will be able to remain in full contact with the central office. Further, the interactive and video capabilities may help reduce some of the feelings of isolation which often affect workers at home (Bleecker, 19; *Technology* 1999).

The fibre optic and broadband capability will increase the capacity for communication to take the form of live presentations, with question-and-answer sessions following. As expertise increases and the application gains greater visibility among managers and others in business this problem will disappear. A second limitation has been the logistical problems involved with bringing the presenter to company headquarters and, more importantly, the audience to designated viewing areas.

The task of bringing the executive to the transmission site may still exist. However, a prerecorded message, videotaped in the person's office or other convenient location, could overcome some of these problems. The executive might then be able to remain in the office, since Q & A could take place via the multimedia computer screen (either with actual voice and, perhaps, a graphic representation of the person, or through text responses by computer).

More importantly, the need for employees to leave their immediate work area would be reduced, if not eliminated.

The growth in use of technology such as multimedia will not increase only because it is available. As the workforce changes, the idea of receiving information from, and interacting with, a "screen" will become increasingly familiar and expected. As author Gwenda Blair says, "My kids are starting out with the assumption that they're going to be looking at a screen. It's a completely different starting point from looking at a page. For them, to look at a page is a step backward. Their neural pathology has been trained in a different way from mine" (Gentry, Kaminsky, and Marans 1990, 26).

The computer-video merger will also affect other operations of FPL's employee information. Most notable, the task of keeping executives informed of outside press coverage and other information will be come easier and more useable by the executives.

In the future, it should be possible to pre-program a computer to "download" and store the incoming feeds, working in the background while other applications occur. Stories can be quickly found, perhaps by asking the computer to list all stories containing key words; by calling up a still-frame sequence of the story, or other means. A copy of the relevant stories can be immediately downloaded or copied to another disk, in the time-frame available for copying even a lengthy written document, today. It may then be possible for the executive to quickly and easily review the story or stories. If the executive so desired, the stored material could be accessed directly.

Of course, we can also anticipate some new problems, as well as the possible acceleration of some existing ones. Employee communication professionals, especially those trained in print-oriented academic public relations departments, will have to develop a sensitivity to visual representation, and the use of graphics and other visuals as informative tools. In other words, an expertise in writing prose may no longer be sufficient.

CONCLUSION

Through a combination of planning and good fortune, FPL has in place the seeds of a technical and human infrastructure to allow it to continue to adequately communicate to its employees. While the systems have not yet been used under extreme conditions of natural disaster or corporate crisis, they have shown their adequacy in routine situations. Recent meetings and a survey of employees indicate increased satisfaction with the mediated information they have received from company executives. The company's own vision of its future will require extensive communication to employees; demography suggests employees will demand it. During the coming period of change, executives will have to maintain a vision of what is necessary to communicate, and what is available to communicate most effectively; only they can create an environment that will allow the technology and their employees to flourish.

REFERENCES

Birkmaier, Craig. "Corporate Broadcasting," *Videography* (January 1991): 81–82.

Bleecker, Samuel E. "The Information Age Office," *The Futurist* (January–February 1991): 18–20.

Broadhead, James. "Perspective," *Synergy* (January 1991): I.

Florida Department of Labor and Employment Security. *Workforce 2000: Choices for Florida's Future.* Tallahassee, Fla.: Department of Labor and Employment Security, January 1990.

Gentry, Ric, James Kaminsky, and Ron Marans. "Video 2000: What Will the Future Bring?" *Corporate Video Decisions* (September 1990): 24–31.

Hellweg, Susan. "Organizational Grapevines," in Brenda Dervin and Melvin J. Voigt, eds., *Progress in Communication Sciences.* Vol. 8. Norwood, N.J.: Ablex, 1987.

"How Our Industry is Expected to Change in the '90s." Special FPL Report, October 1990.

More, E. A., and R. K. Laird. *Organizations in the Communications Age.* Sydney, Australia: Pergamon Press, 1985.

Pincus, J. David, and Robert E. Rayfield. "Organizational Communication and Job Satisfaction: A Metaresearch Perspective," in Brenda Dervin and Melvin J. Voigt, eds., *Progress in Communication Sciences.* Vol. 9. Norwood, N.J.: Ablex, 1989.

"Technology 1999: What's Video's Future?" *Corporate Video Decisions* (April 1989): 36–39, 70–75.

5

Corporate Citizenship and Social Responsibility

I am no loony do-gooder, traipsing the world hugging trees and
staring into crystals. I'm a trader. I love buying and selling. In the past
17 years, I have established England's most successful retailing
company, with 1,000 shops in 45 countries. But I am concerned about
quality in trade, not just quantity.
—Anita Roddick, managing director of The Body Shop

Almost a quarter century ago in the *New York Times*, Milton Friedman
called corporate giving the equivalent of theft, "spending someone
else's money" to solve social problems that are the province of
government. He defined a manager's moral mandate to "make as much
money for the stockholders as they can within the limits of the law and
ethical custom." In the 1990s and into the next century, a generation of
managers views Friedman's position as "not in step with the role that is
expected of corporate management" (Shaw 1993, 747).

Add to this the changes in the nature of stockholders since the 1987
crash from individuals, to institutions such as the enormous pension
funds of TIAA and the states of New York and California, and the
concept of responsibility meets the profit motive in a partnership that
works for The Body Shop, Levi's, Benneton, Tom's of Maine, L. L. Bean,
Apple, Microsoft, and other successful companies.

The message also came from over a decade of financially conservative government that money to support social programs was a
prime candidate in the slashing of public budgets. So if government
was out of the business of solving social problems, who would?—the
members of the community, which has increasingly come to include
organizations and businesses, as well as the individual residents. The
community linked the corporation more strongly, openly, and directly
with its issues and concerns than in the past.

THE CORPORATION AS CITIZEN

To managers educated under Friedman's influence, the concept of corporate citizenship might seem relatively new in American business, even a bit alien to the culture that worships the bottom line. But it has been an element of the philosophy and culture of successful organizations for as long as those organizations have existed. Put simply, corporate citizenship is the acceptance of the corporation's role as a responsible and significant member of its community. The community can be the local towns in which the corporation has its plants and offices, or the nations in which it does business.

Corporate citizenship can also be demonstrated through a traditional relationship with various publics. But in recent times, more often than not, the corporation's citizenship role has been expanded to include philanthropic programs and policy, outreach programs, and government relations: local, state, federal regulators and agencies. For organizations with retail and consumer goods activities, customer relations can take on the visible role of corporate citizenship.

Jerry Anderson, Craig Smith, Jacquie L'Etang, Bernard Avishai, Angelidis and Ibrahim, and others articulate the reshaping of the corporate relationship with the community—a balance between the enlightened self-interest of the members of the organization and an instinctive search to contribute to the larger social good.

Altruism, however, is the least compelling factor in a corporation's commitment to a social responsibility program. No longer can a corporation leave the issue of corporate giving to the whim, or pet charity, of the CEO or strong board members. The combined forces of corporate citizenship and customer expectations have brought about changes in the way companies view their relationship with their communities.

CORPORATE CITIZENSHIP POLICY

What do companies who are good corporate citizens do? A recent study of 160 corporations who defined themselves as good corporate citizens should shed some light on the best practices in this area. (Siccone, "Corporate Social Responsibility, New Ways of Making a Profit," see the commentaries at the end of this chapter.) They overwhelmingly linked their business goals to their giving programs. In addition, their giving programs were linked to the community in which they were located. Such corporate citizens supported education programs, recycling, and other environmental support programs. They sponsored charity events such as walkathons, and they assisted in shelters, centers, and hospitals. Most of the middle and senior managers responsible for the citizenship

efforts in their companies consider their efforts at citizenship to be good
or excellent.

Good corporate citizens measure and report their corporate citizenship activities in the following ways:

- mentioning the activities in their annual report
- publishing a 'Public Interest' report
- mentioning the activities in the company newsletter
- issuing press releases
- mentioning their citizenship actions in advertising and marketing
  materials

International Paper's environmental programs are examples of
"green" corporate actions. These environmentally related efforts are also
considered part of a corporation's social responsibility and citizenship
philosophy. The new approach has had an impact on the way many
corporations give. For example, according to the Foundation Center,
program and capital grants absorb the vast share of grant dollars, 41
percent for special programs and 22 percent for capital grants. Foundations targeted one-third of grant dollars to special groups of people,
including 13 percent for children and youth programs, and 9.6 percent
for minorities (*Foundation Giving*, xi).

New alliances brought on by mergers, takeovers, reengineering,
and restructuring can change the fundamental mission of a corporation's contribution program. Nevertheless, "corporate foundations give
in fields closely related to corporate activities or to strengthen communities in which the company operates" (*Foundation Giving*, 85). Table
5–1 shows the pattern of giving by corporations.

Among the corporations that have changed their philanthropy programs to align their profit-making strategies with the welfare of society
are Eastman Kodak, Allstate, Chrysler, Whirlpool, Citicorp, Reebok,
Johnson & Johnson, Philip Morris, Merck, DuPont, and Coca-Cola
(Smith 1994, 107).

Numerous strong factors and forces have brought about the need
for corporations to change their relationship with the community,
including

- wholesale restructuring within publicly held corporations;
- the blurring of the affairs of business, government, and non-
  profits;
- an overburdened government's seeming inability to meet important
  social needs;

TABLE 5-1
Traditional Corporate Giving Patterns Are Shifting Away from Merely
Sending a "Check" to Linking the Support to Corporate Strategy

Subject Focus Of Grants	% of Grant Dollars	% of Grants	Increase from Previous Year	Decrease from Previous Year
Education	25	23	no change	no change
Health	18	13	yes	
Human Services	16	21	yes	
Arts and Culture	13	15		yes
Public/Society Benefit	11	12	yes	
Environment and Animal	5	5	yes	
Science and Technology	4	3		yes
International Affairs	3	3		yes
Social Science	3	2	no change	no change
Religion	2	2	no change	no change

SOURCE: Foundation Grants, 1994

- the corporation taking over from public education the responsibility for providing the training and education necessary to create in employees the technologically specialized skills required by the changes in the way work is done;

- with decreased regulation and increased litigation, implementing socially responsible programs to create a great deal of good will in the community and with the government and the "social equity" to ward off regulation;

- the social equity creating a positive corporate image that helps the corporation maintain the support of its customers and neighbors during a crisis;

- increased personal liability for individual workers as well as for corporate officers, who no longer can hide behind the entity of a corporation;

- the link between politics and giving, once reserved only for corporate officers, is now being pushed down deeper to the grassroots of the corporation and the communities in which they are located;

- dealing with more educated, aware, and outspoken consumers;

- customers who are constantly in search of quality and information and who want to know the story behind the products they are buying, for example, cosmetics being tested on animals in a humane, civilized manner;

- and, a requirement in schools of business to include ethics and social issues in the curriculum.

In another instance of distinctions being blurred, the hands-off, no-strings-attached relationship among business, society, nonprofit institutions, and government has shifted from a clearly separate to more of a partnership association.

BENEFITS OF CORPORATE CITIZENSHIP

Companies that have a long-term commitment to social responsibility are rewarded, according to Smith (107), with greater name recognition, more productive employees, lower R&D costs, fewer regulatory hurdles, and stronger synergy among business units. Such an approach is much more ethical than the "smoke-filled room."

Acting as a good citizen, modern corporations have provided social services such as health care; or they have funded public facilities such as parks, playgrounds, and recreation buildings; or they have entered a partnership with the community to maintain the infrastructure of highways and bridges.

And in a further instance of blurring, investment strategies of institutions such as pension funds like the California Public Employee Retirement System support corporations that, according to Robert Reich (*New York Times*, September 11, 1994: 9), employ contemporary workforce and workplace practices. These "high performance" companies, which from 1990 to 1994 "outperformed the S&P 500 by an average of 16 percent each year and beat their industry averages by 7.5 percent," value the quality and loyalty of employees, invest in training and retraining, and have clear health and safety strategies.

Investment in these companies, unlike "social investing" which often places altuism over profits, "seeks collateral benefits that are in addition to, not instead of, competitive rates of return." Such an approach strengthens the foundations of the nation and is consistent with the linking of corporate goals and community interests. It is a practice that turns the cynical "What's good for General Motors, is good for the USA" inside out.

More traditionally, companies continue to actively encourage their employees to participate in the local United Way campaigns, the Red Cross, the volunteer fire department, the National Guard, the Little

League, scouting, and scores of other volunteer organizations. But even the volunteer programs are now being linked to the core strategic goals of the company.

For corporations with research and development ties, the corporation often demonstrates its citizenship through the support of its employee membership and participation in professional, scientific, and scholarly societies and organizations. Such support includes attendance at conferences and the encouragement to assume leadership roles in the organizations.

For over twenty-two years, General Motors has published an "annual accounting of its programs and progress in areas of public concern and its efforts to provide its customers with superior products and services that meet or exceed both private and public demands" (*1992 General Motors Public Interest Report*, 1). Their report focused on issues of concern not only to the corporation but to the public as well. It discussed industrial leadership and its importance to the fiscal and social health of the country. It also focused on market issues—the U.S. motor vehicle industry, customer satisfaction, and technology leadership; and social issues—safety, the environment, and energy. Their report contained a discussion on the corporation's role in meeting the needs of people—employees, minorities, and communities. Such an annual accounting of the human side of corporate activity demonstrates corporate citizenship in its best manifestation.

The efforts of McDonald's Corporation illustrate this combination of philanthropy, marketing, and issues management in its building a strong relationship with its customers and the community through the Ronald McDonald houses. The houses are actually a group of locally financed private charities—part of a larger program of charities, not a part of the corporation.

Nevertheless, McDonald's has successfully used these charity programs to meet its goals: to establish itself as a partner in the community, to build a reputation of trust with its customers, to show its commitment to the community, and to influence public attitudes. Certainly McDonald's link to the Ronald McDonald houses is the type of community relations program that, according to Mary Lowengard (1989, 25), is "marketing-driven . . . the primary thrust of the effort is to draw attention to the product."

BUILDING EQUITY THROUGH COMMUNITY RELATIONS

The other type of community relations effort applies to corporations and organizations that seek the support of the community in order to maintain their ability to operate freely. Such companies make products or perform services not clearly understood or valued by the members of the community. Examples include chemical and pharmaceutical manufacturers, utilities, mining and oil companies, and providers of industrial and business services.

Large corporations such as BASF and Allied Signal, compared with Ford and Nabisco, have almost no products the consumer can identify immediately as coming from them. If they have not developed a partnership with the community, if they have not created a sort of equity that does not show up on the balance sheet, a crisis or an emergency could be a potential disaster for the organization. Good companies can be tainted by association if another company in the same industry makes headlines for unethical or illegal practices.

The historical and traditional separation between the corporation and the community contributed to the difficulties in several industries: oil companies after the Cartell-manipulated shortages in the 1970s, chemical companies after the Bhopal disaster, utilities after a nuclear power disaster, military contractors after a congressional investigation, and the savings and loan industry after the nationwide failure of S&Ls and community banks. Such efforts are often a reaction to another company's crisis.

When the *Exxon Valdez* ran aground in 1989, it did more than spill oil; it exposed the weakness in a corporate philanthropy strategy that used a foundation to separate it from important groups, effectively barring it from forming a strategic alliance with environmental groups. Exxon's then Chairman Larry Rawl lacked the "equity" a relationship could have given him. He had no alternative "but to adopt a reactive posture toward environmentalists, thereby making Exxon an easy target for their wrath" (Smith, 108). In September 1994, Exxon was served with a $5 billion punitive damages judgment, the equivalent of a year's profit for the corporation (*New York Times*, September 17, 1994: 1). What might they have saved had they adopted a posture of social responsibility before the accident rather than afterward?

Arco, a competitor, had begun to form strategic alliances with environmentalists beginning in 1971. Arco executives learned from this partnership how to respond quickly and honestly when accidents happened, and the environmental groups depended on Arco's expert testimony to pass clean air legislation that addressed both business and environmental concerns. Texaco also issues a *Community Services Report: Helping Hands*. Their report details that corporation's commitment to its numerous programs in education, the environment, the arts and culture, and civic involvement. It might be argued that its racial discrimination lawsuits in late 1996 might have cost them more dearly had they not had such a policy and built equity in the community.

TABLE 5-2
The Conference Board's List of Largest Industry Contributors Reveals
Companies and Industries with a Strong Need to Create and
Maintain a Positive Relationship with Its Community and Customers

LARGEST GIVERS BY INDUSTRY	# of Companies	Contributions (in millions)
Pharmaceuticals	15	$242
Petroleum/gas/mining	21	217
Computers/office equipment	13	181
Telecommunications	13	172
Chemicals	28	163
Food/beverage/tobacco	17	148
Transportation equipment	13	147
Insurance	45	133
Electrical machinery	19	85
Banking	26	82

SOURCE: The Conference Board

Table 5-2, based on the Conference Board's *Corporate Contributions Report* (1992), indicates which industries use an active contributions program to develop and maintain strong, positive ties with customers and with communities.

THE "NEW ENGLAND APPROACH"

But what happens if you have taken the path of good corporate citizen and you are attacked in the press?

Crises can test an organization's commitment to its citizenship role, as The Body Shop discovered when *Business Ethics* ran an article contradicting its image as being sensitive to the environment, its position on not using animals to test its products, and its efforts as a progressive force in the community (*New York Times*, September 2, 1994: D1,D6). The controversy had a negative impact on the company's stock price, as well as on the socially conscious investing movement begun in 1976.

What can a company do to balance profit and citizenship efforts?

Many companies, including The Body Shop, are now conducting and publicly disclosing the results of an annual social audit similar to the one Vermont ice cream manufacturer Ben & Jerry's has conducted since 1988 (*New York Times*, September 16, 1994 : D6).

We call the practice the "New England Approach."

The New England Approach? Many of our contemporary management actions are based on the practice of democracy and the role of citizens. The roots can be traced to the New England colonies—to town meetings that were held to air differences and make decisions for the entire community, voting, and helping fellow members of the community.

Ben & Jerry's has developed a corporate culture that balances money and good works. A much larger percentage of profits is routinely given to charity. Surplus food stuff is given to farmers in the Vermont countryside and raw products are bought from local dairy farmers to support the community economy. The company limits the compensation of its executives so the differences between workers and managers is never very wide.

The list of its employee- and community-related actions is much longer. In short, the company has put "philanthropic equity" on the balance sheet—a notion that can help even the staunchest Friedmanist see that citizenship can help a strong bottom line, just as other excellent business practices can help a company outperform its competitors. The result has been an influx of investment as the company made the transition to being a player on the world market. Its reputation and resulting equity helped the company through the changes of expansion and the departure of one of its founders in the early 1990s.

Selected Commentary

The commentaries selected for this chapter are from the presentations at the annual Conference on Corporate Communication at Fairleigh Dickinson University. Each of the authors focuses on a part of communication practice in the context of corporate citizenship.

Patricia Siccone presents the results and an analysis of research on approaches to corporate citizenship. The survey of 160 companies identified as good corporate citizens has established a benchmark for identifying the best practices for corporate social responsibility.

Linn Weiss explains how important it is for corporate communication professionals to take an active role in winning public understanding and support of scientific research. He focuses on the efforts of the pharmaceutical industry.

Vaughana Macy Feary recognizes the problem of crime in the workplace and the ineffectiveness of communicating compliance and corporate codes to combat it. She argues that a more effective approach would be to communicate more about philosophically based theories in business ethics.

Corporate Social Responsibility
New Ways of Making a Profit

Patricia Siccone

Understanding the connection between good citizenship, moral worth, and profits has driven corporations to adopt new approaches to doing business. This new approach strives to integrate business and social goals and to promote corporate citizenship.

What Approaches do Corporate Citizens Use to Fulfill Their Partnership with Society?

To provide the answers and establish a benchmark, I surveyed 159 corporations belonging to several industries. Members of the Center for Community Relations at Boston College, companies that already accept their roles as corporate citizens, provided the survey sample. The study was based on the answers of 87 respondents, equaling a response rate of 54%.

This study focuses on corporate social responsibility structures and how they are facilitated and communicated to the organization's internal and external publics. The survey provided key answers to our questions concerning corporate citizenship.

This commentary by Patricia Siccone, a community relations fellow at Becton Dickinson, appeared in the *Proceedings of the Eighth Conference on Corporate Communication*, May 1995. It appears here with her permission.

Industry Participation*	Corporations Surveyed	Percentage Responding
Utility	35	22%
Petroleum/Gas/Mining	14	9%
Telecommunication	12	8%
Computer/ Office Equipment	22	14%
Pharmaceutical/Healthcare	18	11%
Aerospace/Auto/ Transportation	13	8%
Print/Publishing/Broadcast Media	10	6%
Chemical	8	5%
Insurance	7	4%
Consumer Products/Service*	17	11%
Banking	3	2%

*Based on categories from the 1992 Conference Board Report on Corporate Giving

Figure A.
Corporations Identified as Good Corporate Citizens — By Industry

How Do These Corporations Manage Their Philanthropic Initiatives?

Nearly every corporation (97%) surveyed has a corporate giving program, and half (51%) of the companies have a foundation. A very large majority of corporate giving programs (86%) and foundations (73%) integrate their business objectives with philanthropy, supporting the notion of partnership.

How Do Employees Rate Their Corporations as Citizens?

A large majority of senior (61%) and middle management (63%), half of beginning (50%), and a very large majority of non-management (80%) rate their corporations as excellent citizens. Nearly every corporation rated as excellent citizens (98%) and good citizens (93%) have corporate giving programs. More than half of the corporations rated in the excellent category (56%) and nearly half (45%) in the good category support a foundation. Nearly every corporation rated as excellent citizens (91%) and a very large majority rated as good citizens (78%) support business goals with their giving programs. A very large majority of corporations rated as excellent citizens (74%) and a substantial number of corporations rated as good citizens (69%) support business goals with their foundations.

How Do These Corporations Measure or Support Their Citizenship Activities?

Most corporations support their citizenship activities mainly through traditional communication vehicles, which include company newsletters (75%) and press releases (58%). Nearly half of corporations (45%) support their citizenship activities through their annual reports.

What Type Of Services Do These Corporate Citizens Offer to Their Communities?

Educational programs (84%), assistance in shelters and hospitals (76%), and recycling and environmental support programs (70%) are the most popular services these corporations offer their communities.

How Do These Corporate Citizens Support Their Employees' Community Efforts?

Internal publications (91%), matching gift programs (78%), awards/ ceremonial recognition (77%), and educational support through tuition reimbursement (86%) are the most popular ways corporate citizens support the efforts of their employees. Only a minority of companies (24%) show support of their employees' community efforts through merit or promotion for salary increase.

What are the roots of corporate citizenship and how has it become such an integral part of today's work environment and our communities? Reflecting on a strong amount of secondary research, the paper discusses the evolution of philanthropy and the emergence of socially driven businesses. It discusses the two opposite views of Milton Friedman and Peter Drucker and how their views define a middle ground that captures the approach of many socially driven businesses. These companies benefit from customer loyalty related to strong community relationships.

What are some of the challenges and concepts Corporate America must consider into the next century? At the end of the twentieth century, as a more informed, outspoken, and perhaps, distrustful society does not hesitate to question authority, we take the liberty to define the roles needed to make progress in areas of considerable social or environmental decline. Corporate America in the twenty-first century must not only consider profits and productivity, but expand the concept of teamwork into their global and local communities. Corporate America needs to develop partnerships and powerful, tactful promotion of their social initiatives for a vital resource of community support.

To provide examples, I included highlights of such notable socially driven companies as The Body Shop International, Ben & Jerry's Home-made, Levi Strauss, and Tom's of Maine.

Corporate America and governments face the challenge of developing a more advanced workforce and forming productive relationships in a global marketplace. Partnerships of the twenty-first century will strive to establish a more skilled workforce in a technological, service oriented society. Educational initiatives will consider a greater number of non-traditional students who will learn under more mobile and adaptable conditions. The global marketplace presents the challenge to combine profit goals with cultural diversity. Corporations and governments need to develop an understanding of how to respect and benefit from the diversity inherent in a global marketplace.

THE CONCEPT OF CONTEMPORARY CORPORATE CITIZENSHIP

The relationship between business, government, and society has been evolving since the early stages of civilization (Anderson 1989, ix). At one time charitable contributions were made mostly on behalf of wealthy and prominent individuals not tied to their corporations (Smith 1994, 107). Business did not go outside Adam Smith's view of businesses' social responsibility. He believed a company's obligation was to ". . . survive as an originator of wealth" to produce material goods and bring them to market, safeguard capital, maximize profit, and do justice to stockholders" (Avishai 1994, 39). In regard to corporate citizenship, Adam Smith believed companies were not citizens, since according to Bernard Avishai, "their social obligations derive from overt calculations, not a moral struggle."

Milton Friedman, a conservative economist and opponent of corporate social involvement, argued for limited government in the economy by claiming "the forces of a free market will efficiently solve most economic problems" (1974, 459). Friedman believed that corporations have no right to spend shareholders' money to support charitable causes (Anderson, 3). He described this effort as taxing its shareholders without the "elaborate constitutional, parliamentary and judicial provisions to control these functions" (Friedman 1974, 122). In his view businesses need to focus on the bottom line.

Several environmental factors contributed to the changes in how business, government, and society viewed the function and place of philanthropy. The economy was becoming more dependent on industries. Existing as major employers, their presence was a powerful factor in community and government. Business practices directly resulted in positive or negative consequences for internal and external stakeholders.

When factories laid off workers it soared unemployment rates. Unfair working conditions or long hours caused dysfunctional families, and poor production practices meant unsafe consumer products. To control that power, the government set regulations to direct some business practices.

Socially, the growing presence of industry affected the way we lived. A life working in a factory contrasted sharply from working on a farm. Even independent workers were affected by the health of those businesses, since those industries determined the health of their local economies.

According to Michael Goodman, ". . . By the beginning of the 20th century, the company was an integral part of the community. And its presence had a strong impact on the lives of the people, whether or not they took home a company paycheck" (Goodman 1994, 59).

At this time, philanthropy represented what many people view as true altruism. Industries separated their business goals from the nature of their philanthropic initiatives. As Craig Smith, author of an article entitled "The New Corporate Philanthropy" describes, these philanthropic efforts consisted of cash donations to help causes not linked to their industry. Business, government, and society worked within their own limits (Smith 1994, 107). In essence, they basically accomplished the same objective as most modern corporate philanthropy programs. Outside of the moral obligation of the wealthier segment to assist the needier, leaders needed to accomplish a better relationship with their publics. A positive image fostered a community more tolerant of their practices, more loyal to their product or service, and less critical of their faults.

So where is businesses' place in society? Is its primary function to make a dollar or to serve society? When considering such roles, a number of perspectives come into play. Jerry W. Anderson, author of *Corporate Social Responsibility*, introduces both ends of this scale by comparing the philosophies of Peter Drucker, who believed business has an obligation to renourish society, to the more conservative view of Milton Friedman, who advocated businesses' main function is to "do business."

Peter Drucker believes "that business are not created to make money" (Hawkin 1993, 156). The great influence of business on our existence justifies the strong emphasis on human interest objectives. Drucker advocates the notion that focusing on human interest concerns results in a more productive business environment.

However, Friedman's and Drucker's philosophies define a middle ground. This ground marks the social responsibility strategy increasingly implemented by many of today's corporations, who value their role in the local and world community. Anderson notes two exceptions

Friedman makes to charitable efforts: the first exception—closely held businesses should be allowed to make charitable contributions to decrease the tax bite; the second exception—contributions to local institutions and the arts should be made "when they provide marginal return to the company greater than the marginal cost" (Anderson, 19).

Drucker supports a similar effort in stating, "To do good in order to do well, that is to convert social needs and problems into profitable business opportunities is rarely considered by today's advocates of social responsibility" (Anderson, 7). Both philosophies focus on developing a partnership between business, government, and community, striving toward a "win-win" situation. Together, these concepts describe how contemporary companies are combining social responsibility with their business strategies.

Today, the public demonstrates active concern for the power in big business. To have a powerful voice in business's decisions, we must continually educate ourselves, objectively look at our surroundings, develop and promote social visions, and then form alliances with businesses to foster the healthiest local and global communities.

Unfortunately, corporations deal with their own economic hardships. The concept of building strong philanthropic initiatives doesn't depend on an endless supply of economic resources. In an age of downsizing and economic crises, corporations need to find stronger reasons to make donations to needy causes (Smith, 105). With these financial obligations, corporations need to fulfill certain business objectives. By integrating community relations with philanthropy, the needs of the internal and external stakeholders receive fair consideration.

Many experts argue that this approach abandons the meritorious efforts of "true" philanthropy. In supporting this claim, one must consider some underlying concerns of philanthropic efforts. Since the earliest stages, philanthropic efforts have developed more positive relationships between richer and poor classes, between proprietors and their workers, between industry and government. Essentially, the idea of "true" philanthropy has always involved efforts to create more positive relationships.

One of the key distinctions between philanthropic efforts and community relations efforts is the latter's acknowledgement of this vital function to build better relationships. This function comes from both a sense of obligation to its community and its need to gain the support of its stakeholders. Corporations now adopt a more utilitarian perspective of creating the greatest good for the greatest number of people.

Craig Smith's explanation of the function of a corporate citizen supports Drucker's philosophy of "doing good to do better." Smith believes that the ideal situation of corporate philanthropy exists on a "two way street," a dynamic relationship in which neither has the upper hand (Smith, 109).

Corporations are recognizing the benefits of developing strong relationships with their communities. Strong relationships safeguard them from increased regulation, ward off public scrutiny, allow them to take advantage of tax incentives, and to profit financially from a strong image that promotes their role as valuable corporate citizens.

CORPORATE CITIZENS OF THE TWENTY-FIRST CENTURY

As a society, we eagerly search for opportunities to improve labor, environmental, and social conditions. As individuals, we work, pay taxes, and fulfill our roles as a spouse, parent, leader, and friend. Most of us integrate moral codes in our everyday actions and make sincere efforts to correct the mistreatment of ourselves and others. Such behavior defines the notion of a productive citizen. Corporations are community members and paternal figures. We expect them to take initiatives in correcting social wrongs, abandoning markets of social injustice, showing commitment to community's health, and using available resources to protect and assist the less fortunate.

Philanthropy has always been used to acquire an image, but contemporary philanthropy openly demonstrates this concern and is promoted as strategic planning. Forming partnerships with communities plays a vital role in planning a supportive business environment. Society reaps monetary and professional support from philanthropic programs, and corporations form better images and valuable relationships with their stakeholders.

How popular and widely practiced is the idea of integrating philanthropy and business objectives? The benchmark survey of 160 corporations clearly supports the trend of managing philanthropic initiatives with business initiatives as a widely practiced approach among corporate citizens.

The results of the benchmark survey (Table A) show that corporate giving is a norm among corporations who accept their roles as community members. Nearly every corporation surveyed (97%) has a corporate giving program. A very large majority (86%) integrated this function to support their overall mission or business goals. The survey further shows that half (51%) of the corporation support a foundation and a very large majority of those corporations (73%) link their foundation support to business interests. Contemporary corporate philanthropy no longer adheres to the restrictions of traditional philanthropy. In an age of economic hardship and high expectations, companies are making the most of their limited resources.

TABLE A
Managing Philanthropic Initiatives and Linking Giving Programs to Business Goals

Survey Question	YES	NO	No Response
Does your company have a corporate giving program?	97%	2%	1%
Within your company, do giving programs support business goals?	86%	9%	5%
Does your company support a foundation?	51%	47%	2%
Is the foundation linked to your company's business interests?	73%	25%	2%

SOURCE: Siccone Survey

"DOING GOOD BY DOING WELL"

In acting as good corporate citizens, companies benefit from a number of positives. Craig Smith defines these rewards as

- better image

- higher productivity among employees

- ability to overcome regulatory obstacles

- ability to foster synergy among business units, when companies include a interdepartmental decision-making process and effort

Alan Reder, author of *In Pursuit of Principle and Profit*, states "... many managers and company owners who first implemented socially responsible policies and practices, simply as a matter of principle, have reaped awards in the form of improved employee allegiance, productivity and work quality; management insight and creativity; and customer loyalty" (Reder 1994, 7).

To survive the changes of business, corporate giving professionals must strategically engage themselves in promoting their departmental function. In a time of limited resources, cutbacks, and emphasis on gaining efficient work processes, senior management needs to know why an in-house program is useful to the corporation. Since a healthy corporation depends on a productive workforce and strong ties to its internal and external publics, the concept of partnerships plays a major role in developing an effective strategy. To safeguard the existence of a corporate giving program in-house, versus outsourcing to public relation firms, corporations must promote the importance of these partnerships with both its internal stakeholders, its community, and non-profit organizations.

One way corporate giving professionals have accomplished this objective is through increasing the level of participation in the giving process and the use of "time" as a valuable resource to give to communities. As Smith states, corporate giving professionals should make the effort an interdepartmental function. Why should it involve so many people? A number of factors support this strategy: it helps build morale, commitment, understanding of the department's function, a strong network of internal and external support, and a wealthy pool of "time," skills, knowledge, and understanding to commit in developing partnerships with the corporation's community.

Corporations that develop strong internal support will benefit from a loyal source of volunteers and employees who speak positively about their corporation's community efforts. As Craig Smith further suggests, interview the corporation's stakeholders to find a few causes supported by a "corporate family." To make community relations planning an interdepartmental function, a corporation can develop immediate contacts with their community, open effective lines of communication, and by implementing a program developed from employees' suggestions, one can depend on the most committed volunteers. Volunteerism has replaced many community relations efforts formally through financial obligation with the valuable resource of expertise.

The key to successful philanthropic initiatives is effective and continual communication. Corporations should listen and respond to their employees' involvement in developing community relations. When a company listens to the community's needs, assesses its own needs, and develops strategies to meet those goals, harmony can more readily exist between business and society. Anderson explains the question is not whether a company should make these efforts, but how deeply they get involved. When making these decisions, he expains that companies should examine their "physical capabilities, desires, and economic resources" (Anderson, 12).

In an age when corporations face increasing ethical scrutiny, when their success partly depends on their standing as corporate citizens, corporations search for ways to enhance their image. Corporations must adapt, expand, and change their strategies to meet social demands.

SOCIALLY DRIVEN BUSINESS

The benchmark survey (Table B) indicates that employees who work for corporations who seriously consider their roles as corporate citizens rate their companies overwhelmingly high.

TABLE B
How Employees Rate Their Socially Responsible Corporations

POSITION	EXCELLENT	GOOD	FAIR	POOR
Senior Management	61%	39%	0%	0%
Middle Management	64%	32%	2%	2%
Beginning Management	50%	25%	25%	0%
Non-management	80%	20%	0%	0%

SOURCE: Siccone Survey

Among these corporations, a large majority of senior (61%) and middle management (64%), half of beginning management (50%), and a very large majority of non-management (80%) rate their corporations as excellent citizens. Communication is vital in establishing a strong network of support. From the positive response from all levels, these companies have successfully fulfilled the promotion of their programs to their employees.

In response to this change in how business views its connection to society, many corporations are joining organizations "dedicated to advancing socially responsible business practices here and around the world" (Reder 11). Some of these organizations include Business for Social Responsibility, Council on Economic Priorities, and The Center for Corporate Community Relations at Boston College.

Business for Social Responsibility was established in 1992 and has grown in a short time to include 700 member and affiliated companies. According to Kathy Grimes, Vice President of Business for Social Responsibility, this organization is "an alliance that fosters socially responsible corporate policies and brings the unique perspective and resources of the business community to address enormous problems and opportunities confronting both our companies and our society today." In its literature, Business for Social Responsibility promotes its goal of setting high standards for business in the workplace, the community, and the environment.

The Council on Economic Priorities (CEP), formed in 1969, is an independent public interest organization that rates companies' social responsiveness. It researches issues of environmentalism, corporate social responsibility, and conversion to a peace economy (CEP literature). CEP, as noted in its 1993 annual report, is a "centralized source of information for evaluating corporate activities which have an impact on the quality of life . . . information which is either unavailable or inaccessible elsewhere" (CEP 1993 Annual Report).

TABLE C
Services Companies Offer Their Communities

Services Offered By Companies To Communities	Offered
Career Counseling	24%
Business Consulting Services	32%
Educational Programs	84%
Recycling/ Environmental Support Programs	70%
Sponsorship of Walkathons	68%
Assistance in Shelters, Centers, and Hospitals	76%
Other	44%

SOURCE: Siccone Survey

In its 1993–1994 annual report, The Center for Corporate Community Relations at Boston College describes itself as a policy center for corporate citizenship. Its mission is ". . . to provide a forum through which corporations can commit and learn about the best practices related to corporate social responsibility" (1). The Center for Corporate Community Relations accomplishes this mission by acting as a resource of training, consultation, information, and research. It offers a place for corporations to respond successfully to business and community needs.

IMPLEMENTATION OF COMMUNITY RELATIONS STRATEGY

Contemporary corporations can claim they accept their roles as corporate citizens and they integrate involvement at all management levels. To confirm the accuracy of these statements, one can evaluate specific company programs and ways each one supports and encourages the efforts of the employees. Table C shows how corporations internally and externally support community relations efforts.

Of these results the most popular programs were education (84%), assistance in shelters, centers, and hospitals (76%), and recycling and environmental support programs (70%). Education ranked highest, probably as a result of Corporate America's realization that it needs to prepare a more educated and motivated workforce to succeed in a more technological, service-oriented society. Recycling and environmental support programs can range from recycling soda cans within corporate buildings to arranging work groups to clean local beaches. But no matter what degree of involvement it means, companies need to show concern for an issue that the government and public monitors. Sponsorship in walkathons and volunteerism in public care facilities show a corporate focus on developing its citizenship role with the more

TABLE D
Services Companies Offer Their Communities

Ways Companies Support Involvement	
Time Off	55%
Matching Gifts Programs	78%
Awards/Ceremonial Recognition	77%
Recognition in Internal Publications	91%
Merit for Promotion or Salary Increase	24%
Tuition Reimbursement	86%
Other	18%

SOURCE: Siccone Survey

available resources of time, talent, and skills. Business consulting services ranked low (32%) probably because it involves the risk of employees exposing confidential information when offering a personal example for guidance.

The sample of companies shows support in valuable areas, but how do they support those efforts with internal policy and promotion? Table D shows:

A very large majority show support through matching gifts (78%) and awards/ceremonial recognition (77%). Nearly every corporation (91%) shows support through recognition in internal publications and an overwhelming percentage of companies (86%) show educational support through tuition reimbursement. What does this indicate? Companies are demonstrating support and recognition for their employees' volunteerism and educational objectives. However companies are not using the most powerful motivator, money and prestige. Only a minority of companies (24%) have significantly emphasized the importance of a community relations function by integrating its value in its employee evaluations for salary increase or promotion. It is important but not vital enough to place on the companies' top business objectives. With this priority, companies need to provide the resource of time off.

Certain corporations have taken leadership roles in forming the most valuable partnerships with their community. The following corporations have profited from healthy relationships and popularity in this area of social responsibility. Table E describes a few of the companies that deserve special notice.

TRENDS IN PHILANTHROPY AND COMMUNITY INVOLVEMENT

To gain the clearest perspective of corporations who make concerted efforts to form healthy relationships with their community, the 160

TABLE E
Case Examples

COMPANY	SOCIALLY RESPONSIBLE PRACTICES
The Body Shop International (*Body and Soul: Profits with Principles,* by Anita Roddick)	• Measures success by how company supports human concerns • Campaigns: AIDS Awareness Campaign, "Trade Not Aid" Green Campaigns • Established an Environmental Projects Department
Ben & Jerry's Homemade ("Passing the Scoop: Ben and Jerry's," by Claudia Dreifus)	• Respects the concept of partnerships with its employees and community • Strives to maintain fair employee policies • Hires Greystone Bakers, a supplier that hires the unemployable • Gives 7 $\frac{1}{2}$% of its profits to its foundation
Levi Strauss ("Managing by Values: Is Levi Strauss' Approach Visionary or Shaky," by Russell Mitchell & Levi Strauss Literature)	• Aims at being a responsible corporate citizen to all of its stakeholders, fulfills this role through partnerships • Leadership Efforts: volunteerism and community service, cash and non-cash donations, advocacy of non-profits • Promotes diverse workforce at all management levels • Harassment and exploitation of labor is a serious violation of culture
Tom's of Maine (Tom's of Maine Annual Report 1993)	• Focuses on partnerships • Established Community Life Department • Earthkeeping Campaign: partnership with National Wildlife Federation and CVS • Community efforts include: protecting the rainforest, indigenous cultures, funding for summer camps for children of migrant workers, support of Harvard's Divinity School's Center for Values in Public Life, and a strong emphasis on volunteerism

SOURCE: Siccone Survey

corporations surveyed acknowledged the importance of being good corporate citizens. The survey (see Table F) shows the following percentages from cross-variable ratings of "good" and "excellent" versus the support of foundation or corporate giving programs, and offers a benchmark for other corporations.

TABLE F
Rating of Corporate Citizenship

SURVEY QUESTIONS	EXCELLENT	GOOD
Does your company have a corporate giving program?	yes 98%	yes 93%
	no 0	no 7%
Within your company, do giving programs support business goals?	yes 91%	yes 78%
	no 6%	no 15%
Does your company support a foundation?	yes 56%	yes 45%
	no 42%	no 52%
Is the foundation linked to your company's business interests?	yes 74%	yes 69%
	no 23%	no 31%

SOURCE: Siccone Survey

The benchmark survey supports the notion that corporate citizens with high ratings support foundations or have established corporate giving programs and have linked those objectives to meeting business needs. Contemporary philanthropy integrates the concept of partnership. This may explain why more than nine out of ten companies in the excellent (98%) and good (93%) categories have corporate giving programs and a lower percentage of excellent (56%) and good (45%) support a foundation. Perhaps corporate giving programs offer a more functional system to form partnerships with limited resources. Historically, foundation interests were kept separate from business objectives and this traditional philosophy may still represent the function of this arrangement.

The survey (see Table G) also shows that most corporations promote their citizenship efforts mainly through traditional communication vehicles. The most common vehicles used by corporations in this sample included company newsletters (75%) and press releases (58%). Realizing that corporate citizenship is a necessity for corporations has led a large minority (32%) of corporations to publish a public interest report that promotes their community efforts. A public interest report establishes an image of serious commitment to important issues. By promoting this commitment in a separate report, it gives the public a stronger, more comprehensive view of how the community benefits from a partnership.

Education has become a main concern of employers as we enter the twenty-first century. When companies depend upon more advanced

TABLE G
Company Approaches to Measure or Support Citizenship Activities

APPROACH	PERCENTAGE
No Measurement Approach	10%
In the Annual Report	45%
In a Public Interest Report	32%
In a Company Newsletter	75%
In Press Releases	58%
In Advertising and Marketing Material	35%

SOURCE: Siccone Survey

skills, businesses are now making efforts to increase the level of education among the masses. This contradicts Adam Smith's philosophies of management and education focused upon basic training. At this time, corporations did not depend on a workforce composed of empowered individuals, striving as team players. Workers did simple tasks over and over, both a cause and result of their limited ambition or opportunity.

As we progress into a new century, companies have realized we need a different type of worker to reach productivity goals and maintain a healthy bottom line. With a global economy allowed by the efficiencies of technology, corporations need workers that can communicate effectively, grasp concepts, and apply their training to their present situations creatively. Corporations need workers who are technologically smart and creatively challenged. They have implemented programs to develop these skills and perceptions during students' earliest elementary years. New minds, not bound to traditional communication vehicles and thought, present companies with an opportunity to mold and enrich the young, uninhibited minds of the twenty-first century.

As companies combine business and philanthropic initiatives, non-profit professionals will need to develop their awareness of corporate "know-how" or etiquette in selling or promoting their programs. As this sector and the corporate world collaborate to form programs that provide mutual benefit, it would serve both parties to gain experience in the other. Community relations professionals' understanding of non-profits increases the level of community awareness, therefore developing a more powerful analysis tool in setting business objectives. The non-profit professional's exposure to corporate life allows a greater refinement in corporate etiquette and an advantageous mind-set to sell their concept as a "building block" of corporations' community relations objectives. Toward the future, a resume that shows experience in both worlds, a clear understanding of economics, and an ability to package information will have great value to the non-profit and for-profit employers.

WORKING AND LEARNING IN THE
TWENTY-FIRST CENTURY MARKETPLACE

The communities of an organization encompass local, national, and international communities. Access to more efficient communication vehicles, our ability to travel faster, and our televisions linking us to even the most primitive cultures has allowed us to form a competitive and promising global market. As we enter the twenty-first century, we will increasingly conduct business in small communities that stretch globally. Finding productive partnerships will present a challenge for multi-national and domestic corporations.

A key to having a healthy local community is developing an economy partly based on international trade. Foreign nations have become a part of our community in an age when governments recognize the value of participating in free trade. Businesses dealing with global markets use corporate citizenship efforts to win shares in international markets (Smith, 112). Meanwhile many foreign investors have begun to adopt a similar strategy (112).

The presence of foreign companies in the United States has steadily increased over the last two decades (Pinkston and Carroll 1994, 157). As the United States invests in foreign nations and vice versa, the global community needs to assess the concerns of differences in culture and regulations.

Pinkston and Carroll note the differences in views of certain countries when considering the connection to business and society or community. "England has shown to emphasize economic responsibilities to owners in its business community. France, on the other hand, has been understood to focus on company employee relations, as has Germany. The Japanese environment has appeared to nurture the business-community relationships" (Pinkston and Carroll, 161). However, in their study of 131 chemical facilities, which had certain limitations to consider, these scholars found that foreign affiliates had "similar corporate citizenship orientations and priorities" as the domestic facilities in the United States (166).

Since U.S. corporations perfected this model, they are most able to grasp this competitive advantage. However, in an age of downsizing and budget cuts, there is competition within the corporation for financial resources. "Figures released in October 1993 show that 1992 giving fell 1% to $5.9 billion, the first decline in giving since the Great Depression" (113). The concept of corporate citizenship has become a common practice and expectation among U.S. companies.

This new relationship has gained popularity for the business of foreign competitors (114). ". . . Surveys conducted in Canada, the

United Kingdom, Australia, France, Germany, Spain, and Japan show that corporate giving increased considerably even though each of these countries was mired by recession" (114).

With the advancement of technology in an increasingly service-oriented work environment and its necessity to communicate in a global marketplace, corporations are forming partnerships with educational institutions to prepare for the twenty-first century. According to the benchmark survey, a very large majority of the corporations offer educational programs to their communities. Among these corporations a great number offer tuition reimbursement, promoting a more highly educated workforce.

Future business environments will demand specialized skills, the ability to apply theory and knowledge to resolve present problems, and proficiency in using computer software. Unfortunately, corporations are finding themselves at a disadvantage with a workforce not familiar with technology and not able to perform successfully in this environment. ". . . Twenty percent to 30 percent of U.S. workers were deficient in skills that make it possible for them to do their current jobs efficiently, use new technologies, or participate in training programs" (Avishai, 46).

Louis Harris and Associates' study further shows a decline in computer accessibility as salary decreases (Rose 1994, 25). So as information steadily progresses into our workforce, it will create a serious disadvantage for the less economically secure. This shows corporations need to make great strides in remedying this situation. In addition to developing a workforce from the start of educational careers, corporations need to continue focusing on more culturally diverse student populations. Our knowledge of the information technology gives us mobility, a political and community voice, convenience, and a wealthy resource of information and services in both our leisure and work lives. However to gain access to these channels, we need to reeducate ourselves on how to use these networks most cost-efficiently, creatively, and functionally.

Bernard Avishai, writer of an article "What is Business's Social Compact?" discusses taking education out of its old paradigms or framework with technology. Places for secondary education, "could well become networked hives of specialized, team-based, computer-supported mentoring (47). Primary schools may remain with classroom-based teaching to help children gain "simple courtesies" (47).

Educational institutions and nations of the global marketplace strive to redefine traditional roles and define their new places in the global marketplace. Educational institutions debate over the value to the traditional curriculum versus one that develops more specialized skills to prepare for the demands of the future workforce. Markets must focus on valuing profits with diversity in cultures and the workforce. As we enter the twenty-first century, we will see partnerships focused on making positive changes in how we work, communicate, and learn.

CONCLUSION

The concept of corporate citizenship has become a common practice and expectation in business environments. In an age in which markets cater to informed and outspoken consumers, corporations concern themselves with image. Positioning themselves as valuable community members allows them to secure themselves with the asset of public support.

Because government is strained by overwhelming debt and limited resources, we look toward corporations as community members and paternal figures to initiate social change. To react to these demands during a difficult economy, corporations look toward opportunities to develop partnerships with the non-profit sector. By integrating philanthropy with business objectives, Corporate America has found a productive way to allocate resources. These valuable resources include money, time, and expertise.

Corporations' willingness to foster community growth has established a more committed workforce, a healthier community, and better relationships with governments. Corporate citizenship allows a new paradigm to exist. This paradigm allows business, government, and society to exist as partners working toward common goals and shared visions.

REFERENCES

Anderson, Jerry W. Jr. *Corporate Social Responsibility: Guidelines for Top Management*. Westport, Conn.: Quorum Books, 1989.

Avishai, Bernard. "What is Business' Social Compact?" *Harvard Business Review* (January–February 1994): 38–48.

Business for Social Responsibility Literature 1993. Washington, D.C.: Business for Social Responsibility.

The Center for Corporate Community Relations at Boston College, Annual Report 1993. Chestnut Hill, Mass. The Center for Corporate Community Relations at Boston College.

Corporate Contributions 1992: A Research Report. New York, N.Y.: The Conference Board.

Council on Economic Priorities Annual Report 1993. New York, N.Y.: Council on Economic Priorities.

Council on Economic Priorities Literature 1993. New York, N.Y.: Council on Economic Priorities.

Dreifus, Claudia. "Passing the Scoop: Ben & Jerry's," *The New York Times Magazine* (December 18, 1994): 38–41.

Friedman, Milton. "The Social Responsibility of Business is to Increase Profits," *The New York Times Magazine* (September 13, 1970) 32–33; 122–26.

"Friedman, Milton." *World Book Encyclopedia*, 1974 ed.

Goodman, Michael B. *Corporate Communication: Theory and Practice.* Albany: State University of New York Press, 1994.

Hawkin, Paul. *The Ecology of Commerce: A Declaration of Sustainability.* New York, N.Y.: HarperCollins, 1993.

Pinkston, Tammie S., and Archie B. Carroll. "Corporate Citizenship Perspectives and Foreign Direct Investment in the U.S.," *Journal of Business Ethics* 13, (1994): 157–69.

Reder, Alan. *In Pursuit of Principle and Profit: Business Success Through Social Responsibility.* New York: G. P. Putnam's Sons, 1994.

Roddick, Anita. *Body and Soul: Profits with Principles—The Amazing Success Story of Anita Roddick and the Body Shop.* Crown, 1991.

Rose, Ed. "The Haves and the Have Nots," *Communication World/* IABC 11 (1994): 22–25.

Smith, Craig. "The New Corporate Philanthropy," *Harvard Business Review* (May–June 1994): 105–16.

Tom's of Maine Annual Report 1993. Kennebunk, Me.: Tom's of Maine.

Selling Science to Society

Linn A. Weiss

We are living in a truly revolutionary age—one in which the pace of technological innovation has led many American businesses to shift from high-volume, standardized production to a high-value, more specialized market niche orientation. Science and technology have become of critical importance to the progress of society and hold the key to understanding the accelerating changes in our world. We are not only beginning to gain insight into arcane technologies, but we are seeing their immediate applications as well.

The research-based pharmaceutical industry is a leading indicator of scientific change, as emphasized by a demonstrated willingness to risk capital for technological advancement and high returns. Dedicated to expanding the frontiers of medical science and health care, it is clearly one of America's most important technologically driven industries. No other high-technology industry devotes as high a percentage of its sales to research and development. In 1991, the research-based pharmaceutical industry reinvested 16.1 percent of its sales in research and development, compared to an average of 4.5 to 5 percent for all other industries. In the past four decades, America's pharmaceutical companies have invested more than $37 billion in research, representing a doubling in research

Linn A. Weiss is staff vice president, corporate communications at Schering-Plough Corporation. His commentary appeared in the *Proceedings of the First Conference on Corporate Communication*, May 1988. Shirley Boyden Maxwell, associate editor at Schering-Plough Corporation, collaborated in the research and writing. A revised version appears here with Mr. Weiss's permission.

investment every five years since 1970. Research and development expenditures were about $9.6 billion in 1991 and are expected to reach a record-breaking $10.9 billion in 1992.[1]

Today, the pharmaceutical industry is poised to revolutionize health care, with research and development programs leading to novel therapeutic agents that will prevent, cure or treat diseases heretofore untreatable by science. New understanding of human biology at the molecular level is providing keen insights into human disease. This, coupled with modern technology such as genetic engineering and computer molecular modeling, is enabling scientists to "design" new pharmaceuticals to attack specific diseases. The promise of medical science is real. The challenge is to create and sustain a public environment of trust that will permit that research promise to be fulfilled—one that will ensure the continual provision of life-saving and life-enhancing drugs to the people who need them.[2]

PUBLIC UNDERSTANDING MUST KEEP PACE

To extrapolate from the novelist C. P. Snow's idea of "two cultures" (the sciences and the humanities), it is vitally important, as the frontiers of medicine are being extended by researchers and corporate managers, that public understanding keep pace. We must recognize that along with public excitement over technological progress comes a good deal of uncertainty.

Public knowledge of science and technology is critical in a society increasingly affected by their impacts and by policy decisions determined by technical expertise in such areas as environmental quality and public health, regulation of food additives and drugs, the siting of large-scale technical and research facilities, and the impact of new medical techniques.[3]

As scientific change further unfolds, communicating the potential of "the new research" to the public is imperative. The public's support of research depends on how well they are informed. In other words, "what is explained to the public is generally believed by the public, and what the public believes, they may support."[4]

Traditionally, the pharmaceutical industry hasn't actively sought public visibility. Communications efforts have involved the transfer of medical and scientific information solely to medical professionals—primarily, physicians, pharmacists and nurses. While this customary role of pharmaceutical companies in imparting product information to practitioners has not faded in importance, it has become apparent that drug-related information supplied only to medical professionals fails to serve society's—and the pharmaceutical industry's—needs today.

To achieve important medical advances rapidly in a public climate of goodwill, effective communication is imperative between the laboratory scientist and layperson; between the scientist and business person; and between business and its various constituencies.

PUBLIC RELATIONS
THE CONDUIT OF INFORMATION

Within the pharmaceutical industry, one of public relations' functions is to plan and execute a program of action to earn public understanding and acceptance.[5] The job of a corporate public relations director today in the pharmaceutical industry involves, in part, informing the public about products, ideas and services and bringing together the scientist, business manager and lay public to enhance communication, understanding and cooperation among these diverse individual groups.

Public relations, having taken the time to master the fundamentals and the language of the new technologies, is in an optimal position to interact with, to understand and to address each constituency's needs and to foster a free exchange of ideas among them.

The Management Challenge

Business leaders must not only acknowledge the increasing importance of science and technology, but they must also understand the active role they play in scientific work. They must find ways to release the creative energies locked in the laboratory and the marketplace and unite them towards common goals.

Corporate management is responsible to the public, its shareholders and its scientists to manage the research and development process effectively, while creating an overall environment conducive to scientific achievement and communication. Consideration must be given to the public's demands for breakthrough products and improved deliverability and quality; to the shareholders' demands for profits; and to the scientists' need to confer openly with colleagues and to pursue the serendipitous process of scientific discovery. It is public relations' task to orchestrate communications among these sometimes disparate and conflicting enterprises.

For example, a partnership that has adapted itself successfully to bridge the traditional communication gap between science and commerce is one that emerged in 1982, when Schering-Plough Corporation, a research-based pharmaceutical and consumer products company, acquired DNAX Research Institute, a basic molecular biological research organization in Palo Alto, California.

The relationship was structured to preserve, to the greatest degree possible, a university-like setting free from corporate restraints. Scientists remain closely linked to academia through collaborative efforts, participation in colloquia and scientific publications, and to the corporate world by periodic meetings with the advisory committee that governs the institute.

Schering-Plough's internal communications process has been invigorated by its involvement with DNAX. The scientists there, engaged in pioneering research work, are attuned to the company's long-range strategic goals, many of which they help formulate. What's more, they frequently interact with the bench scientists at Schering-Plough's other laboratories and discuss how those projects complement and can be facilitated by their ongoing research work in Palo Alto. They have opportunities to convey formally and informally their desires, aspirations and hopes to the most senior levels of management and, in the process, have forged a bond of understanding, trust and commitment.

The Scientist's Challenge. There was a time when scientists and technologists lived in a world apart from the rest of society, when the term "ivory tower" was an appropriate description of their domain.[6] The traditional perception of the scientist is the "mad scientist" image of a figure in a rumpled, ill-fitting white coat, locked away in a lab, hunched over an array of test tubes, bubbling over with murky, mysterious substances. While we do not hold this as our serious vision of science, the scientist—and particularly the academic researcher—has traditionally cultivated separation from the world where practical application is the method and profit is the motive.

Businessmen and women traditionally have not tried to bridge the two worlds. Rather, they've been stymied by a lay view that the scientist speaks a language that those without training can never understand.

C. P. Snow, one of the most widely read scientists of our time, used the term "the two cultures" to describe this gap. He said, "Somehow we've made ourselves believe that the whole of technology was a more or less incommunicable art."

It's clear that this gap is beginning to close, because news about technology is in increasing demand, and we are all becoming—if not fluent—at least familiar with languages that once were foreign to us.

Due to a variety of influences, the scientist is becoming increasingly involved in the public and political sectors of our society. The scientist and technologist definitely no longer live in an ivory tower but must, of necessity, deal with social and political forces that are not only looking over their shoulders but, in some cases, telling them how to go about accomplishing their goals.

There has been a steady, but relentless, encroachment by public interest groups and individuals into the daily life of a working scientist—groups that are intensively concerned with the impact of scientific and technological developments on society—particularly, environmental and public health impacts.[7]

The inhibiting effect that public misconception and intervention often have on scientific progress accentuates the value of effective communication between the scientist and the layperson.

The public expects the scientist to deal comprehensively with the negative, as well as the positive, aspects of technical development. In many such cases, scientists are called upon to participate in briefings, public meetings and public hearings and provide background studies needed to dispel public concerns and fears regarding sometimes controversial research studies. The scientist then must come out of the laboratory and interact with various interest groups in society using terms, apart from their standard technical jargon, that will be understandable and acceptable to the lay public.[8]

Many scientists, however, have not been formally trained with the type of communications skills required for such interactions. To mitigate the problem, a number of scientific journals and organizations have published guidelines for scientists on how to respond to and communicate with the media. Corporations such as Schering-Plough often arrange for communications consultants to assist scientists in developing their presentation skills. Non-profit organizations such as the Scientists' Institute for Public Information and special media/scientific referral services have emerged to assist comprehensive reporting of scientific information and current issues.

The Public Relations Challenge. Serving as a conduit for information from the laboratory to the outside world, public relations develops new channels of communication to bring management in more direct positive contact with the scientist, the layperson, the investor, the reporter and all other parties. What's more, public relations is playing an increasingly active role in taking investors and journalists "up the learning curve" of new science, explaining how the industry has reached the most important step in its history—the great leap from treatment to prevention—and squaring the often serendipitous, "impractical" discovery process with the company's strategic progress on a business plan.

A concerted, judicious, long-term communications effort is required to sustain public interest in a company's projects over a considerable span of time. Public relations representatives are aware that "you can't expect to win by the method of chuck-wagon technology, where you cook something up in your lab, dish it out and yell, 'Come and get it!' That simply doesn't work."[9]

For the long years of pharmaceutical research and development, clinical testing and regulatory review that frequently precede new product introductions merely envisioned therapeutic compounds must be adequately portrayed. Public relations must make each step in product development both understandable and interesting to the public—steadily striving to educate. In addition to portraying the pharmaceuticals and drug-delivery technologies of a company's research and development, public relations is assuming a more active role in explaining, photographing and illustrating arcane science and developing sound strategies to win public understanding and support.

CASE STUDY
SCHERING-PLOUGH COMMUNICATIONS PROGRAM ADDRESSES NATIONAL HEALTH CARE DEBATE

As the debate over national health-care coverage intensifies, the relationship between drug pricing and medical progress needs to be better understood. The pharmaceutical industry view is: a public policy that focuses on the price of drugs without considering the cost-effective benefits that they offer to society, as alternative treatment measures to hospitalization and surgery, is shortsighted.

To enable the pharmaceutical industry to make its case that pharmaceuticals are not part of the problem of health-care costs in the United States, but are a vital part of the solution, Schering Plough in 1990 and 1991 commissioned two studies from the Battelle Medical Technology Assessment and Policy (MEDTAP) Research Center of Washington, D.C. The more recent study was disseminated publicly via a communications program.

The first study, commissioned in mid 1990, was entitled *The Value of Pharmaceuticals: A Study of Selected Conditions to Measure the Contribution of Pharmaceuticals to Health Status.* Looking back over the past 50 years quantitatively, it demonstrated how pharmaceuticals had helped avoid enormous economic costs that disease imposes on American society.[10]

In early 1991, to demonstrate that prescription drugs will be a good economic and social value over the next 25 years, the company commissioned the second study, entitled *The Value of Pharmaceuticals: An Assessment of Future Costs for Selected Conditions.* The study employed a qualitative forecasting methodology using experts to "crystal ball" 10 to 25 years into the future, and projected what the world would be like without the anticipated new pharmaceuticals and what it would be like with those pharmaceuticals.[11]

The study focused on five disease categories: two types of cardio-vascular disease, three types of cancer, two forms of arthritis, Alzheimer's disease, and HIV infection (AIDS). Conclusions for all the diseases studied were remarkable—that advances in medical care and changes in lifestyle will save millions of lives and hundreds of billions of dollars in the next quarter century.

To communicate the industry's message effectively to public policy decision makers, the company took a proactive role in the public dissemination of the latter study by convening back-to-back news conferences in Washington, D.C., attended by major media, congressional and executive branch staffs, physician organizations and voluntary health-care groups.

As the debate over health-care costs intensifies in the early 1990s, it is imperative for the pharmaceutical industry to take proactive steps in communicating the value of science and of its industry to all sectors of society.

MULTI-COMPANY R&D COMMUNICATIONS SURVEY

The concept of producing research brochures to portray research activities, achievements and products in the pipeline has been pursued by Schering-Plough and a number of other pharmaceutical companies, as evidenced by an informal confidential telephone survey conducted in the summer of 1987 by Schering-Plough's Corporate Communications Department.[12]

With the purpose of determining how other companies give publicity and recognition to their research and development activities and scientists, the survey explored both the internal and external research and development communications efforts of 42 research-based, high-tech companies (35 of which are pharmaceutical companies/subsidiaries) (see Appendix A).

Nine of the companies polled have published research brochures. Schering-Plough's 48-page pharmaceutical research brochure contains numerous high-gloss, laminated photographs supportive of a text that is technical enough to be of value to the scientist, yet comprehensible enough to be of interest to the layperson. The brochure discusses Schering-Plough's research and development achievements and the future course of research. It features a message from the president of Schering-Plough Research Institute, a historical profile of the company's research organization, and individual sections devoted to chemical research, biological research, biotechnology, worldwide operations, pharmaceutical sciences, process development, pre-clinical and clinical trials, the future and Schering-Plough Research Institute awards.

Other vehicles that are utilized to convey information about a company's research progress include annual and quarterly reports, reprints of research-oriented executive speeches and newsletters. Three of the companies polled periodically feature research in their employee video newsletters. Some companies publish separate annual reports for their research institutes, while others dedicate a section of their regular annual report or, sometimes, the entire report to a particular area of research. Schering-Plough's 1982 annual report, for example, was devoted to the new age of biotechnology and the company's progress in developing its genetically derived alpha-2 interferon product *Intron A*. It utilized photomicrographs of biotechnological organisms to reveal and explain genetic engineering. The company's 1989 annual report used photomicroscopy to illustrate its leading compounds in development.

Six of the pharmaceutical companies included in Schering-Plough's 1987 survey said they issue press releases in connection with the publication of scientific papers and/or the discussion of important drugs at scientific symposia and financial analyst meetings. One of the companies makes scientific papers available to the investment community. More than 50 percent, though, refrain from issuing press releases about unapproved products (for proprietary and regulatory reasons as well as concern about "overpromising" the public and investment community about drugs that may not come to fruition). Three of the companies said they issue press releases on broad research concepts, as opposed to specific unapproved products.

Twenty-five of the companies surveyed communicate research and development news via their regular company newsletters, and a few of them sometimes run special multi-part series dedicated to research. Eight of the companies have research and development newsletters and magazines that contain research status reports on products in the research pipeline; information about specific drug/research areas; scientist profiles; articles written by scientists; and news about scientific awards, promotions, etc. Most of these publications are prepared by specialized in-house research and development communications departments.

To encourage prevalence of a "pro-research" environment, some companies arrange scientific lecture programs, whereby company scientists (and, sometimes, outside scientists as well) make presentations to employees, during normal work hours, regarding specific areas of research. Seven of the companies in Schering Plough's survey that have such programs reported that they have been successful in boosting morale among employees while fostering a better understanding of where the company is headed in terms of research and development and products in the pipeline.

One company in the survey holds periodic luncheons for groups of company researchers to discuss with research executive management research projects, strategies, issues, etc.; and another holds luncheons to honor recipients of scientific awards. Seven of the companies polled said they encourage their scientists to publish their research papers.

Eight companies have a scientific honors program that rewards scientists for outstanding achievements in the field of research. Such scientific awards and achievements are usually recognized with internal publicity (e.g., company newsletters and bulletins) and external publicity (press releases).

As a novel approach to handling scientific recognition, one company acknowledges scientists who have participated in the development of an approved product in a commemorative booklet about the product.

As revealed by respondents' telephone survey comments, a company's public relations function not only must supply reliable, useful information about products, markets and technologies to its employees, the public and investment community, but must also help bridge the communication gap between scientists and the media by bringing scientists and journalists together to discuss current scientific issues. Special media/scientific referral services have been designed for the purpose, as well as periodic media roundtable discussions and publications.[13]

According to the Scientists' Institute for Public Information, the media normally favor stories that emphasize the end products of science—the practical results, the new techniques, surprising phenomena—rather than the process by which science develops. Yet, in order to make intelligent decisions concerning science, the public needs to know something about the process by which it advances; i.e., the fumbling trial-and-error, the logical way in which a scientist devises tests to choose between alternative hypotheses, the long chain of small advances gradually leading to new understanding, and the unexpected discoveries.

Schering-Plough's telephone survey showed that, to maintain a healthy relationship with the media, three of the companies surveyed by Schering-Plough have adopted the practice of keeping key media contacts (e.g., science writers/health editors) informed, on a regular basis, about progress in various areas of research. One company's approach to prompting media interest is to arrange medical writers' seminars to educate the media about particular therapy areas of interest, with reference to relevant company products. Other companies sponsor their own symposia, to which the media are often invited.

Such a dialogue serves to address the concern of elevating public understanding and support of science and technology.

In an attempt to quantify respondents' input from Schering-Plough's multi-company R&D communications survey, a programs matrix (see Appendix A) has been devised to reveal corporations' most prevalent current activities. Examination of the matrix reveals that 60 percent of the firms called publicize scientific achievement in some way. In terms of the number of different corporate activities pursued (11 categories; 128 programs), the mean score was 12; the median was 9; and the mode P.R. activity, 25, [which] involved R&D-related stories in a company newsletter.

It should be emphasized that this was an unscientific and informal "pilot" study. As the Schering-Plough interviewer Shirley Boyden Maxwell learned during the course of the telephone interviews of additional types of R&D activities, they were added as survey subjects during each succeeding phone interview. Therefore, total corporate R&D activities may be somewhat higher than the matrix reports. What would appear to be important about this informal survey, though, are: (1) The broad spectrum of R&D communications activities being undertaken by corporations and (2) the weighted trends that emerge from even this unscientific polling.

While some companies promote their research and development efforts more actively than others, they all share an acute awareness of technology's impact and the recognition that making technology's complex messages clear is vital to scientific progress. Only with the positive communication of goals, products and programs will companies be able to usher in a new pro-research era.

CONCLUSION

From gene-splicing in laboratories to artificial intelligence in computers, technology-oriented companies must have two-way communication with a broad public, from Wall Street to Washington to Main Street. Whether a small start-up concern or an established corporation, firms are looking to media and investor relations to help carve out product niches, attract funding, and win general public approval.[14]

The public's greater awareness of technology's impact and value, along with technology's high visibility among educated audiences, puts a premium on effective communication. In essence, a company that can't communicate its mission to a reporter, an analyst, or a consumer will see the impact on the bottom line.[15]

In dealing with the expectations, fears, and demands of the industry's various constituencies, the corporate public relations function must help orchestrate these sometimes disparate and sometimes conflicting interests into a congruent corporate rationale for action. This requires mastering the fundamentals and the language of the new technologies to interact effectively with, understand, and address each constituency's needs. Public relations then must develop new channels of communication—both outside and inside the company—to bring management in more direct positive contact with the scientist, the layperson, the investor, the reporter, and all other parties.

To face the future with confidence, it must be recognized that progress does not come at the hands of the business manager, nor does it occur in the laboratory of the so-called "mad scientist." Only those who interact, who communicate, who understand each other's needs, and who rely on the free exchange of ideas will turn the scientific revolution into substantial progress and change that will benefit all.

NOTES

1. Pharmaceutical Manufacturers Association, *Modern Medicines: The Case for the Pharmaceutical Industry* (Washington, D.C., 1992), 1.

2. Ibid, 4, 5.

3. Dorothy Nelkin, *Selling Science: How the Press Covers Science and Technology* (New York, N.Y.: W. H. Freeman and Company, 1987), 2.

4. Sheldon G. Gilgore, M.D., Chairman, Pres., & CEO, G. D. Searle & Co., "A Time of Challenge: A Time of Change" (remarks delivered before the Pharmaceutical Advertising Council, New York City, February 19, 1987).

5. Definition formulated by the editors of *Public Relations News*, New York, N.Y.

6. Neal E. Carter, Vice President, Battelle Memorial Institute and Director, Columbus Division, "The Political Side of Science" (remarks delivered before the Town Hall of California, Los Angeles, Calif., April 22, 1986, reprinted in *Vital Speeches of the Day*, July 1, 1986, 558).

7. Ibid.

8. Ibid.

9. Dr. Roland W. Schmitt, Senior Vice President, Corporate R&D, General Electric Company, "R&D in a Competitive Era" (extracted remarks, reprinted in *The Executive Speaker*, January 1987).

10. Batelle Medical Technology and Policy Research Center, *The Value of Pharmaceuticals: A Study of Selected Conditions to Measure the Contribution of Pharmaceuticals to Health Status* (Washington, D.C., 1990).

11. Battelle Medical Technology Assessment and Policy Research Center, *The Value of Pharmaceuticals: An Assessment of Future Costs for Selected Conditions* (Washington, D.C., 1991).

12. Schering-Plough Corporation, "Research and Development Communications" (unpublished telephone survey of corporate communications/public and media relations departments within 42 research-based, high-tech companies, 35 of which are pharmaceutical companies/subsidiaries; survey conducted by Schering-Plough's Corporate Communications Department, July–August 1987; companies included in survey: Abbott Laboratories, Allied Signal, American Cyanamid, AT&T/Bell Labs., C. R. Bard, Becton Dickinson, Beecham Laboratories, BOC Group, Inc., Bristol-Meyers, Burroughs-Wellcome Co., Carter-Wallace, Inc., Ciba-Geigy Corporation, Forest Laboratories, Genentech, General Electric Co., Glaxo, Inc., Hewlett-Packard, Hoechst-Celanese Corp., Hoffman-La Roche, IBM, ICN Pharmaceuticals, ITT, Johnson & Johnson, Eli Lilly and Company, Marion Laboratories, Merck & Co., Merrell Dow Pharm., Inc., Miles Laboratories (Bayer), Monsanto, Mylan Laboratories, Pfizer, Inc., Proctor & Gamble Co., Sandoz Pharm., Corp., Searle Pharm. (Monsanto), SmithKline Beecham Corp., Squibb Corp., Sterling Drug, Inc., Stuart Pharmaceuticals, Syntex Corp., Upjohn, Warner-Lambert, Wyeth Labs (Am. Home Prod.).

13. Neal E. Miller, D.Sc., Ph.D., *The Scientist's Responsibility for Public Information: A Guide to Effective Communication with the Media* (New York, N.Y.: The Media Resource Service of the Scientists' Institute for Public Information), 18.

14. Mark Forster, "Breaking the Technology Barrier," *Public Relations Journal* (July 1986), 10.

15. Ibid., 12.

APPENDIX A

Schering-Plough Corporation's R&D Communications Survey

[Forty-two companies surveyed include: Abbott Laboratories, Allied Signal, American Cyanamid, AT&T/Bell Labs., C. R. Bard, Becton Dickinson, Beecham Laboratories, BOC Group, Inc., Bristol-Meyers, Burroughs-Wellcome Co., Carter-Wallace, Inc., Ciba-Geigy Corporation, Forest Laboratories, Genentech, General Electric Co., Glaxo, Inc., Hewlett-Packard, HoechstCelanese Corp., Hoffman-La Roche, IBM, ICN Pharmaceuticals, ITT, Johnson & Johnson, Eli Lilly and Company, Marion Laboratories, Merck & Co., Merrell Dow Pharm., Inc., Miles Laboratories (Bayer), Monsanto, Mylan Laboratories, Pfizer, Inc., Proctor & Gamble Co., Sandoz Pharm., Corp., Searle Pharm. (Monsanto), SmithKline Beecham Corp., Squibb Corp., Sterling Drug, Inc., Stuart Pharmaceuticals, Syntex Corp., Upjohn, Warner-Lambert, Wyeth Labs (Am. Home Prod.)]

R&D PROMOTIONAL ACTIVITY	Number of Companies Participating
• Press Release (R&D-Pre-approved Products/ Scientific Advances)	15
• Press Release (Scientific News of General Interest with only Peripheral Tie to Company Products)	3
• R&D Brochure	9
• R&D Magazine/Newsletter	8
• R&D Featured in Company Newsletter	25
• R&D Featured in Company Video	3
• R&D Featured in Annual Report	20
• Scientific Honors Group	8
• Publicize Scientific Achievement	21
• Symposia/Seminars	9
• Lecture Program	7

Crime, Business Ethics, and Corporate Communication

Vaughana Macy Feary

CRIME, BUSINESS, AND SOCIETY
THE SCOPE AND MAGNITUDE OF THE PROBLEM

Crime is an increasingly serious problem in, and for, American business. There has been an upsurge of violence in the workplace. Fifteen percent of workplace deaths among men and 40% of workplace deaths among women are due to murder. A government study suggested that the difference in the percentages was attributable to the dangers confronted by the large number of women who work at night. As of 1989, occupational crimes defined as crimes which involve "offenses committed by individuals, for themselves, in the course of their occupations and the offenses of employees against their employers" were increasing (Croal 1992, 11). In 1990, companies found that such crimes might account for as much as 2% percent of their annual sales, a staggering $40 billion annually. As of 1989, white collar crime (crime encompassing both organizational and corporate crime), which includes everything from simple pilferage to fraud and embezzlement, was increasing at the alarming rate of 15% a year and was estimated to account for 30% of business failures. At least half of such crime consisted of pilferage (Leipzig 1992, 305).

Drug and alcohol offenses are also serious problems in the American workplace. According to Mathea Falco (1992):

This commentary by Dr. Feary, of Fairleigh Dickinson University, appeared in the *Proceedings of the Seventh Conference on Corporate Communication*, May 1994. It appears here with her permission.

Two-thirds of all adults who used illegal drugs in 1991 were employed, a total of about 15.6 million people. The National Institute of Drug Abuse (NIDA) estimates that 10% of the work force is drug addicted or alcoholic. Illegal drug use varies by industry, ranging from 13% in transportation, and 14% in retail to 22% in construction. . . . . The costs of drug use in the workplace including lost productivity, absenteeism, accidents, medical claims, and thefts amount to $60 billion a year. (91–92)

Corporate crime, defined as "illegal corporate behavior, which is a form of collective rule breaking in order to achieve the organizational goals," is also increasing (Croal, 11). This type of crime involves socially injurious acts, which cause financial, physical, or environmental harm; it is committed by corporations and businesses against workers, consumers, the environment, the general public, and government(s). Two-thirds of the companies on the Fortune 500 list have been found guilty of corporate crimes (Leipzig, 305). Amitai Etzioni (1993) reports that criminal fraud was discovered in 60% of the savings institutions seized by the government in 1989, and that a study of 600 of the largest U.S. publicly owned wholesale, retail, and service corporations with annual sales of $300 million or more found that over 60% had at least one enforcement action taken against them. More than 40% had engaged in repeat violations, but the conviction rate was well below one percent (Etizioni, 153–54). An earlier 1983 study had found, in examining adverse legal decisions against 70 of America's largest corporations, that as many as 98 percent were recidivists (Frank and Lynch 1992, 118). Etzioni also reports that the U.S. Sentencing Commission collected data which showed that in large publicly owned firms 25 percent of the time a top executive knew of the criminal activity, while in 34 percent of the cases a manager knew of it (156).

Crime is not only a major problem in American business, it is also a problem for American business. It can be argued that the health of American business depends upon the economic health of the society within which it operates. A cover story in *Business Week* (December 13, 1993) estimates that rampant crime costs America $425 billion a year. In 1990, annual spending for maintaining state and federal correctional facilities reached $11.4 billion. At a time when most major corporations are downsizing, and most new jobs are provided by small business, such expenditures drain the pool of state resources available for small business loans and consume a major portion of the corporate tax dollar. Furthermore, the new U.S. Sentencing Guidelines make it very apparent that the decade of greed during the 1980s is over, and that an effort is well underway to initiate a decade of retribution for those corporations which have made no effort to reduce corporate crime during the 1990s.

BUSINESS RESPONDS TO CRIME IN THE EARLY 1990S

In response to the staggering costs of crime for American business, one might have expected the business community to launch a sustained, multi-faceted attack on crime comparable to the campaign business and the Centers for Disease Control (CDC), have initiated against AIDS in the workplace. Unfortunately, however, for the most part, current corporate communication about crime seems largely confined to the sort of communication which is designed to preclude lawsuits or to reduce corporate liability under existing sentencing guidelines. The focus is on corporate crime, rather than on crime per se.

Demonstrating the existence of "an effective" compliance program to the courts is not simply a matter of producing a written code. Rather the four mitigating conditions are integral parts of an "effective" compliance program.

First, the organization must have policies defining the standards, rules, and procedures to be followed by its employees. Second, the organization must communicate its policies effectively to employees, for example, by training programs and publications. Third, the organization must use due diligence to ensure that its policies are complied with, for example, by utilizing a monitoring system reasonably designed to ferret out criminal conduct by its employees and by having in place and publicizing to employees a reporting system whereby employees can report criminal conduct within the organization without fear of retribution. Fourth, the polices must be enforced, for example, through disciplinary mechanisms.

The first two components of an effective compliance program deserve comment because they have radically transformed traditional conceptions of business ethics.

The first requirement of an effective compliance code accounts for the current emphasis on corporate codes among so-called business ethics consultants. As a result of their advice, undoubtedly communication specialists will be devoting a great deal of time to drafting, revising, and communicating corporate codes.

Certainly, corporate codes are important. An adequate corporate code demonstrates both the commitment of the CEO to a set of values and greater professionalism and accountability on the part of management. A corporate code also seems to afford some protection against improper employee conduct, especially in cases where there is reason to suspect that misappropriation of funds, conflict of interest, improper gifts, or theft of proprietary material may become serious problems. Changes in corporate structure and culture as the result of downsizing, mergers, and acquisitions, as well as changing laws or social standards, also suggest that codes may be necessary to incorporate ethical considerations into decision making at all levels under changing conditions (Berenbeim 1993, 1–8).

Codes usually address three areas of concern: the corporate mission, constituency relations, and corporate policies and practices. Adequately formulated, they may provide some minimal basis for making decisions in cases where there is genuine moral uncertainty or serve to redirect muddled value assessments in cases where managers know what constitutes ethical conduct in a given situation, but fail to do the right thing because of trying to meet performance objectives. An adequate code must take into account the particularities of the specific corporate culture for which the code is formulated, a culture shaped by a specific history, specific industry practices and standards, specific regulatory challenges, and specific past problems and legal challenges. Then, and only then, is a code at all likely to deter criminal conduct and thus constitute a truly effective compliance code (7,16).

Subjects addressed by codes include: (1) equity—considerations of fairness vis-à-vis salary or price; (2) rights—justifiable claims of employees, customers, and suppliers under various circumstances, such as health screening, sexual harassment, whistle-blowing, etc.; (3) honesty—matters concerning conflicts of interest, conflicts between company ethics, and common practice in foreign countries, gifts, advertising, etc.; (4) social responsibility—matters concerning plant closures, environmental and product safety, corporate philanthropy, etc. (17–19).

Finally, while in the past, codes were usually couched in affirmative language, an effective compliance program involves sanctions for improper conduct. As a result, an effective code must now include some specific enforcement language (Berenbeim, 22).

The second component of an effective compliance program consists of communicating the code through compliance and ethics training and through disseminating publications about the compliance code couched in language easily understood by employees. The specifics and methodologies of compliance training need not detain us here. Suffice it to say that the goal of compliance training is to provide employees with specific information about laws, regulations, and policies which affect their work lives or about sources from which they can obtain such information. The objective of such training is to deter crime through teaching employees to clearly distinguish between lawful and unlawful conduct and through teaching employees to understand the importance of compliance for both the company and the individual desirous of avoiding legal penalties.

According to Mazur (1993), there are three general approaches to ethics training which are compatible with the objective of demonstrating the existence of an effective compliance program. The first is rule-based ethics training in which "employees are informed of and asked to understand their responsibilities for a variety of rules and regulations that, more so than compliance, specifically address what are traditionally considered ethical issues." The second approach is "ethics awareness" training which involves introducing "ethical concepts" to employees and also making them aware of the organizational support available for their newfound sensitivities such as ombudspersons, ethics officers, values statements, open-door policies, and ethics hotlines. The third approach, and presumably the best, according to Mazur, is the "grander" Systems Approach to Managing Values (SAMV) developed by Kirk Hanson of Stanford University and The Business Enterprise Trust. This approach consists of a suggested seven-step process for creating "an ethical work environment," which includes:

1. Clarifying organizational values—integrity, customer satisfaction;

2. Communicating values and principles through management speeches, training sessions, and stories—an example of a "principle" is "We hold ourselves accountable for the quality of all the work we produce";

3. Designing systems to support values and principles—credos, value-driven performance evaluations, etc., must be consistent with values and principles;

4. Applying values to decisions at each level of the corporation;

5. Setting up systems to monitor, audit, and impose sanctions;

6. Establishing procedures for resolving difficult cases and for learning from mistakes;

7. Setting up periodic feedback loops so that values and principles can be renewed and reinforced. (45–47)

Communicating about issues of ethical concern such as privacy, sexual harassment, discrimination, freedom of commercial speech, AIDS in the workplace—in terms of normative ethical theory—is rapidly giving way to communicating about such issues in terms of corporate codes. Communicating about ethics has become little more than training employees in the values of specific corporate cultures. Business Ethics has been effectively separated from its traditional philosophical base, and communication about ethics now seems to amount to little more than conversations between business practitioners.

CRIME, BUSINESS ETHICS, AND CORPORATE COMMUNICATION
RECOMMENDATIONS FOR CHANGE

There are at least four major reasons why the current popularization of Business Ethics is a mistake. First, the 1991 Sentencing Guidelines are not engraved on a stone tablet; they can and probably will be further revised. Second, laws are not written in stone. They also can be, and probably will be, radically revised. Third, the confidence that business practitioners display in the idea that creating an ethical environment is largely a matter of rearranging flow charts is wholly misplaced. Fourth, even if there were good empirical evidence to support the assumption that current compliance and ethics codes would reduce crime in business, such an approach leaves most of the problems crime causes for business wholly untouched. Each of these points deserves brief comment.

As William W. Wilkins Jr., chairman of the U.S. Sentencing Commission, notes, guidelines are not "set in stone." The Sentencing Reform Act (SRA) established the Commission as a permanent agency charged with the ongoing task of eliminating sentencing disparities and recommending amendments on the basis of advice from the criminal justice sector. Although members of the Commission shared a basic philosophy, enunciated in the introductory commentary of the 1990 draft, which holds that corporations should be provided with incentives for self-regulation because organizations are in a better position to detect and deter crime within their own ranks than any outside enforcement agency, there was considerable skepticism about the effectiveness of compliance programs in achieving these objectives. Judge MacKinnon, for example, cited numerous cases in which corporations with compliance programs had committed crimes, and he argued that compliance programs should not be weighted heavily in assessing culpability scores (Clark 1993, 33). Chairman Wilkins also makes it very clear that compliance programs will not continue to reduce corporate liability if good empirical evidence emerges which show that they are not serving to increase detection and prevention of corporate crime. Still another indication that compliance programs may be weighted less heavily in reducing culpability scores is the fact that they carry already vastly diminished weight in anti-trust and environmental cases.

More significantly, there are deep philosophical problems with current sentencing guidelines. One motive for the new guidelines was to eliminate gross sentencing disparities. Another motive was to give recognition to good corporate citizenship. The eventual importance attributed to compliance codes in determining corporate culpability scores was justified by considerations about the alleged unfairness of the rule of vicarious criminal responsibility (respondeat superior) under which even corporations, which are good corporate citizens, could be held liable for the actions of lower level employees, even when those employees acted against express corporate policy and against explicit instructions (Perry and Dakin 1993, 1–2). The problem with this line of argument is that it introduces considerations of equity and fairness; such arguments are an open invitation to compare sentencing guidelines determining individual criminal liability with those determining corporate liability. Business ethicists, who are business practitioners rather than philosophers, blandly assume that, given the differences between corporations and real persons, different sentencing guidelines are justifiable. This assumption has no basis, however, because the real issue is whether the differences between corporations and people are the sorts of morally relevant differences which justify differences in treatment.

One could argue that, from the legal perspective, corporations are very much like people. Certainly, with respect to First Amendment rights (freedom of commercial speech), the Court seems to be moving in the direction of holding that corporations are sufficiently like people to be accorded the same rights. To accord corporations the rights of persons but to exempt them from the responsibilities of persons seems contradictory and self-serving.

Retribution for individuals convicted of street crime, but utilitarianism for corporations and individuals convicted of suite crime, seems not only contradictory but unjust. If indeed sentencing guidelines should be based upon considerations about what is likely to deter crime, as the Commission seems to have concluded, then presumably individual sentencing guidelines should follow the same approach, but the punishment accorded offenders convicted on drug charges, for example, is based on retribution rather than deterrence; drug addicts are sentenced to prisons under mandatory minimums, not to in-patient substance abuse centers, and they are not regarded as any less culpable if they can demonstrate that they have tried to be "good citizens" by getting treatment for their addictions in the past. By contrast, white collar criminals are less frequently incarcerated and more frequently paroled or assigned community service.

Suffice it to say here that radical differences in treatment resulting from our present dual approach to sentencing can only result in disparities which will ultimately be regarded as unjust by the general public. Suite crime does more damage than street crime. There are no morally relevant differences between suite crime and street crime. People incarcerated for street crime are racial and ethnic minorities; they are suffering from inequalities in sentencing which are ultimately attributable to inequalities in wealth and power. The general public is in a "tough on crime" mood, inimical to big business, and increasingly angry over seeing white collar criminals get light sentences (Braithwaite and Pettit 1990, 186–89).

The attenuated version of ethics training currently being promoted by business practitioners is unlikely to promote the ethical workplace the business community wants to promote. Whether virtue can be taught, and how it is to be taught, is a philosophical issue as old as Plato and as new as the numerous new studies of moral education and moral responsibility. The most widely recognized psychological theory of moral development associated with Lawrence Kohlberg (1971) is based upon a philosophical conception of morality. The most serious challenge to Kohlberg is Carol Gilligan's (1982) theory, which is interwoven with feminist philosophical traditions. Of course, corporate credos are useful! Of course, ethics should be institutionalized! The attempt to substitute Johnson and Johnson's credo, however useful, for moral theory, and to reduce moral development to a set of corporate values, is to mistakenly assume that organizationally necessary requirements for creating an ethical corporate climate are sufficient to the task.

Mazur mentions two troublesome cases. The first case involves complex ethical issues about which managers are genuinely perplexed (as in studies of privacy at IBM). Such issues must be considered in terms of philosophical theories. The second case is when an employee knows the right thing to do, but fails to do so because of wishing to comply with performance objectives (as in the recent Sears scandal). Obviously, institutionalizing ethics can be helpful in these cases, but, at best, the kind of ethics training suggested by Mazur can promote only the lower stages of moral reasoning and may not be effective with women for whom an emphasis on caring as opposed to principles may be more effective. Furthermore, a great deal of occupational crime, such as pilferage, may be attributable to deficiencies in critical reasoning skills. People who do poor consequential reasoning or exhibit cognitive rigidity frequently commit such crimes, and there is impressive empirical evidence that programs based upon Kohlberg's and Edward De Bono's theory of critical reasoning can reduce recidivism by as much as 76% (Ross and Fabriano 1985, 73). In the case of upper management, one would expect that some minimal education in philosophical theory (provided by a philosophically based Business Ethics class required by most universities) would enhance ethical sensitivity and promote the kind of autonomy so lacking in Mazur's second case.

Finally, the attenuated version of business ethics now being promoted by business practitioners will do nothing to alleviate the major costs of crime for American business. Many criminal offenders are unemployed when they commit crimes. According to a Report to the Nation on Crime and Justice (2nd ed., Washington, D.C.: USGPO 49), forty-five percent of all males in 1983 were unemployed at the time they entered jail. Fifty percent had annual incomes under $5,600; the crimes committed by the unemployed probably, indirectly, cost American business billions of dollars each year. Recidivism rates are high, in part, because ex-inmates can seldom find jobs. Frequently, telling their employers the truth is made a condition of parole, but if ex-offenders tell the truth, employers will find excuses not to hire them. If they lie, they are later exposed, fired, and in violation of parole.

The solution to the problem of recidivism lies in promoting individual and social responsibility. Offenders need rehabilitative programs, including programs which improve their moral and critical reasoning, while they are incarcerated. Corporations, like other social institutions, must play a role in funding them. Offenders also need tutors and mentors from the business community to teach them to relinquish the expectations of an essentially socialist system of prison, a system in which all decisions are made for them, and all essentials—food, clothing, and shelter—are provided for them. Finally, on release, ex-offenders need jobs and support systems which are currently unavailable. The current emphasis on effective compliance programs can only reduce the willingness of the business community to hire ex-offenders or to demonstrate social responsibility in support of rehabilitative efforts. As a consequence, recent approaches to business ethics will probably contribute more to perpetuating the costly cycle of crime and recidivism than it will to reducing it.

CONCLUSION

Part of resolving the problem of crime in and for American business involves communicating about both crime and ethics. The messages of today's communication specialists about compliance and corporate codes are necessary, but they are only a part of the messages which should be sent through the business community. Corporate criminal liability is only a small part of the total cost of crime, just as compliance and corporate codes are only a very small part of business ethics.

REFERENCES

Berenbeim, Ronald E. "Codes of Conduct." In *Compliance Programs and the Corporate Sentencing Guidelines, Preventing Criminal and Civil Liability*, New York: Clark Borardman Callaghan, 1993.

Braithwaite, John, and Philip Pettit. *Not Just Deserts, a Republican Theory of Criminal Justice*. Oxford: Oxford University Press, 1990.

Clark, Nolan Ezra. "Corporate Sentencing Guidelines: Drafting History." In *Compliance Programs and the Corporate Sentencing Guidelines*, 1993.

Croal, Hazel. *White Collar Crime, Criminal Justice and Criminology*. Philadelphia: Open Court Press, 1992.

Etzioni, Amitai. "The U.S. Sentencing Commission on Corporate Crime: A Critique." *White Collar Crime: The Annals of the American Academy of Political and Social Sciences*. London: Sage Periodical Press, 1993.

Falco, Mathea. *The Making of a Drug Free America, Programs That Work*. New York: Random House, 1992.

Frank, Nancy K., and Michael J. Lynch. *Corporate Crime, Corporate Violence*. New York: Harrow and Heston, 1992.

Frey , R. G., and Christopher W. Morris. *Liability and Responsibility: Essays in Law and Morals*. Cambridge: Cambridge University Press, 1991.

Gilligan, Carol. *In A Different Voice, Psychological Theory and Women's Development*. Cambridge, Mass.: Harvard University Press, 1982.

Hills, Stuart, ed. *Corporate Violence, Injury and Death for Profit*. Savage, Maryland: Rowman and Littlefield, 1987.

Kaplan, Jeffrey M. "Corporate Sentencing Guidelines: Overview." In *Compliance Programs and the Corporate Sentencing Guidelines*, 1993.

Kaplan, Jeffrey M., Joseph Murphy, and Swenson Swenson. *Compliance Programs and the Corporate Sentencing Guidelines*, 1993.

Kohlberg, Lawrence. "From Is to Ought: How to Commit the Naturalistic Fallacy and Get Away with It in the Study of Moral Development." *Cognitive Development and Epistemology*. New York: Academic Press, 1971.

Leipzig, John S. "Ethical Dilemmas Related to Perceptions of Corporate Message Inconsistency." In *Communication in Uncertain Times, Proceedings: The Fifth Conference on Corporate Communication*. Madison, N.J.: Fairleigh Dickinson University, 1992.

Mazur, Timothy C. "Training." In *Compliance Programs and Corporate Sentencing Guidelines*, 1993.

Perry, William K., and Linda S. Dakin. "Compliance Programs and Criminal Law." In *Compliance Programs and Corporate Sentencing Guidelines*, 1993.

Ross, Robert R., and Elizabeth Fabriano. *Time to Think, A Cognitive Model of Delinquency Prevention and Offender Rehabilitation*. Johnson City, Tenn.: Institute of Social Sciences and Arts, Inc., 1985.

Steer, John R. "Sentencing Guidelines: In General." In *Compliance Programs and the Corporate Sentencing Guidelines*, 1993.

Swenson, Winthrop M. "An Effective Program to Prevent and Detect Violations of Law." In *Compliance Programs and Corporate Sentencing Guidelines*, 1993.

Wheeler, Stanton, Kenneth Mann, and Austin Sarat. *Sitting in Judgment, The Sentencing of White Collar Criminals*. New Haven, Conn.: Yale University Press, 1988.

Wilkins Jr., William W. *Compliance Programs and Corporate Sentencing Guidelines*, 1993.

6

Corporate Communication and Meeting the Press

You've had a very productive day at your office in the corporation's headquarters of an internationally known maker of low-fat additives for the prepared food industry, and you are leaving for the day.

As you unlock your car in the parking lot you are approached in a nonthreatening way by an individual who says she represents the local newspaper. She has some concerns about the report she received over the wire service, and which she heard repeated that afternoon on CNN, about a research laboratory in Sweden that has found a link between no-fat oil substitutes and heart disease in its latest experiments on rats.

What do you do?

How you respond in such a hypothetical situation has a lot to do with corporate identity and corporate culture, the issues covered in the previous chapters. These two forces will guide you to the action you take, no matter what the experts say is the best way to handle relations with the press.

If your corporate culture says your day ends when you leave your desk, you might shrug and say you are going home for the day, offering to see the reporter about the issue tomorrow. The reporter of course has a deadline and knows that tomorrow will be too late. The other paper in town will have had the story and some comment from the company by then. You meant not to be a block, but the reporter certainly considers you one, or at best a non-source for the story. Frustrated, she is determined to find out what you are hiding.

On the other hand, if your company has made a point of creating a professional and productive relationship with the press, you might look up a bit puzzled and say you have been buried all day in an industry analysis report. Nevertheless, you ask the reporter to follow you back to your office. There you place a few calls—to the R&D department and to the public affairs officer to see if the reporter can go to the lab and ask a few questions related to the news wire report and the CNN broadcast.

In the second instance, your organization is seen by the press as a source of information and expertise on the topic. Your company becomes a part of the solution, not the problem.

Creating such good relations with the media requires constant effort and attention.

MEETING THE PRESS
GENERAL CRITERIA

Having a sound, mature corporate attitude toward the public and the media is of primary importance.

The contemporary business environment is awash with media—newspapers, magazines, professional and industrial journals, TV, business radio, multimedia, the Internet and the World Wide Web. Corporations spend millions of dollars on marketing and advertising so their message can reach their current and potential customers.

If the press views a corporation's product or service as news, it will write or broadcast a story. Many organizations measure media coverage in terms of the equivalent cost to purchase space in the newspaper or air time on TV or radio. Such coverage is almost universally the goal of any media relations plan. Media relations is now a routine part of an organization's strategic planning.

In spite of this, some corporations still cling to the notion that the less that is communicated to the press the better. Their non-press relations policy creates an unnecessary barrier with representatives of the media. So in the event that a corporation or the industry of which it is part makes headlines, the company with poor or no contacts with the press is likely to see itself described in inaccurate or negative terms.

Good relations with the press often results in the reporter checking with the corporation to validate statements and facts. This contact affords the opportunity to set the record straight, or put the facts into a clearer, more objective context. Rumors and inaccuracies can be corrected.

It also is important to prepare wisely for a press interview. Take the same care in preparing to meet the press as you would with an advertising or a marketing campaign.

MEETING THE PRESS
SOME GUIDELINES

The suggested actions that follow comprise some guidelines for meeting the press that are most often cited by scholars and practitioners.

1. *Be prepared.* Make sure you have all the facts you need. In an information society such as ours, having accurate data and timely statistics is expected. Not only are you giving your valuable time to discuss issues and events with the press, but their time is valuable as well, so do your homework.

2. *Make your points.* Have three main points you wish to get across. Just as you would in an executive summary of a report, or in a marketing communication, identify clearly the main ideas that make up the message you want communicated.

3. *Be concise—but avoid yes and no answers.* Show you are aware of the space and time limitations of the media by presenting your position clearly and concisely. Even though brevity is a virtue, the press also looks for interest, so yes and no answers often make the story difficult to write and uninteresting for TV or radio.

4. *Get comfortable.* Remember that your body movements and eye contact also communicate on a nonverbal level. When meeting face-to-face with the media, prepare for the discussion by making sure you will not be interrupted by phone calls or colleagues. It is a good idea to meet in a conference room or lounge set aside for outside guests. Comfortable chairs, availability of refreshments, and a quiet, professional environment allow for a comfortable meeting.

5. *Tell the truth.* Building credibility with the media begins with their perception of you as a source of accurate and truthful information. Integrity is a valuable attribute and one that is difficult to attain but quick to disappear at the first sign of deception.

6. *Use the printed word.* Be prepared for any press encounter with a printed statement or press release to help reporters get their facts straight—figures, statistics, the spelling and titles of people mentioned. Remember, the reporter's job is to report the facts, and getting accurate information often includes complex and detailed data.

7. *Keep your composure.* The media must also sell newspapers or attract viewers to sell advertising. Such pressure often translates into the search for an unusual or a controversial angle. Journalists call this the "hook," the means to capture the audience's attention. So you might be confronted with offbeat, even offensive questions in an effort to elicit an emotional reaction that would make a good headline. Be cool under pressure.

8. *Be yourself.* People react positively to people they perceive as genuine. Being yourself is linked with telling the truth and is another part of building corporate integrity. Of course, ignore this advice if you are a grumpy introvert who hates being around others.

9. *Think of the reader or viewer.* In the first part of this book (see chapter 2) the importance of considering the audience in any communication was discussed. When in a press interview, think of how your responses would appear on the front page of the *New York Times* or the *Wall Street Journal*, or on the local TV news at 6 P.M. or the national news that follows.

10. *Forget "off the record."* If you do not want something to appear in print, or to be broadcast, do not say it in the first place.

11. *Avoid repeating loaded questions.* A loaded question can be a trap to put words into your mouth. Use your own words, or ask the reporter to rephrase the question.

12. *"Stopped beating your wife?"* Often reporters will ask an outrageous question just to get your response. Respond professionally rather than emotionally. React calmly and avoid a personal confrontation with the reporter.

13. *Say you don't know.* When asked a question that stumps you, or requires information or data you do not have at hand, say you don't know. Follow up immediately with the way in which you plan to get the information and offer to contact the reporter later, preferably before his or her deadline.

14. *Assert company policy in response to thirdhand information.* If the reporter cannot identify the source of his or her information, politely decline to discuss rumor and hearsay because of your company's press policy.

15. *Be aware of leading or hypothetical questions.* In an effort to elicit a statement from you, a reporter might ask a question that leads you into speculation. Such questions are particularly common when corporate officers are asked to comment on possible mergers or acquisitions, anticipated layoffs or restructuring, or planned change efforts such as reengineering.

16. *Be sensitive to deadlines.* The daily production of newspapers and TV or radio broadcasts places strenuous demands on reporters to file their stories on time. It is a common courtesy to ask at the beginning of an interview what the reporter's deadline is. Time is a valuable commodity.

17. *Be accessible.* Give reporters a contact number, an E-mail address, and a fax machine number to indicate that you will be available for follow-up questions as the story is being written and later as a source for other stories.

18. *"No comment."* The response "no comment" is now almost universally interpreted by the press as a corporate ploy to hide something.

If you cannot talk about a proprietary issue or a matter that might have a personal impact on an employee, say so.

According to *Fortune* magazine (Stratford, 1989)

- make the CEO responsible for press relations

- face the facts

- consider the public interest in every operating decision

- be a source before you are a subject

- if you want your views represented, you must talk

- avoid TV unless you feel free to speak candidly

- respond quickly

- cage your lawyers

- tell the truth—or nothing

- be human

WALL STREET
THE FINANCIAL PRESS

What is the relationship of corporate communications and the company's bottom line? Most experts and practitioners have come to agree that good corporate communications can improve the company's financial position, keep managers out of trouble with the Securities Exchange Commission, and help protect against unfriendly takeover attempts.

Companies must communicate clearly their financial expectations and long-term outlook. Investors and investment analysts are interested in just such information in making a decision about investments for themselves and their clients.

Annual reports, 10-K and 10-Q reports, and quarterly reports are among the documents required by law for the SEC and the stock exchanges, and stockholders. These fundamental documents can be used to communicate the corporation's vision for the future, while providing the detailed financial analysis needed by stockholders, regulators, and the financial press.

The legal policy of "materiality" has evolved through regulatory changes and decisions. It requires that a publicly held company disclose all information that may have an impact on the profit or financial position of the organization. Such disclosures are done through information wire services—Dow Jones and Reuters.

Communication with individual investors and institutional investors such as pension plans and annuities is also done on a daily and periodic basis through the business and financial press. Relations with the financial press usually means the *Wall Street Journal*, *Business Week*, the *Financial Times*, *Barrons*, *Forbes*, and other periodicals devoted to general business news.

Firms invest a great deal of effort to develop positive relations with these media, so reporters and editors come to them for information about the company or the industry. Also, corporations place ads in these periodicals for a variety of reasons, from greeting a new corporate officer to setting the record straight for investors on issues and rumors about the company.

Placing articles that explain a corporation's position on a merger, acquisition, restructuring, or downsizing can have a positive impact on the image the company creates in the minds of the investor community. These management decisions reflect how well the organization manages change and the stress that accompanies it. A solid relationship with the press can benefit the organization through an objective report in the press.

MAIN STREET
THE HOMETOWN MEDIA

The newspapers and local radio and TV stations will cover your company for the local angle. If your organization has a substantial presence in the community, any slight change in the size of your national workforce or global strategy will make the front page on Main Street, U.S.A.

With this in mind, make sure the corporation's representatives in the community and the ones at the home office have had substantial contact with one another before the information is reported. Such conversation ensures consistency in information given to reporters. The implication is for careful planning. Good relations with the press are nurtured.

A local media strategy is just as important as a global one. A process approach can be applied locally as well as globally. The process follows a problem-solving model and is simple to remember.

First, define the problems or issues. Write the problem down as a statement and analyze the situation. The analysis requires research—the gathering, processing, and interpretation of information. The most fundamental research method is listening and observing. Many change programs are based on the dictum, "Listen to your customer," and your customer may be a fellow employee as well. Everyone you contact should be considered your customer.

Other research methods include

- Delphi groups (experts in the field)

- surveys

- interviews

- focus groups

- advisory committees and boards

- media content analysis

- analysis of incoming mail

- government or commercial poll results

Your interpretation of the information you gather helps you confirm the problem statement or restate it in light of your interpretations. The results of your analysis should lead to planning the next step in the problem-solving model.

Second, articulate goals and develop a program of actions and activities to achieve those goals. Planning consists of identifying the audiences or "publics," the goals for each, the message and media strategies determined to meet those goals, and the budget schedule and other resources that must be committed to the program. Planning also involves preparing for the evaluation of the performance of the program.

Third, implement the plans and communicate the messages. Here the fundamentals of the communication process offer the key to successful implementation of the plans. Understanding corporate goals, matching them with audience needs and expectations, and being mindful of the context in which the communication occurs applies here and in all communications efforts.

The objective is to change the thinking and behavior of the audience. To meet that goal, the audience

- becomes aware of the idea or message;

- becomes interested and seeks more information;

- evaluates the pros and cons of the idea and decides to try it;

- applies the idea on a trial basis;

- and, if the idea is acceptable, adopts it into normal behavior or practice.

Fourth, evaluate the process. The evaluation of the effectiveness of the program can vary from the number of column inches or the number of minutes on the air the effort generated to the increased awareness of the issues measured in the target audience to changes in attitudes, opinions, or behaviors to evidence of economic, social or political change. The criteria and evaluation methods must be determined as the program is planned and as it evolves.

PARK AVENUE
NATIONAL NEWSPAPERS

We have only a handful of national newspapers, that is, daily print media that claim reporting U.S. and world news as their mission. The *New York Times* and the *Washington Post*, and to a lesser degree the *Los Angeles Times*, consider themselves newspapers of record. They report any event of importance for the country and the world and generally make their reports available to the world through their wire services. The *Wall Street Journal* is included in the financial press, but it could easily be included in the general news category since business is involved in everything and its coverage of events is certainly global in scope.

These few national newspapers have enormous impact on public opinion and on general attitudes. The stories they run tend to set the agenda for other media, particularly television news programs and cable network programming. Even though broadcast media cover late-breaking stories very well, they are weak in business, economic, and financial news coverage.

Corporations of any size scan these newspapers every morning for stories and information. They create a company briefing book of the clips and circulate it among their officers, alerting them of any news related to the corporation, its products, the industries of which it is a part, or stories related to its core business strategy.

On-line technologies allow individuals within corporations to program software to call up articles in fields in which they are interested. The process is driven by a search for key words or names, in exactly the same way you might search an on-line database for information. In this way, finance and marketing professionals can obtain the stories related to their field of expertise.

How often do you see on TV news of trade negotiations such as the GATT (General Agreement on Tariffs and Trade) or the International Monetary Fund (IMF) discussions of loans to Russia. Even scandals such as insider trading and the S&L failures are often reduced to pictures of the defendants arriving at or leaving a courtroom or hearing.

However, it is the print media that still covers business in depth, with the exception of cable news programs devoted to business issues. Even *USA Today*, as a national newspaper, is more like a series of sound bites or headlines that you might see on CNN Headline News.

INDUSTRIAL BOULEVARD
THE TRADE PUBLICATIONS

Trade- and industry-specific newspapers and periodicals offer businesses a medium specific to their business. These publications are mainly closed circulation periodicals. That is, the people who receive the publications are involved in the industry in some way. Further, these publications have either paid or free subscriptions.

The free subscription periodicals are generally regarded as promotional vehicles for the industry or trade, providing advertisers with a controlled audience. Literally hundreds of magazines on electronic media, Internet access and marketing, and communication technologies now flood traditional and E-mail boxes in large and small companies. Changes in communications and in the process of marketing and advertising have fueled this outpouring of promotional material thinly presented as news and information.

The paid publications generally work with a clear journalistic separation between the editorial content of the reporting and the advertising department. Such publications are seen as being more objective, thus containing more reliable information. Examples include *Aviation Week and Space Technology* for the aerospace industry and *Publishers Weekly* for the book and magazine industry.

RESEARCH PLAZA
PROFESSIONAL JOURNALS

Professional journals have long been the main vehicle for the communication of research findings in every field. Their very existence and value depend on objective editorial policies. Most do not accept advertising because of a hint of bias.

Some however accept ads from professional organizations and groups for conferences, books, and other publications. This might include *Harvard Business Review* for general management theory, even though it runs ads for upscale automobiles and liquor.

The best way to develop relations with such publications is through general support of professional societies and organizations that in turn promote the publications. The accountants, lawyers, writers, journalists, psychologists, engineers, and scientists in your company can identify the journals in their field.

Support of a company professional in the preparation of an article for such a publication was considered to be of great value. However, as organizations reengineer and downsize, the long-term value of a corporation's support of the professional community of which it is part, through publication in professional journals, has taken a backseat to the bottom line. Such shortsightedness misses an economical long-term investment of the company's intellectual capital.

A long-term investment in the intellectual output of its professionals is certainly at the foundation of the success of Lucent Technologies, the corporation formed in 1996 as AT&T implemented its "trivestiture" plan. Lucent was the beneficiary of decades of research and techno-logical success at Bell Labs. As a totally new company, it was able to use its corporate identity equity from Bell Labs to create a similar identity for the new corporation.

BROADWAY
ENTERTAINMENT MEDIA

Social events related to charity functions are often the only time a corporation appears in the entertainment media, unless of course the corporation is part of the entertainment industry.

Corporations are often included in the entertainment media if they become sponsors of media events such as the local opera, Philharmonic, or Shakespearean company; nationally televised cultural events; or the Super Bowl, Olympics, or other sporting events.

Case Studies

The case studies selected for this chapter are based on graduate seminar case studies presented at Fairleigh Dickinson University in 1995 and 1996. The first graduate seminar looked into the unethical and illegal practices of a utility's vice president of corporate policy and external affairs. The case study presents the corporate document sent to shareholders and, by extension, the media. It represents a clear indication that decisive action was taken to face the past and usher in a new era for the future.

The second case study invloves an example of "Not in My Back Yard" (NIMBY) syndrome. It is a narrative of the difficulties a municipality encountered in its efforts to find an appropriate site for a jail.

The Case of the VP for External Communication

ORANGE AND ROCKLAND UTILITIES, INC. AND SUBSIDIARIES
SUMMARY OF THE REPORT OF THE SPECIAL COMMITTEE
OF THE BOARD OF DIRECTORS

Dear Shareholders:

During the past year, we have kept you informed about the activities of the Special Committee of the Board in its investigation in connection with the alleged criminal activities of James F. Smith, the company's former chairman and chief executive officer, and admitted criminal wrongdoing of a then-vice president and two former employees of the company.

It is unfortunate that the types of events occurred as these did. But once uncovered, the Board of Directors took immediate and effective action to investigate and correct the situation. The Special Committee of the Board—created almost from the first moment that allegations emerged—consisted entirely of outside directors and was delegated responsibility to conduct an independent investigation. Recognizing that the integrity of the corporation was at stake, the Special Committee's primary objective was to do whatever was necessary to determine all the facts and to recommend remedial measures to restore that integrity.

To ensure a full, thorough and impartial investigation, the Special Committee retained the law firm of Stier, Anderson & Malone, headed

---

This public record document was presented as part of the graduate seminar that looked into the unethical and illegal practices of a utility's vice president of corporate policy and external affairs.

by former federal and New Jersey state prosecutor Edwin Stier, and the accounting firm of Price Waterhouse & Co. The investigators examined over 200,000 pages of documents and over 60,000 expense transactions during the past year, and the Special Committee's conclusions were based on the investigatory work performed by these firms.

The guiding principles were to insure that the investigation be conducted fairly and with the utmost objectivity, to pay meticulous attention to detail and to apply uncompromising standards of integrity to the entire process.

The Special Committee has fulfilled its mission. It has done what it set out to do. With the public issuance of its report, Orange and Rockland has provided full disclosure as promised.

Our shareholders and our customers had been ill-served by a few individuals and by a system that permitted those individuals to operate. We truly regret the turmoil these events created over the past year, and we pledge that it will not happen again.

We now have all the facts. We know what went wrong. And we know how to fix it. We have already taken a number of concrete steps to control business expenses and to clearly define ethical standards. This Report, directly or by inference, may suggest the need for other changes in how we manage our business. If so, we will change.

As we put the events of the past year behind us, we look forward with enthusiasm, energy and confidence as we enter the new competitive era. Orange and Rockland is fundamentally a good company, with strong prospects for the future. We are confident that we are fully capable of providing shareholders with the value they demand and customers with the service they deserve.

[SIGNED BY]
Chairman of the Board
&
Vice Chairman and Chief Executive Officer
September 1994

SUMMARY OF THE REPORT OF THE
SPECIAL COMMITTEE OF THE BOARD OF DIRECTORS

The Special Committee of the Board of Directors of the corporation issued its final Report summarizing the findings and conclusions of its investigation on August 22, 1994.

The investigation concentrated on three principal problem areas

- The misconduct of James F. Smith, the company's former Chairman of the Board and Chief Executive Officer

- The misconduct of Linda Winikow, the company's former Vice President of Corporate Policy and External Affairs, and others in the corporation's Corporate Communications Department

- The subversion of the corporations' internal controls

The Special Committee has concluded that Mr. Smith and some other key officers undermined the corporation's internal control mechanisms, interfered with the corporation's internal audit procedures, and actively concealed information from the Board which would have brought the misconduct to light. As a result, Mr. Smith, Ms. Winikow, and others were able to systematically misuse and misappropriate corporation assets and resources and engage in certain other improper transactions.

JAMES F. SMITH

The Special Committee concluded that Mr. Smith abused his authority during his tenure as Chief Executive Officer by

- systematically engaging in the misappropriation of corporation funds and resources for his personal benefit;

- subverting the corporation's internal controls and violating many of its corporate policies;

- fostering and encouraging an environment in which there was pervasive evasion and abuse of internal controls and concealment thereof from the Audit Committee and the Board of Directors;

- failing to properly supervise, and encouraging misconduct by Ms. Winikow and other subordinate officers; and

- concealing information from the Board and its committees. The Special Committee concluded that, while some other officers were also at fault, Mr. Smith must be held ultimately responsible for the misconduct described in the Report, the loss of the corporation's credibility with its state utility commissions, and the other adverse consequences to the corporation which directly flowed from his failures to supervise properly the affairs of the company and its officers.

RESTRICTED DISBURSEMENT ACCOUNT

The investigation uncovered that, beginning in 1977, business expenses of Mr. Smith and other officers began being processed through a restricted disbursement account which was not subject to the corporation's normal accounting controls and beginning in 1982, the corporation's Internal Auditing Department was not effective in implementing the corporation's internal controls and preventing the misuse of the corporation's assets. The evidence obtained from the investigation indicated that for the period 1976 through 1993, an aggregate of approximately $402,842 of improper expense and an aggregate of approximately $1,340,279 in inadequately documented expenses were paid by the company through the restricted disbursement account.

COMMUNICATIONS DEPARTMENT

Ms. Winikow and others in the department engaged in various improper and illegal political fundraising activities, including requiring vendors to make political contributions and reimbursing the vendors through payment of falsified invoices for services. Ms. Winikow and others also charged the company for various personal projects performed by O&R's vendors, and members of her department used vendors to embezzle funds from the company. The investigation has determined that an aggregate of approximately $482,776 was improperly paid by the company to vendors for the foregoing purposes.

In addition, questions were raised as to the number of other payments to vendors aggregating approximately $1,762,355, but the investigators were unable to quantify the amount of any improper payments based on the evidence available. Further, the investigation found that internal controls were extremely weak in the Department and that the facilities of the Department were used for personal projects of Mr. Smith, Ms. Winikow, and others at an aggregate cost to the company which the investigation could not quantify based on available records.

OTHER FINDINGS

The investigation also found that other company facilities, including the Conference Center, as well as company employees, had been used for personal purposes by Mr. Smith, Ms. Winikow, and others at an aggregate cost to the company which the investigation was not able to quantify based on available records.

UTILITY COMMISSIONS

The company has not yet determined what portion of the amounts referred to above may have been improperly charged to accounts and used in setting rates, and is unable to predict what action, if any, the New York, New Jersey, or Pennsylvania utility commissions may take with respect to past, present, or future rates, or the imposition of penalties, on the basis of the findings and conclusions of the Special Committee's investigation or their own investigation. The company has already refunded an aggregate of $439,100 to ratepayers.

REMEDIAL ACTIONS

As a result of the investigation, the corporation has

- terminated the employment of six officers and employees, including Mr. Smith, Ms. Winikow, the controller, the former controller, and the internal auditor of the corporation;

- brought suit against Mr. Smith, Ms. Winikow, and others to recover damages;

- cooperated with the New York, New Jersey, and Pennsylvania utility commissions by providing them access to evidence accumulated by the investigation;

- agreed to rebate to ratepayers misappropriated monies that are found to have been charged to accounts and used in setting rates;

- agreed to establish the position of an independent Inspector General for a period of seven years; agreed to discontinue for five years all political contributions and the activities of all political action committees;

- abolished the restricted disbursement account;

- hired a new outside auditor; and

- instituted new policies regarding the internal audit function and internal controls.

Shareholders wishing a copy of the Report of the Special Committee may obtain one by writing:

Manager of Financial and Executive Communications
Orange and Rockland Utilities, Inc.
One Blue Hill Plaza
Pearl River, NY 10965

"Get Tough on Crime: But Don't Lock 'em in My Back Yard"

Diana Vance

Since 1988, the Morris County Board of Chosen Freeholders has been attempting to site and construct a new jail. Since that time, a minimum of $1.5 million dollars has been expended in this effort and the County has yet to break ground for a new facility.

A variety of factors have impacted upon this situation: consistent turnover on the Freeholder Board during the past five years resulting in new criteria for jail site selection established with each new Board, and a desire of elected officials to appease all constituents in an attempt to gather or maintain voter support. This last factor is important as the Freeholder Board has regularly bowed to public pressures, the NIMBY syndrome, from constituents when considering sites for the new County Jail. As early as 1989, the Freeholder Board admitted "that the pressure from citizens living near the sites had taken its toll." It appears that politics and public pressure played important and intrusive roles in ruling out several sites (*Morris County Daily Record*, April 30, 1989: B4).

There is unanimous agreement that the existing County jail facility is overcrowded and antiquated. Mandatory jail sentences for drug offenses, motor vehicle violations, and more stringent domestic violence laws have dramatically impacted upon increased inmate population in recent years.

The current facility in Morris County was originally built in 1932 to house 107 inmates. An addition in 1984 brought the capacity to 144 inmates. The average population of the jail is 294 inmates. The current facility has inadequate housing capacity, ventilation and temperature control, open space, meeting room and handicapped access. Based on a projection done by a criminal justice planning firm, the County could expect approximately 800 inmates by the year 2010.

MORRIS COUNTY JAIL SITING EFFORTS

In 1988, a Freeholder appointed Jail Siting Committee was charged with the task of developing jail site selection criteria. The criteria were categorized into four areas: Essential; Very Important; Important; Desirable.

Essential Criteria

1. at least 75 acres

2. allow for future expansion

3. provide adequate parking

4. topography conducive to construction

5. should relate well in scale, natural screening, and aesthetic quality to the surrounding area

Very Important Criteria listed 19 items, including

- not more than ten minutes from firefighters, police, local hospitals

- not located in close visual proximity to existing neighborhoods

- served by public transportation, with access to major traffic routes

- capacity for expansion and improvement

- site owned by a governmental agency

- site acquisition should not require a lengthy hearing or negotiation process

- reasonable development costs

- refuse service available to the site

- support of County government of the site

Important Criteria included

- centrally located with regard to population density

- site access has high snow removal priority

- telephone service, sewer lines, and natural gas should extend to the property line

- access roads are adequately maintained

Two Final Criteria

- local government and contiguous municipalities should be supportive of the location

- citizenry in relative proximity to the site should be supportive of the location

SUMMARY OF SITE SELECTION AND REJECTION ACTIVITIES

A. *Greystone Park Psychiatric Hospital*—This is a state run psychiatric hospital located on 1,100 acre grounds in the municipalities of Parsippany and Morris Plains. The original facility was built in the late 1800s and by the 1940s housed almost 7,000 people. By the early 1980s that population had decreased to approximately 700, and the majority of the massive buildings on the hospital grounds were no longer in use, and in serious disrepair.

The Jail Siting Committee had selected a 250 acre cornfield parcel of the property located at the southern tip of the Greystone complex. Residents of four surrounding municipalities formed a citizens group against the plan in early 1988, saying they feared that the jail would add traffic to local roads, stigmatize Greystone patients, and threaten the safety of the neighborhoods. Former State Senator Leanna Brown introduced a bill prohibiting jails or prisons on the grounds of state owned psychiatric hospitals. The local Mental Health Association publicly opposed the site. A statement was issued by the State Department of the Public Advocate indicating that the close proximity of the jail would cause patients to perceive themselves as prisoners. It was also stated that the presence of the jail would increase the likelihood of violence and drug use. The Advocate dismissed Greystone Site proponents contention that the Advocate was taking a NIMBY stance by referring to problems at Ancora Psychiatric Hospital where a minimum security state prison was built in the 1970s. An escaped inmate had been convicted of raping an Ancora nurse at the location.

Freeholders voted 6 to 1 to remove the Greystone site from consideration.

B. *Washington Valley Site*—This area, located within Morris and Mendham Townships, is County owned property. While most of the area had been reserved for a reservoir, it was felt that there was enough high ground (about 40 acres) to accommodate the jail. Although the site lacked immediate sewer access, it met most of the other criteria: close to Morristown, adequate size, lightly populated area, county owned with a buffer area.

Local citizens formed the "Coalition for Sane Jail Site" and claimed that this site was inappropriate because of the close proximity to residential housing; concern for the historic nature of the area; the importance of the site as a recreation area for hikers, horseback riders, and nature lovers; the existence of endangered wildlife and concerns over the impact to environmentally sensitive wetlands. Following the submission of a report by an environmental consulting firm which identified further concerns regarding the wetlands, the site was eliminated from further consideration.

C. *Wharton Site*—In April of 1991 the Freeholder Board appointed a Committee of senior county staff in its most systematic effort at site selection. Thirty (30) responses were received to a notice requesting offers of privately owned land of approximately 20 flat acres, with utility access, close to Morristown. The responses were reviewed for a general adherence to the criteria. After eliminating a number of sites, the Committee focused on one located in the municipality of Wharton. Although there were major problems with the site—questionable sewer capacity, well water contamination, and debate over ownership—the Freeholder Board pursued the site. There was a massive community outcry with literally hundreds of concerned citizens attending Freeholder meetings to voice their opposition. The citizens expressed concern regarding the safety of their children; the potential for inmate escape; increased traffic; decreased home values; and an overall deterioration on the quality of life. The site was eliminated from consideration.

D. *Morristown*—An architect was retained to determine the feasibility of constructing a jail on the somewhat limited space available near the courthouse complex. A review team of county administrative officials advised against accepting the architect's proposed schemes, citing extreme disruption to ongoing County operation, historic preservation issues, difficulty in acquiring air rights, loss of existing parking, restrictions on future expansion options, and extreme construction conditions. Further, there was also an outcry from the town government. The mayor of Morristown indicated that this was not a "Not In My Back Yard" response on the part of the town, but claimed that the town had already assumed more than its fair to share County faculties. The plan was abandoned.

E. *John Street Site, Morris Township*—While obviously not the County's first choice, this site provides a number of advantages. The wetlands appear to be of a far lower quality than those encountered on other prospective sites; it is in close proximity to the courthouse complex; emergency services are close; it is not visible from any local road and is located in a basically industrial area and is accessible to local public transportation routes. It is a swampy, wooded area behind a gravel pit, adjacent to Rt. 287, as well as close to a sewage plant.

There were two major obstacles to be addressed with this property. The first issue had to do with wetlands mitigation. Following lengthy negotiations, a new wetland designation strategy was approved by the DEPE.

Secondly, the County had to relocate affordable housing units that had been planned for the site. The County proposed a three tiered plan. Aggregate housing would be built for low income elderly and handicapped individuals; $250,000 in low cost loans would be provided to renters in public housing to buy their apartments and $300,000 would be allocated to upgrade area homes. This plan was acceptable to the Public Advocate, but not to the local citizens.

"The residents are not going to be bought off," said Alice Kaswan, the attorney representing the community. "They don't believe that a jail is appropriate for their neighborhood." The Morris County branch of the NAACP and the Morris County Fair Housing Council jointly decided to reject the new housing plan. The joint declaration was based on the contention that there were other suitable sites for the jail in Morris County. Describing the Freeholders as "champion mind-changers" about potential jail sites when opposition rose in the other municipalities, the two organizations said they "are asking the Freeholders to simply change their minds one more time and put affordable housing, not a jail, on the site" (*Morris County Daily Record*, July 29, 1994).

On July 28, 1994, the County filed a suit to remove the affordable housing obligation from the site to allow the building of the jail. The suit requested that the "siting of the correctional facility be allowed despite the site being zoned for low cost housing." The need for a new jail should supersede the need for housing, the suit contends. A hearing date has not yet been set.

7

Corporate Communications and Crisis

It is 7:00 P.M. on a wintery Thursday evening. A light snow has fallen, not sticking to the sanded roadways which surround The GCOP (Giant Chemical, Oil, and Plastics) Company hydrocarbon chemical complex in Donnelsville, a quiet community of 50,000 in southern New Jersey.

The plant, the largest hydrocarbon chemical complex in the world, produces 40 percent of the world's supply of hexo dexolene—a new product which has revolutionized paints by increasing viscosity by 100 percent. Hexo dexolene, a petroleum derivative, is highly caustic in concentrated form; it turns to a highly toxic, colorless, and odorless gas when it mixes with salt and water. It dissipates very slowly in a gaseous state, but halogen can contain the gas. The product is harmless when mixed with other chemicals in a controlled manufacturing environment.

The forecast is for fair conditions through Sunday, highs in the 30s.

A tank truck leased to GCOP Co., loaded with 12,000 gallons (U.S.) of its GCOP HEXDEX Brand hexo dexolene pulls out of the plant gate bound for a delivery in Eastern Connecticut. The sign over the gate reads: "1,793 Days Without a Fatality."

The driver, Al Benson, is 38 years old and a professional driver with Ace Trucking for ten years. A Vietnam vet trained in the U.S. Army as a tank commander, he has been married to his second wife for five years. They have a 4-year-old son. Al has a safe driving record—no history of substance abuse, mental illness, or physical impairment.

He is driving a White/GM/Volvo Diesel Cab. It was last inspected in October and approved by all local, state, and federal highway safety standards. The cargo tank was manufactured to GCOP standards for the transportation of HEXDEX. The corporation's specifications exceed all ICC, OSHA, ANSI, and other applicable standards.

Al pulls the rig onto the New Jersey Turnpike heading north. At the George Washington Bridge he turns and stops at the toll for an inspection and waits until after midnight to cross.

He then passes over the Hudson River then through the maze of roadways under the residential towers on the Manhattan side and onto the elevated roadway bridge over the East River, heading into the Bronx.

186

Suddenly, a van swerves in front of the truck from the left lane, cutting it off. The truck driver slams on the brakes and turns hard to the right, hitting the passenger car in the right lane.

Both vehicles slide solidly into the guardrail and concrete barrier. The cab and trailer jackknife, severing the air brake lines and locking all the tires. The truck shudders to a stop, overturning on the roadway.

Air hisses from the lines to the cab, fuel flows from a ruptured tank on the cab, the cargo tank has split along a welded seam—the contents flowing onto the roadway and into the storm drains which empty directly into the river.

Police arrive at the scene within minutes.

It is now 1:00 A.M. Friday morning. New York Police Department Officer Alvarez of Highway 1 calls GCOP to inform the company of the accident.

What do you do now? What steps do you take?

A panel of corporate officers and media representatives were faced with the situation just described, and the questions started a panel discussion titled, "When Disaster Strikes" as part of the Schering-Plough Executive Lecture Series on Corporate Communication at Fairleigh Dickinson University in March 1990. (The script was written by Michael B. Goodman and Tom Garbett.)

Corporate representatives included: Moderator David E. Collins, Corporate Executive Vice President of Schering-Plough, who handled the Tylenol scare as president of MacNeil; Robert Berzok, Director of Corporate Communications for Union Carbide; S. C."Duke" Watkins, Manager—Hazardous Material Transportation and Chemical Recovery for Allied-Signal; Gregory L. Johnson, Corporate Vice President and General Counsel of Warner-Lambert; and Tom Garbett, Distinguished Visiting Professor at Fairleigh Dickinson University and corporate advertising consultant.

Media representatives included the environmental reporter from the local newspaper, the business reporter from the state's largest daily, and the news director from WWOR-TV, a regional independent station syndicated nationally on cable.

David Collins asked each panelist for observations and statements on the situation. Each panelist was asked to offer a summary on what to do when disaster strikes. Much of the discussion covered planning, preparing for, and handling a crisis, which will be discussed later in this chapter in the selected commentaries.

The panelists seemed to agree, which for a group of journalists and business representatives was unusual since the relationship between the two is usually adversarial. Both maintained that the situation required cooperation among everyone involved. Then moderator David Collins was handed a note with the following information directed toward the press:

At 7:00 A.M. you receive a call from the Green Group, a small radical environmental organization that began in the late 1980s in Western Europe. The caller—William James—informs you of the incident, saying it was no accident, that he personally drove the van, cut off the tanker to show the world how vulnerable all human beings are to industrial poisons in our water, air, and soil. Your story has hit the street. What do you do now?

The new complication, according to the newspaper reporter, changed the character of the situation from "an accident to an incident." The TV news director said she would not go on the air with the news before she checked out the call. In the context of broadcast journalism's sensationalism, several people considered the comment to be somewhat at odds with the way stations have behaved in the past.

The hypothetical situation demonstrated the continued need for corporations to understand the nature of crisis, its impact on the health of the corporation and its employees, the strategic nature of communications in times of corporate stress, and methods for communicating during a crisis.

The first part of this chapter discusses understanding the stages of a crisis, planning and managing a crisis, and responding during the crisis and after. The remainder of the chapter discusses crisis preparation through issues management, particularly environmental or "green" issues.

STAGES OF A CRISIS AND THE CORPORATE RESPONSE

Many people who write about crises and management use a medical analogy. The comparison is fitting. During World War I, medics developed the triage technique for rendering aid on the battle field.

- those not seriously wounded could be treated and released with little effort and time

- those near death for whom no amount of effort could make a difference

- those who would most likely recover if something were done immediately

The triage model applies to communications and actions during the crisis itself, when time to contemplate and analyze is all but nonexistent. This approach fits the management principle of applying limited resources for their greatest impact.

The other model borrowed from medicine is the development of disease through the stages of

- prodromal,

- acute,

- chronic, and

- resolution to a normal state.

In practice, you can refer to

- the precrisis stage,

- the clear signs of a crisis,

- the persistent reemergence of the crisis, and

- the resolution.

Often companies do not see a potential for crisis in the normal course of business. For example, the W. R. Grace Company ignored for a long time the need to plan an orderly succession of its CEO until it became clear that nature would force such an action. The public became aware of the problem when the nightly news reported the chairman's comment in 1992 that the governor of New York was "Mario the Homo."

Another example is the owner of the chicken processing plant who kept the fire exits of his plant bolted shut until a fire at the plant killed several workers. An analysis to develop a crisis plan would have spotted that gross violation of the law as a potential crisis of major impact to the company and its people.

Airlines, utilities, computer operations, and hospitals plan for the unthinkable because they have learned from painful experience that the unthinkable has a nasty habit of happening.

CRISIS COMMUNICATION PLANS

In the past, what happened in a business was literally no one else's business. Corporations cut off questions with a curt, "No comment." Such closed door policies create an information vacuum. Investigative reporters of the 1990s and beyond, like their muckraker ancestors almost 100 years before who spawned the practice of public relations, want to fill that vacuum. With the trend toward sensationalism, many reporters will do just that, often in ways that are damaging to the organization.

Employees also fill the information vacuum, fueling the rumor mill within an organization. Combine one disgruntled employee and one ruthless reporter and the result is at least a major headache for the company; at worst it can be the catalyst in a media feeding frenzy with an unpredictable outcome.

Cooperation with the media and employees is a much more prudent and mature policy for any organization to take in normal times and in times of crisis.

Planning for a crisis as a fact of corporate life is the first step in its resolution, and a subsequent return to normal operations. No one can predict when the event will occur, only that sometime in the life of an organization a product will fail, the market will evaporate because of a new invention, the stock will fall, an employee may be caught doing something illegal, the CEO will retire, the workforce will go on strike, a natural disaster will occur, or a terrorist will plant a bomb.

It is perfectly normal for executives to avoid thinking about a crisis. Positive thinking is embedded in the way managers are taught to be effective. Problems are opportunities; one man's misfortune is another's fortune—and so it goes. Admitting that a crisis could occur is to entertain the worst of all corporate sins—the notion of failure.

The tendency to ignore the worst also recognizes that people cannot control events. Being unable to control the forces of nature certainly does not mean weakness on the part of managers. It merely indicates that people must plan to deal with emergencies and their consequences. Weakness comes only when people do not prepare for events. Companies that get into trouble are often the ones that never considered that bad things would happen to them.

Emergencies, disasters, bomb threats, criminal charges, executive misconduct—none of these may happen, but a well-run corporation develops plans in case the unthinkable occurs. Even the best-run companies can and do have difficulties.

Gerald Meyers, in his book *When It Hits the Fan*, identifies nine types of crises.

1. public perception

2. sudden market shift

3. product failure

4. top management succession

5. cash flow problems

6. industrial relations

7. hostile takeover

8. adverse international events

9. regulation and deregulation

Planning for a crisis implies that the people in the company can recognize a crisis when it occurs. People experience generally the same stages when faced with adversity or catastrophic loss.

- denial or isolation

- anger

- bargaining for time

- depression and grief

- acceptance

An organization is no different since it is made up of people. Organizations experience

- shock,

- a defensive retreat,

- acknowledgment, and

- adaptation and change.

RESPONDING TO PRESSURE GROUPS

More and more interest groups make corporate life difficult for some companies, either through public demonstrations staged to capture media attention, through announced boycotts of company products and services, through out-and-out harassment of company executives and employees, or through terrorist acts directed at the corporation.

Ask yourself what you would do in a similar situation the next time you see a Greenpeace boat being rammed by a Japanese fishing boat for trying to stop a shipment of nuclear reactor fuel at sea, or AIDS sufferers in ACT-UP in death costumes outside a drug company protesting the price of the experimental drugs for treatment, or pro-life groups demonstrating in front of a multinational organization that makes RU-486, the "morning after pill" available only in Europe until the late 1990s.

Your answer, of course, is that if you look out your window and your first notion is that there are folks out there who have ideas drastically different from yours, you are way behind in dealing with the immediate situation on your corporate doorstep. Planning for the inevitable can be good business.

"GREEN" ISSUES AND CRISIS PREPARATION

The fast food industry provides an excellent illustration. People on New York's Long Island live in a fragile seacoast environment and are concerned with all types of pollution. Fast food restaurants began to hear calls for the ban on Styrofoam cups and other Styrofoam wrapping for hot food because the business use of that material was literally only minutes, while it would take centuries for the Styrofoam material to break down in landfills.

Instead of considering these comments as being those of radical environmentalists, the corporations decided to join the people and return to the use of paper products made from recyclable and recycled materials. The message: "We listen to you and we are all part of the community. As good citizens, we are doing our part."

The fast food restaurant operators saw the protest as a message from their customers, as well as a comment on their products and services. Their response made good business sense. The decision resulted in prudent actions to turn a potential crisis into an opportunity for the organizations to work with the community, and for them to get closer to their customers.

Nowhere do the "M" forces clash so clearly as they do over the environment. The conflicting power of money and morality is at the heart of understanding the social and business fabric of contemporary America. Freedom of choice, freedom of religion, free markets pull and tug at one another over the issues of the environment, sexual behavior and practices, and behavior that could corrupt the individual and the community. These issues represent the sharp edge of social change, potentially valuable in a dynamic free society, or a grave danger to the health of the corporation.

People on their own and in organized groups have been, and continue to be, extremely vocal on these social issues. Often they express their position with their pocketbooks, as Exxon found out after its oil tanker the *Exxon Valdez* went aground in Prince William Sound and fouled the Alaska coast with thick crude oil.

Why be concerned about "green marketing"? Are they indicators of shifts in attitudes or signs of a decaying society? Should reaching these new markets be part of a corporate strategy?

The communications solution: *find out from your audience*—survey customers, stockholders, and employees to see what they think.

Any corporation or organization that chooses to ignore the environment does so at great risk. These are the facts of social life, and like prohibition and segregation was, and drugs are, the company that ignores these realities of the workplace may be so ill prepared for them that the impact could be catastrophic. These issues may become mainstream, such as the treatment of alcoholism and drug addition among the workforce; or, they may fade away over time.

No one can predict, but we feel that monitoring the changing social landscape is just as important to the bottom line as watching the daily stock price, or the rise and fall of interest rates.

Monitoring social change is the best way a company can prepare itself for new markets and for changes in existing customers' attitudes. Social change is often not indicated on the traditional balance sheets and financial statements, but its power can be felt as such changes influence the culture of the corporation and of the community it serves.

Concern over the quality of the air we breathe and the water we drink has become a mainstream concern. Reflecting that concern in the communications of the corporation allows you and your organization to keep existing customers. For a company to ignore environmental concerns at the end of the century would be an invitation to even its most loyal and conservative customers to place their business elsewhere.

Green marketing represents a corporate response to the financial pressures brought on by competition, worldwide environmental regulations, customer demands that the companies they do business with act positively and responsibly toward the environment, and the demand for quality in the way all of us live.

Try this. Take any document you have received from a Fortune 500 company in the last few weeks—a letter, a brochure, an annual report. More likely than not, somewhere on it you will see the following symbols:

Why? Customers expect it. And if they do not, they are not put off by the notion that a company recycles. It has become part of the mainstream behavior of a good corporate citizen, and in most states and cities across the country, it is the law.

What was a battleground only a few years ago, and still is for a few laggards, has become the norm. Every organization has some tangible sign in its offices and facilities—from recycling bins to green folders for recycling office papers to the packaging it uses for its products (*Institute of the Packaging Professionals Packaging Reduction, Reuse, Recycling &*

Disposal Guidelines, 1993 Revised Edition) to the marketing claims for a product's environmental benefits ("Guides for the Use of Environmental Marketing Claims: The Application of Section 5 of the Federal Trade Commission Act to Environmental Advertising and Marketing Practices," Federal Trade Commission, July 1992).

So when experts say that the "green" movement in marketing is dead, is it?

No, it is not.

It has just become part of the expected behavior for corporations, not a major or competitive advantage. It is not dead by any means—just business as usual. What contemporary corporation would be openly and publicly anti-environment and expect to keep its customers?

How should companies exploit or not exploit their "green" activities? During the "greed" decade of the 1980s, the drive for profit forced many companies to rank very low the impact of their actions on customers, employees, and the greater social good. Driven by corporate councils and a philosophy that adhered to the letter of the law rather than its spirit, many corporate leaders asked "Can we do it?" as opposed to "Should we do it?" The environmental icons and popular culture symbols of disaster such as Cherynobel and Bhopal are the result of such an attitude. Well-meaning companies can have their image tainted and, by extension, their brands, through a simple act of indifference.

Companies like Levi's, Ben & Jerry's, and The Home Depot reflect an attitude that people want to like your product and your company, and know your story. It is more than social responsibility or a reason to develop a cause-marketing strategy. It is a customer's passion for your product. According to Jackie Ottman, "In this new marketing age, products are being evaluated not only on performance or price, but on the social responsibility of manufacturers." (Ottman 1993, 8).

The customer now perceives the value of a product to include its environmental soundness, as well as its package. Consumers now look at the long-term impact of the product on society after it is used. The concept of quality in products now incorporates its environmental impact.

Customers' needs, laws and regulations, and the reality of technology to simultaneously create new solutions to clean up the mess and also to cause a new mess are the forces driving companies to include a "green position" in their marketing, advertising, and corporate communications.

Why the shift? Baby boomers have grown up with an environmental sensibility, a health and fitness consciousness, and an activist spirit. Also, in 1970, along with the first Earth Day, the Clean Air Act

TABLE 7-1
Different Attitudes Toward Environmental Issues

SHADES OF GREEN—
PROFILES OF ATTITUDES TOWARD GREEN ISSUES

True-Blue Green	20%	ACTIVE
Greenback Green	5%	
Sprouts	31%	SWING
Grouses	9%	NOT ACTIVE
BASIC BROWNS	35%	NOT ACTIVE
(disproportionately male, southern, blue-collar, and economically downscale)		

SOURCE: Ottman, *Green Marketing*

was passed; and in 1972 the Clean Water Act was passed. Concern for the environment had become the law of the land. Table 7-1 offers a profile of attitudes toward environmental issues.

Add to the pressure from consumers the force of law and regulation, a global marketplace, and the ability of engineers using the latest technology to design products that are "green."

In the future, your products will be fitted with a "green port," an electronic memory that a technician can access quickly to find out the materials and components in the product, its service records, and perform a quality check (*IEEE Spectrum*, August 1994). All of this to determine if the appliance can be reused, repaired and resold, or dismantled and some parts reused. Hype?

Don't bet on it.

In Europe, the lack of landfill space and increased waste from electronics and household appliances are driving regulations on the recycling of products from refrigerators to cars to personal computers to fax machines to TV sets to stereo equipment.

In the past, the product user and the local municipality have been responsible for waste disposal and recycling. In the industrialized countries, however, that process now requires fundamental changes in the way products are designed.

New products must use less material, last longer, be made of recyclable materials, contain fewer hazardous constituents, and incorporate recycled materials. Design changes such as these require the active involvement and innovation of manufacturers so that product function and quality, as well as business competitiveness, are maintained, while environmental concerns are addressed. (Dillon 1994, 18)

In response to these forces, Germany, Japan, Austria, Italy, Switzerland, France, and the Netherlands have begun to articulate guidelines for "producer responsibility." Their efforts indicate a new era of environmental accountability, "one that directly impacts core business strategy." (Dillon, 18) Companies who wish to conduct business in these countries will have to meet an array of regulations, as well as comply with strict standards called ISO 9000. If you do not meet the criteria, you cannot sell your products and services in the European Union.

How permanent is "green marketing"? Even though membership in such environmental groups as The National Audobon Society, Greenpeace, and The Sierra Club has shown a steady decline since 1989, it would be a serious miscalculation for any business to assume that consumers are any less committed in their support of a clean environment. "Many former backers say green awareness is integrated into their lives, and other issues such as crime and health care now take precedence. Most say they're still vigilant about the environment and would balk if businesses took the withering of the movement to mean they can be careless about their pollution" (Aeppel 1994, B1; see also Kevles, *The New York Review of Books*, October 1994, and Maddox, *Financial Times*, November 1994). The environmental issue is even now mainstream for opponents such as the pro-extraction, anti-regulation Wise Use movement. They do not attack the idea of protecting the environment, they attack government and regulations.

Positioning your company in this context requires some careful balance between projecting the corporation's image as a supporter of the environment and as a supporter of the middle and working class. Many Americans perceive the environmental movement as being elitist, one that is indifferent to the working class and to people in general, and a firm ally of big government.

Once you stake a claim on the "good," any negative news may have an impact on both your image and your stock price. The Body Shop is a case in point. An article in the journal *Business Ethics* called into question some of the company's claims of environmentally friendly manufacturing practices. The company responded aggressively to the story in the *Wall Street Journal*, and though the stock price fell the company met the crisis in a positive way (Adelson 1994; Stevenson 1994). It also weathered a storm over its relationship with the Kayapo Indians of Brazil, a supplier of Brazil nut oil for hair conditioner. It seems the Kayapo's simple life in the rain forest was changed by the lure of the money and gadgets of the modern world (Moffett 1994). But any first-year anthropology student could have predicted that anything new in a culture changes the culture.

How do companies organize for "green marketing"? General Motors, as part of its efforts to reorganize and meet its corporate vision as being the world leader in transportation products and services, issued in 1994 its first ever *General Motors Environmental Report*.

> We are striving to provide economic benefit to our society while minimizing the environmental impact on our activity. We recognize that we have many challenges to address, including consumer preferences, competitive markets, and limits on financial and human resources. Achieving the nation's economic goals in an environmentally sustainable manner will require teamwork and partnership with numerous stakeholders. As an example of this new collaborative approach, GM was proud to endorse the CERES Principles, a code of corporate environmental responsibility, in February 1994. CERES, the Coalition for Environmentally Responsible Economies, is an organization of national environmental and investment groups focused on social responsibility. GM is the first major manufacturing company to endorse the CERES Principles, as well as the first Fortune 50 company whose own environmental principles have been endorsed by CERES . . . (*GM Environmental Report*)

Is the effort GM has focused on environmental issues mere compliance with the law? Yes, but GM, by endorsing the CERES Principles, has pledged to "go voluntarily beyond the requirements of the law." In that spirit, GM demonstrates its environmental performance by setting measurable goals, such as: "eliminate chlorofluorocarbons (CF-12) from vehicle air conditioning systems by the end of 1994; eliminate ozone-depleting solvents by the beginning of 1995; continue to reduce SARA Title III Toxic Release Inventory emissions; increase plant audit frequency from four to two years; and sponsor two new GREEN environmental programs per year" (*GM Environmental Report*, 28).

Of course, anyone would agree with these principles (see Figure 7-1), but is there a commitment at GM to back it up? Is the environmental policy tied to people and resources? If we can believe their report, the corporation has made such a commitment: "Commencing in 1994 environmental performance of operating units, along with other criteria, will be considered in compensation reviews and promotional opportunities" (GM Report, 4). The corporation has numerous initiatives for research and development, pollution prevention and materials recycling programs, reduction of toxic chemical use programs, goals for the replacement and phase-out of ozone depleting chemicals, programs for workplace safety and health, plans for emergency response and public disclosure, strategy to emphasize waste minimization and

Figure 7-1
General Motors Environmental Principles

As a responsible corporate citizen, General Motors is dedicated to protecting human health, natural resources, and the global environment. This dedication reaches further than compliance with the law to encompass the integration of sound environmental practices into our business decisions.

The following environmental principles provide guidance to General Motors personnel worldwide in the conduct of their daily business practices.

1. We are committed to actions to restore and preserve the environment.

2. We are committed to reducing waste and pollutants, conserving resources, and recycling materials at every stage of the product life cycle.

3. We will continue to participate actively in educating the public regarding environmental conservation.

4. We will continue to pursue vigorously the development and implementation of technologies for minimizing pollutant emissions.

5. We will continue to work with all governmental entities for the development of technically sound and financially responsible environmental laws and regulations.

6. We will continually assess the impact of our plants and products on the environment and the communities in which we live and operate with a goal of continuous improvement.

---

pollution prevention, and a commitment to energy conservation. GM, as a member of the global community and a research consortium to explore further improvements in vehicle recycling, also has a commitment to "product stewardship." It is committed to issues such as product life cycle, vehicle recycling, automotive emissions, fuel efficiency, and alternative fuels.

Let's look for example at some companies that are sure bets to win the environmental contest for the hearts and minds of the consumer, as well as those that must work mightily and constantly, with slow, if no progress.

The winners are easy to spot, thanks to the Council on Economic Priorities, "a public service research organization dedicated to accurate and impartial analysis of the social and environmental records of corporations" (*Council on Economic Priorities 1993 Report*). It publishes an environmentalist version of consumer reports, *Shopping for a Better World*. In it are company profiles of twenty companies (see Figure 7-2) out of 191 rated for the book that earned a grade-point average of 3.5 or

Figure 7-2
Council on Economic Priorities Honor Roll Companies

Adolph Coors	Grand Metropolitan PLC
Anheuser-Busch Companies, Inc.	Hewlett-Packard Company
Aveda Corp.	Johnson & Johnson
Avon Products, Inc.	S.C. Johnson & Son, Inc.
Ben & Jerry's Homemade, Inc.	Kellogg Company
Colgate-Palmolive Company	Levi Strauss & Co.
Dayton Hudson Corporation	Nordstrom, Inc.
Digital Equipment Corporation	Rhino Records, Inc.
General Mills, Inc.	Tom's of Maine
Giant Food Inc.	Warner-Lambert Company

SOURCE: *Shopping for a Better World*, 1994

better. Companies were rated in eight categories: Environment, Charitable Giving, Community Outreach, Women's Advancement, Advancement of Minorities, Family Benefits, Workplace Issues, and Disclosure of Information.

Of course you might question whether or not companies such as Coors and Anheuser-Busch that make a product like beer that can potentially cause harm and death belong on this list. In CEP's 1993 Annual Report it recognizes its Silver Anniversary Award Winners, Xerox Corporation, and Shorebank Corporation for "exceptional, broad and sustained commitment to superior social and environmental performance." It also honored these companies "for outstanding achievements or initiatives in specific areas of social responsibility": community involvement—Brooklyn Union Gas; environmental stewardship—S.C. Johnson & Son, Inc.; responsiveness to employees—SAS Institute; international commitment—Levi Strauss & Co.

The CEP Annual Report also listed the following corporations as "egregious environmental offenders": Commonwealth Edison, E.I. DuPont de Nemours, Exxon, General Electric, International Paper, Louisiana-Pacific, MAXXAM, Rockwell International, Texaco, and Texas Utilities. Even a casual comparison between this list of sinners and the list of saints indicates a clear pattern. If your core business is related to the finding, recovery, or harvesting of resources from the environment, you have a more difficult case to make for environmental stewardship than an ice cream manufacturer or a service company.

Let's look at International Paper since it is on the CEP environmental sinner list. If you are the largest paper maker in the world and the organization that rates your performance can trace its beginning to *Paper Profits* (MIT Press), a major environmental analysis of the pollution control records of the twenty-four largest companies in the pulp and paper industry, what can you do? Most likely, you cannot hope to win the CEP, but you can influence the rest of your stakeholders, which is what International Paper has done. It has stepped up to the issue of its role in the environment, in a fashion similar to General Motors. It has combined its core business strategy with its corporate communication efforts. It has addressed its social responsibility to the environment in its Annual Report (1993).

> The environmental challenges facing the paper and forest products industry take many forms, from endangered species and wetlands issues affecting our forestlands, to air and water emissions and solid and hazardous waste disposal at our manufacturing facilities, to recycling and packaging reduction initiatives focused on our products.
>
> For each of the last several years, International Paper has spent $100 million or more addressing these issues—and made excellent progress. For example, we have voluntarily
>
> - reduced the already small amount of dioxin in the water discharged from our bleached pulp mills by more than 95 percent;
>
> - slashed air and water emissions of 17 toxic chemicals specifically targeted by the Environmental Protection Agency (EPA) by 72 percent;
>
> - cut solid waste going to landfills by more than 50 percent;
>
> - converted one of our paper machines to make 100 percent recycled printing papers from old newspapers and magazines; and
>
> - established an innovative and widely applauded habitat conservation plan for a threatened species—the Red Hills salamander.
>
> International Paper intends to continue its leadership role in proactively developing environmentally sound forest management practices, and in promoting or requiring the use of these practices by our suppliers and contractors. Our goal is to be—and to be recognized as—the most responsible steward of our nation's forests in our industry. (*International Paper Annual Report 1993*, 33–34)

Cynics might charge that this effort is hype, but International Paper does not just devote a paragraph or two to the topic in the Annual Report. It backs up its commitment in its position papers, its issue briefs, and its *Environment, Health and Safety Progress Report*.

In stating its commitment to the environment, it recognizes its responsibility as a large forest products company to take a leadership role in protecting the environment, while adapting to continually stricter rules and increased public expectations about the environment.

As a corporation, it admits, "Regrettably, we do not always meet those expectations. Yet our responsibilities to our customers, our employees and our neighbors remain clear and constant. We take these responsibilities seriously because we have a stake in the world around us, and we want to pass on a legacy of commitment to make the world a better place than we found it" ("A Commitment to Environment, Health and Safety Excellence by International Paper," 1993:28). The company's effort does not stop there. It has tied its TV commercials, print ads, and programs with schools in an effort to develop a greater understanding of environmental issues for all Americans, rather than perpetuating the old notion that environmental issues are too complex and technical to explain.

Global Green and the European Union? Europe has been a significant part of the environmental movement in this century, as well as in the past, because it has limited land and depleted natural resources. Europeans are, in general, very concerned about quality of life issues. If the *IEEE Spectrum* (August 1994) issue on the greening of home electronics is any indication, the draft legislative initiatives in Germany and the Netherlands underscore the importance of environmental concerns in the design, use, reuse, and disposal of products. The Netherlands objectives include the following:

- prevention—achieve as much quantitative prevention as possible by reducing materials use and increasing the product's useful life

- recovery—achieve 100 percent differentiated collection by the year 2000 for optimal product and materials reuse

- product reuse—achieve as much reuse as possible of collected equipment

- materials reuse—for waste remaining after product reuse

- processing of residues—incineration with energy recovery is preferred

In addition, a study by the British Royal Society for the Encouragement of Arts, Manufactures & Commerce (RSA) "Tomorrow's Company: The Role of Business in a Changing World" (1994) recognizes the importance of the environment in the conduct of business. Over the last twenty years the pressures have been profound. Now companies must consider the life cycle of their products, from manufacture to disposal and potential reuse. They too recognize that customers the world over include environmental factors in defining quality. The RSA also notes that exposure to possible fines for environmental violations could have a negative impact on a company's ability to secure financing. And in Europe too, companies are joining cooperatively with each other and with environmental groups and government agencies to approach environmental issues.

> Tomorrow's company will continue to be challenged by the rising cost of protecting the environment, and the inevitable tensions between ethical considerations and the need for business competitiveness. In the face of increasing pressure from government, consumers, employees and the community, businesses will only compete successfully if they internalise (sic) environmental objectives. (RSA, "Tomorrow's Company," 23)

Selected Commentary

The commentaries selected for this chapter are from the presentation at the annual Conference on Corporate Communication at Fairleigh Dickinson University. The authors focus on understanding crisis communication, planning for crises, and communicating in a crisis.

Marion Pinsdorf concludes after analysis of numerous crises that personality, management style, lack of information, and insensitivities to the environment are usually the explanation for an executive's poor performance in a crisis. In short, people supply their own banana peels.

Linda Dulye advocates the use of two-way, face-to-face communications as the best way for information to flow during times of rapid change in an organization. Her case study describes how an internal communications process improvement effort can achieve positive outcomes.

Supplying Your Own Banana Peels

Marion K. Pinsdorf

KEEPING SECRETS—DON'T EVEN TRY

Is it hubris, illusions of omnipotence, blindness or just plain stupidity which convinces anyone, anywhere they can keep secrets? Politicians and scientists try it. Corporate executives and governmental agencies try it. Individuals try it—all resulting in expensive revelations. Why?

It's not just the tell all time we're in, or that privacy is an increasingly endangered value, or that listeners and participants attempt to elevate their own importance by revealing secrets of the newsworthy. Former President Richard M. Nixon asked former Secretary of State Henry Kissinger to pray with him. A very painful and private moment at the height of Watergate, but Kissinger prayed and probably told.

It's not just investigative reporters seeking secrets so they too can star like Bob Woodward and Carl Bernstein (*All the President's Men*). They changed, importantly, how information is gathered—talking to secretaries at home, midnight is best, to disgruntled employees, to power seekers and the low-level worker who knows that small but vital piece of information. The invisible employee in front of whom you've talked or handed over sensitive information to be duplicated may be the very person to pass along the secret.

It's not just the mean and litigious time, when anyone seems anxious to sue the "deep pockets" at the drop of an insult. Or, when

This commentary by Marion Pinsdorf, of Fordham University, appeared in the *Proceedings of the Seventh Conference on Corporate Communication*, May 1994. With some editorial changes, it appears here with her permission.

media leaks are used to dissolve a marriage to the advantage of the leaker (the House of Windsor), to knock out competitors for high positions (too numerous to detail) or to scuttle or advance a policy (gays in the military). It's not just compassionate friends thinking they can spare families pain. Undoubtedly, the White House had the very best of personal intentions in not immediately announcing details of the late Vincent Foster's pressures, depression and suicide, but as each detail was revealed, stories, and speculations metastasized.

All these reasons apply, but the greatest surprises come from the perverse nature of secrets themselves to surface at exactly the worst, most embarrassing and expensive moment. Think of research data ignored, not rechecked, hidden or dismissed that brought great grief and costs to DuPont, Dow Coming, A. H. Robins, and Allied Signal.

Consider these secrets not kept:

- Nuclear power design and operational difficulties, disasters in the Urals, even problems at Three Mile Island that surfaced fatally at Chernobyl.

- Remember former Missouri Senator Thomas Eagleton, whose nomination as running mate for George McGovern in 1972, foundered on hospitalization for alcoholism secret no longer.

- Did Zoe Baird ever think she would lose the chance to be Attorney General because of the very private matter of paying Social Security for household help? Perhaps women are more vulnerable to secrets surfacing because they may not, like President Clinton, have considered staying politically viable.

- Remember E. F. Hutton attempting to keep secret its check kiting, even as the information was leaking out. Now when E. F. Hutton speaks the SEC listens—not just its customers.

- [Remember] how Iran Gate emerged from secrecy through a Beirut newspaper.

- Perhaps the clearest expression of secrets surfacing inopportunely was Dan Quayle's. When questioned about his National Guard service he replied, "I never thought 20 years ago, I would be here" (nominated as vice president).

Both the public and financial stakes of attempting to keep secrets are high. Four corporations illustrate this.

First, a tragic case of a good company making a greedy mistake and trying to smother effective communications is that of A. H. Robins, producer of *Dalkon Shield*. The great respect and financial strength

Robins enjoyed were the very attributes that blinded it to the need for scrupulous self-examination and to an understanding of how quickly a good name can be tarnished. Robins fell into a trusting trap of believing an acquisition shared its values. Many companies slipped that way during merger frenzy.

After all the costly public disasters, many managers still neglect to factor possible public liabilities into their product and other planning. Attempts to hide or stonewall especially once the press focuses in on product problems and consumer complaints is a prescription for serious, long-term trouble.

Second, hot topics exacerbate media relations when the corporate issue is as controversial as contraception, as in the case of Robins or Dow Corning's silicone breast implants. A scare word, even misapplied, only inflames the media frenzy. Cancer, incorrectly associated with silicone implants, caught public attention easier and faster than the complex issue of an immune system disorder. It surprised experts actively involved with the implants. That scientifically the data revealed no convincing link between breast implants and cancer almost didn't matter.[1] It must be addressed.

Even a minor non-issue can become the issue that frames and drives the crisis. The public understands bounced checks in the U.S. House, but not budget intricacies; meltdown not in terms of telephones, about which it was initially used, but about nuclear reactors at Three Mile Island.

Ironically, companies not sensitive to their past mistakes are doomed to repetition. Dow Corning's parent company was attempting its public relations rehabilitation at the time from *Agent Orange* and Napalm with warm fuzzy advertisements. Also, breast implants were losing money and held a small market share. Now, manufacture has stopped, but product liability continues.

Third, keeping verbal secrets is bad enough, but writing them down doubles the trouble. DuPont is being hoisted on the petard of litigation and death of a product, *Benlate*, by its own documents and "for making nice."

Although DuPont "repeatedly denied" *Benlate* harms plants "or that it covered up any evidence about the fungicide," few are listening, fewer believing, but many are suing. Documents supplied many banana peels on which the company slid into continuing and costly litigation. *Benlate* is a case study in how to get yourself in expensive trouble.

Keeping secrets is neither time nor cost efficient and, to mix a metaphor, it gives respected white hat companies like DuPont a very black eye. The "worm in DuPont's pyrrhic court victory" was the release of millions of documents to nearly 500 other litigants who claimed *Benlate* damaged their crops as well. And as a classic crisis pattern, *Benlate's* problems "have escalated worries" about other DuPont "ultra potent weed killers." If the company cannot stem these complaints, "*Benlate* may look like small potatoes."

And fourth, initial warnings and first squashing may be internal, but often they are missed by others as well. That essentially was how *Keypone* became a costly problem for Allied Signal. Although developed in the late 1940s as an active ingredient in insecticides, it was not until two decades later that a large market developed. The danger signals, so called *Keypone* shakes, flashed only in 1974. Complaints were downplayed, evidence ignored. Despite complaints within the plant, management "denied anything was really wrong." But they didn't take time to gather data.[2]

Why? Sheer demand for *Keypone*? Did even they not know the degree of toxicity? Allied stressed the dust was harmless, only later to discover it was dangerous, life threatening. The problem illustrates the slowness of lag between producing a product and understanding the full range of its dangers.

Allied's carefully earned reputation for environmental safety and responsibility was severely shaken with the general public and with the EPA, OSHA and other agencies. Belatedly, Allied realized it must assume fault (partially) and address the problem. Allied showed support for workers, their families, the community, funded medical research and set up multimillion dollar foundations that would help in cleanup. The costs were great—more than $20 million in fines, settlements, and legal fees, but costliest of all a badly tarnished reputation.

Procedures were changed, incentive-compensation ratings included social and environmental responsibilities, but all too late this time. Keeping secrets Allied learned is very, very costly and just plain impossible.

Ironically, but typically, a chance to interdict the chain of causation presented itself early on, when an outside ethicist was conducting a seminar during which a participant mentioned a small chemical spill. Should we discuss that? Oh no, it isn't terribly important. All assumed it was minor and would never go public. It did. It was *Keypone*.

AT WACO EVERYTHING WENT TRAGICALLY WRONG

ATF's tragic raid on the Branch Davidian compound outside Waco, Texas, is an awesome cautionary tale of making your own trouble again and again—rushing past factual check points, hearing selectively, and basing operations totally on the element of surprise; and then proceeding even when that key element is lost.

Normally, cases of crisis communications present some mitigating might-have-beens. Or armchair analysts, with all the advantage of hindsight and free of responsibility or danger, cavalierly criticize participants for what they could not possibly have seen. At Waco the chain of causation was flawed from the very beginning. No one attempted to question or intercept faulty decisions as they were being made. Although the official Department of the Treasury report[3] repeatedly honors the "spectacular courage" of agents "in the face of gunfire," the overall judgement is unremittingly harsh. The investigation "found disturbing evidence of flawed decision-making, inadequate intelligence gathering, miscommunication, supervisory failures, deliberately misleading post-raid statements about the raid and the raid plan by certain ATF supervisors (Report, 7).

Two major points suggest the extent of flaws and myopic thinking—surprise and the media. Many incorrectly linked the two—that the media gave away the surprise. The media is often whipping boy of choice by executives facing disaster. At Waco that was unfair.

Surprise: After perhaps too quickly dismissing the idea of capturing David Koresh away from the compound or besieging him—fearing mass suicide, an expensive and protracted standoff, opportunity to destroy evidence, and testing the patience of the U.S. public—ATF leaders decided on an assault. Surprise was key—but it was lost early. Lacking contingency plans and filled with unwarranted optimism, the raid proceeded with all the rigidity of German troops on trains heading for the front in 1914. Visions of a short war seemed more realistic than reversing the operational plan. ATF at Waco was just as rigid.

Media: Part of the rush was a series "Sinful Messiah" planned by the *Waco Times-Herald.* ATF met with editors and the paper's security chief, even offered reporters "front-row seats" during the "execution of a contemplated law enforcement action" (Report, 68–69). Attempting to hide the raid from reporters and the Branch Davidians was like hiding a mongoose in a python. Military helicopters, Bradley fighting vehicles, provisions for medical support, ambulances, and medivac helicopters, even a reservation of 153 rooms in Waco hotels for agents alone, was enough to blow the surprise. But, to ensure good coverage, an ATF press officer contacted Dallas newspapers and radio stations for weekend contact numbers, advising that ATF might have something going on that weekend. Waco media were not contacted "out of concern that the raid's security might be threatened" (Report, 79).

Lapses in intelligence gathering and evaluation, casting the informational net too narrowly, flawed oversight, even operational mistakes, complete perhaps the most costly ever, in lives, dollars, and image, case of making your own trouble.

CONCLUSIONS

The cases analyzed are merely a small representation of how politicians and academicians, business executives and sports superstars repeatedly make their own trouble. With good sense and communications counseling, thoroughly checked and grounded in reality, anyone usually can avoid slipping on his own banana peels. Techniques include: seeking out and heeding early tracelines of change or trouble, looking beyond the numbers, beyond quantification to understand the greater complexity of any public problem, understanding the vast differences invisibility and criticism when a very private life goes very public, not trying to keep secrets, even potentially damaging ones, thinking with vision but minding the nitty-gritty, the details, and always attempting to see the problems as others do, not as the executive would like them to. The great scholarly challenge of crisis communications is simply that tomorrow's news will produce yet another example.

NOTES

1. Comments made by Barbie Carmichael, U.S. Vice President for Communications, Dow Corning, during a Fordham University seminar, "Managing Crisis, The Role of Real Time Response," in New York City, April 27, 1992.

2. The author acknowledges information from private conversations and from Gerard Waldron's "The *Keypone* Contamination of Hopewell, Va." presented as a partial requirement for MBA, Graduate School of Business, Fordham University, December 1990, p. 3, and C. Brian Kelly, "Who's Poisoning America?" Chapter 3.

3. "Report of the Department of the Treasury on the Bureau of Alcohol, Tobacco, and Firearms Investigation of Vernon Wayne Howell, also known as David Koresh," Washington, D.C.: Government Printing Office, September 1993.

Toward Better Two-Way

Why Communications Process Improvement Represents the Right Response During Uncertain Times

Linda M. Dulye

Communications during tough times necessitates response. More appropriately, it necessitates continuous response.

Tough times—indeed, the status quo of American industry today—shouldn't be a drain on the internal communications vigor of an organization. To the contrary, when conditions on the outside are strained, the communications process inside should be energized even more.

Information gaps cause employees to *misinterpret* changes in the workplace, *mistrust* management for mandating the changes, and *polarize* themselves from management and the organization. The net effect is disruptive to morale, productivity, and, ultimately, the organization's competitiveness for winning in a tough market.

Regardless of how bad the news is, people need to hear it. They deserve to be informed about all aspects of their organization—bad and good. Workforce reductions and income misses are as important to discuss as contract wins and health care benefits. By arming employees with facts *and* the rationale behind the what, where, when and how, the internal communications network redirects a work force's energy away from anxiety toward action.

This case study by Linda Dulye, of PSEG (formerly of GE Aerospace), appeared in the *Proceedings of the Fifth Conference on Corporate Communication*, May 1992. A revised version appears here with her permission.

Toward achieving that result, the information exchange must be candid, continuous, and two-way (emphasizing face-to-face communications between a manager and his or her direct reports). The benefit of this strategy for organizations facing uncertain times is evidenced by the case study that follows. Conducted over a six-month period, the study focuses on internal Communications Process Improvement (CPI) within the manufacturing division of a Fortune 100 firm. The division, referenced hereafter as AEB, produces sophisticated electronics products for the international aerospace market. With a customer base that is strictly military, AEB has undergone an internal upheaval in response to cutbacks in U.S. defense spending and the end of the Cold War. Over a two-year period beginning in December 1990, AEB employment shrunk by some 45%—a stark contrast to the workforce expansion that accompanied the Reagan military buildup of the 1980s. Of the eliminated jobs, about 70% affected hourly, represented employees. The remaining 30% affected salaried and nonexempt workers.

It was within this climate that the CPI initiative, called Toward Better Two-Way, was introduced in AEB. Toward Better Two-Way developed an active, two-way communications channel in a setting where communications exchanges between managers and employees were infrequent and ineffective (molded by the "information = power" management theory).

The need for communications lines to open wider than the information flow from employee newsletters was necessitated by the speed of change, internally and externally. Inside the business, layoffs, reorganizations, and management changes were occurring quarterly. Budgets for supplies, travel and living, and other discretionary expenses were being slashed by as much as 50%. Even the traditional December holiday party was axed in response to across-the-board spending cutbacks. Employees were being challenged to find better ways of doing their jobs that would improve quality, speed up processes, and lower costs. "Work smarter, more efficiently, together as a team" was the new challenge before the AEB workforce. Yet, the momentum of teaming efforts—through empowerment initiatives— was being thwarted by layoffs. Teams lost members weekly, forcing continuous regrouping and regauging.

Externally, the marketplace was shrinking by an average of 10% annually. Projections showed that pace to continue over the next five years. Yet despite the smaller market, more and more companies were vying for a piece of the action. Competition had gone global, thanks to the entry of foreign firms, particularly European and Asian manufacturers.

This environment of constant change and uncertainty posed the right opportunity for the Communications Process Improvement. AEB employees needed to know what was happening, why it was happening, and what it meant to them. They needed the information delivered differently than during boom times. Internal communications had to be faster, more interactive, and more personalized. Toward Better Two-Way responded with a three-prong strategy: change the internal communications process, introduce the new process, and measure its effectiveness. Let's examine each of these steps more closely.

CHANGE THE PROCESS

Regardless of the type of organization, the purpose of communications remains constant—to relay information, back and forth, or up and down. Critical to the success of that information exchange is the media (that is, the communications tools and processes) used to convey the message.

In the vast majority of organizations, the traditional media for communication is print. Newsletters, bulletins, magazines, brochures, posters, and annual reports carry the news of a business's performance and its people. This media is directly one-way only, toward transmitting information. Additionally, the information being relayed is general in nature—that is, geared to a large audience, rather than tailored to a specific group. Transmission of the information is fixed, not flexible, occuring weekly, monthly, or quarterly, depending on the publication schedule.

Amidst a business climate of uncertainty, this communications approach falls short in effectiveness. The print mode is too slow in delivery, too general in content, and one-way only in transmission. Faster delivery of information is needed on a continuous, more personalized basis to address the issues, questions, and rumors that escalate with change in the business. To support this communications climate, the lead role of communicator must shift from the internal communications office to the management team. Managers must become the primary information source by relaying important business messages to their employees and, even more important, listening to their employees comments and questions. It's this latter element—the feedback from employees—that distinguishes the communications flow as two-way and enhances the effectiveness of the communications exchange (versus a one-way media).

The Toward Better Two-Way process at AEB facilitated an active two-way communications exchange through a medium known as a communications cascade. The cascade created a communications domino effect: information flowed from top management and then cascaded through each management layer below until it reached employees. The length of time for the communications cascade was designed around several factors: the size of the organization (approximately 2,500 employees), the number of management layers (four layers between the vice president and employees), and logistics (two facilities located 15 miles apart). The AEB business adopted a "48-hour rule," whereby key messages were disseminated from management's weekly staff meeting and were communicated to all levels of the organization within 48 hours.

Here's how the communications flowed through the four layers of AEB management and ultimately to employees:

Tuesday morning: General Manager meets with immediate staff (Section Managers); key messages for the week are defined

Tuesday afternoon: Section Managers meet with their management teams (Sub-Section Managers)

Wednesday morning: Sub-Section Managers meet with their Supervisors and Foremen

Wednesday afternoon–Thursday afternoon: Supervisors and Foremen meet with employees

The delivery vehicles for messages in the AEB communications cascade were no-frills, on-the-spot team meetings called Stand-Ups. These weekly sessions lasted about 20 minutes—enough time for a manager to gather the team informally in his or her office, or an open area of the factory floor to review key messages for the week, talk about issues pertinent to the group, and elicit feedback.

INTRODUCE THE NEW PROCESS

Educating users is paramount to the success of any new process. Once developed, the action plan for rolling out the AEB Toward Better Two-Way initiative was presented to upper management for buy-in. Endorsement from high management was absolutely imperative for communications change. Upper management defined the tone and pace of internal communications. If information wasn't disseminating regularly from high management, middle and lower management had little data to absorb and share with employees. The information vacuum became filled with rumor, speculation, and anxiety. The goal, then, was to fill the pipeline—continuously and with accurate information.

The need for improved two-way communications was defined by the AEB vice president as a goal for the year. In a letter to all employees distributed prior to the debut of Toward Better Two-Way, the vice president stated: "In the coming months, I look forward to meeting you during roundtable dialogs and walks through office and shop areas. As we get to know each other, you'll see that I advocate candid, meaningful two-way communications. It's important that we understand where we are going as a business."

AEB upper management further endorsed the process by holding regular all-manager meetings and employee roundtables to share information about business performance and challenges; listening to and responding to employee feedback; identifying communications skills as a requirement for managers; and including communications effectiveness in manager performance ratings.

As part of the Toward Better Two-Way launch, all AEB managers and supervisors participated in an in-house, six-hour Communications Skills Training course. The course reinforced effective presentation, listening and interpersonal skills. Additionally, it defined the new communications tools and processes being introduced via the Toward Better Two-Way initiative. Each training class began with a half-hour commentary by the vice president and general manager reaffirming the commitment to more and better two-way communications.

Supplementing the skills training was a weekly key message sheet prepared by the general manager and distributed to all managers to assist them in their weekly Stand-Up sessions. The sheet highlighted four or five business concerns, such as missed schedule commitments, quality issues, customer comments, employee recognition, and organizational changes. A recurring message was the importance of Toward Better Two-Way in fostering a more informed and involved workforce which, in turn, would leverage competitiveness.

The AEB management team also set aside time each week for spontaneous (unannounced) walks through office and factory areas to talk with employees. The routine helped to "humanize" management, especially upper management, by making them more visible and approachable to employees. Additionally, it connected management to the real issues and questions circulating through the workforce. For employees, the weekly walk-abouts further supported management's role as their primary information source. Finally, the walk-abouts served as "checks and balances" to ensure that all managers were fulfilling their new two-way communications commitments. An upper manager could easily check the regularity and effectiveness of a lower manager's communications efforts by asking employees for their comments about the new two-way process.

The net result was a visible commitment never before seen in the AEB workplace. Management was walking the talk with employees; employees were talking more than ever with management. The communications process and, more importantly, mindset, was clearly changing.

MEASURE EFFECTIVENESS

Effective communications is never static. It continually evolves to fit the needs of its organization and its users. Therefore, a measurement tool was integral to the Toward Better Two-Way process for periodic evaluation of the new communications tools—much like the use of Statistical Process Controls in the AEB high-tech manufacturing environment. This measurement was essential for two reasons: first, it prodded reluctant managers into action, and second, it identified strengths and weaknesses from which ongoing improvements in the process were designed and implemented.

AEB measurements of communications effectiveness were taken prior to the onset of Toward Better Two-Way and repeated six months after its launch. More than 400 employees (about 20% of the workforce) were randomly selected to attend focus sessions conducted by the internal communications office to canvas opinions about how employees found out and felt about the business. Employee reaction was captured in two ways: through informal discussions and in a written communications survey.

The results of this assessment process show a dramatic reversal in communications trends. Employees believed they were informed about business goals. Prior to the Toward Better Two-Way process, 67% of the sample group responded they never or seldom were informed about goals. Six months later, only 23% of AEB employees said they never or seldom were informed about goals. More than half of the surveyed employees said they were well informed about business goals.

Target Groups A and B represent employees from two AEB functional areas heaviest hit by restructuring. (Target Group B, in fact, are employees from a manufacturing facility to be closed during the following year.) Despite these adversities, Target Groups A and B experienced a turnabout in how they felt about the business and management. When initially asked whether or not they were informed about business goals, Target Group A respondents indicated a 75% showing in the never or seldom response, while Target Group B showed a 68% response of never or seldom. Six months after the Toward Better Two-Way launch, responses of never or seldom to that question were sliced to 6% for Target Group A and 15% for Target Group B. The leading response for both Target Groups was often or always—50% of Target Group A respondents and 53% of Target Group B respondents.

Equally important, the credibility of management was enhanced through the Toward Better Two-Way Process. Six months into its implementation, the two-way CPI helped to cut the AEB grapevine. As the survey results indicate, employees now looked to their immediate manager as their information source of choice. Prior to the Toward Better Two-Way process, 67% of surveyed employees identified the grapevine as their primary information source. Within Target Groups A and B, the showing was even higher—70% and 75%, respectively. Six months after CPI initiatives were implemented, the grapevine share had eroded substantially. Just 26% of employees said they heard first about the business from the grapevine. Within the Target Groups, that share was virtually eroded. Only 5% of Target Group A respondents and 0% of Target Group B respondents said the grapevine was their top information source. Rather, 56% of Target Group A employees and 46% of Target Group B employees said their immediate manager had become their primary information source. Within the AEB group at large, managers were identified by the majority of respondents—44%—as their primary information sources.

The Toward Better Two-Way process gelled an information bond between AEB managers and employees. Face-to-face exchanges became the norm rather than exceptions. The survey results highlight this transformation. Prior to the Toward Bettter Two-Way initiative, 27% of AEB employees said they were meeting regularly with their work group. Six months into the intiative, 79% of AEB employees said group meetings were happening often or always. The increase in meeting frequency is captured by each of the Target Groups: Target Group A frequency (regularly held meetings) increased from 10 to 85%, while Target Group B climbed from 0 to 65%.

The most profound testimony of communications improvement was registered in employee responses when asked to rate the overall communications effectiveness of the Toward Better Two-Way process, using a 1 to 10 rating guide with 10 being the highest rating. Prior to the Toward Better Two-Way start, communications efforts were poorly regarded. The majority of respondents—37%—were assigned a rating of 1. (Some 5% of employees gave their own rating of 0.) The highest rating—6 of 10—received a 3% response. Within both Target Groups, the effectiveness ratings were even lower, with 47% of A respondents and 56% of B respondents assigning a rating of 1.

Communications effectiveness ratings after the first six months of CPI escalated. Some 87% of the total AEB group gave a rating of between 5 and 10, compared with only 17% assigning a 5–10 rating prior to the CPI process. The highest rating—8 of 10—was registered by 24% of the AEB group. Within Target Group A, some 38% of employees gave a rating of 8. Clearly, the responses indicated a reversal in opinion.

Communications effectiveness had become positively weighted. Employees were more informed about business goals and the external market than ever and, subsequently, more involved in the business. A dedicated effort on the part of management in opening up dialogs and communicating candidly had struck an appreciative chord in the workforce.

SUMMARY

Communications Process Improvement demands alterations in the management fabric of an organization—from rigid and tight–lipped to open, candid, and receptive to interaction. Because the change is so profound, snags will arise in the process. For example, the Communications Skills Training integral to the Toward Better Two-Way process at AEB helped managers fine–tune their style.

However, the training didn't change everyone into a communicator. Some individuals weren't able to surrender their power hold on information. Others couldn't hone their interpersonal skills to fit a less formal work environment. Still other managers stumbled in personalizing messages—that is, relating the impact of external and internal changes to their employees' roles in the business. Some also were guilty of information dumping, whereby data simply strews out indiscriminately without sensitivity to the audience or union issues among the represented workforce. Individualized training and refresher courses helped reform some of these communicator hold-outs. Others still resistant to change to the new, more open and empowering management style were reevaluated through annual performance ratings and, in some cases, reassigned to nonmanagement positions.

Overall, however, Toward Better Two-Way dramatically changed the communications culture and climate of a business wrestling with uncertainty. The need for this communications change was equally recognized by management and employees as essential for winning in a tougher competitive market. Total workforce commitment to the new two-way communications strategy combined with specially designed tools and processes yielded impressive gains in the speed and quality of communications over a relatively short period of time. Toward Better Two-Way—with its proven results—is a change process that can be successfully adapted to any organization.

8

Corporate Communication and Technology

The issues that face technical communications professionals focus on human interaction—both with machines and with other people. The use of contemporary communication technologies in an environment of accelerating change, political uncertainty, economic stress, and uncertain corporate direction places new demands on the communications professional. No longer is mere superior talent with the written word sufficient. The need to understand the ethical conflict of individual rights and corporate goals is now necessary for survival. With increased emphasis on team action and the proliferation of empowerment programs through Total Quality Management (TQM) and reengineering, the need to work effectively with others, rather than in isolation, is also a necessity in corporate life for communications professionals.

In meeting challenges in a dynamic world, professional communicators and managers need more information about how to interact with machines and with others in an increasingly interdependent network of ideas, people, and machines. Scarce resources have forced managers and professional communicators to depend on global computer networks as both information resources and communication tools; to consider interpersonal skills as being essential in reaching corporate objectives; and to think ethically in response to increased economic pressures brought on by the forces of change in international business activity.

Information technologies have changed the way we create, archive, access, and distribute information. New technologies have made the access to and use of information more egalitarian, less proprietary. Gatekeepers have been eliminated and new classes have emerged—the information *haves* and the information *have nots*.

Some experts, such as Marvin Zonis of the Chicago Graduate School of Business, noted in his "Business Forecast '97" (New York, December 5, 1996), a global destabalization as a result of these technical advances—a rapid breakdown in the power structure of business, the family, and political organizations. However, the equalizing power of information has flattened the hierarchical nature of organizations. With hierarchies disappearing, egalitarian and collaborative structures are emerging.

It is now very difficult to identify an agenda. The workplace, the nature of work, and the fabric of our society entered a change cycle that is rapid and unrelenting. Once the relationship between individuals and the institutions of our culture could be relied upon; a bond existed that engendered trust and loyalty. Increasingly, people find trust and loyalty rare commodities indeed.

Stock Price vs. Workforce Commitment. In March 1996, in my graduate seminar discussion on ethics and technical communication, one of my students recounted that in her organization downsizing was accomplished on a Friday afternoon with armed guards watching over employees who were told to pack personal belongings and leave the building within a few hours. The move had been rumored for a few weeks, and several clerks in response to the company's actions had shredded the orders that had come in by fax for the week that preceded the downsizing. My student, a loyal employee who was shaken by her company's move, said she could not trust her employer again after that.

If that is the case, then what happens to the relationship between the individual in times of great change, particularly when the corporation is doing well and profits are up?

Just when you thought you had adapted to change, along comes the AT&T announcement in late 1995 that it is breaking up into three companies and eliminating 40,000 jobs. Stock prices rose with that news. The reaction from the community was anything but positive. What looked like a brilliant business decision placed in stark contrast the divergent agenda of Main Street and Wall Street. In early 1996, "AT&T once known warmly as Ma Bell, has become vilified as an icon of American corporate greed" (*Wall Street Journal*, March 18, 1996: B1).

But the latest episode in the change revolution is much larger than AT&T's action. The public rage that was released is yet another symptom of the impact the transformation of our society is having on the individual. It is comparable to the upheaval in personal lives of the industrial revolution in Europe and the United States in the last century. The pace, the rules, the cycles of civilized life, are all up for grabs. The digital information revolution has simultaneously empowered the individual and made each of us incredibly vulnerable.

So just when you thought you lived in a world in which organizations put the customer first, recent events underscore the reality that today the influence and power of stockholders has superseded the power of labor, management, and the community. The irony is the power of stockholders is also the power of organizational employees whose pension plans, 401Ks, IRAs, and mutual funds are all going up. At the turn of the last century, powerful individuals—Vanderbilt, Getty, Rockefeller, Ford—influenced public policy with their economic clout; and later corporations—G.E., G.M., AT&T—and government agencies— Defense, Education—took over.

UNDERSTANDING INFORMATION AND TECHNOLOGY

Have you ever heard someone in your organization explain a strange decision or event with, "That was just political"? You might have shrugged and gone off shaking your head thinking you could not do much in that case. Well, Thomas Davenport, Robert Eccles, and Laurence Prusak think you can do a great deal. In their *Sloan Management Review* article, "Information Politics" (Fall 1992: 53–65), they describe the following five political models that help explain an organization's approach to information:

- technocratic utopianism

- anarchy

- feudalism

- monarchy

- federalism

Technocratic utopianism, according to the authors, is a heavily technical approach to information management stressing categorization and modeling of an organization's full information assets, with heavy reliance on emerging technologies. In such organizations, both IS (Information Systems) professionals and users work under the assumption that technology can solve all the problems. Issues that might be considered political or organizational are ignored because they are either unrecognized as a force or considered unmanageable and therefore dismissed. Instead of focusing on the information content and its use in the organization, people in technocratic utopias concentrate on the technologies used to manipulate information.

Anarchy can be used to describe organizations that have no overall information management policy. People in such organizations gather and manage their own information. Few companies set out to achieve such a state; rather, anarchy develops in the wake of a breakdown in centralized information management, or in the absence of a key company executive who considers common, shared information important to the health of the organization. Technological breakthroughs such as the personal computer made this state of anarchy possible. Anyone could create and manage a database, then generate a customized report in record time and at minimal cost. In the long term, the impact of such an information state leads to redundancy and information discrepancies. Most organizations cannot function for long in a state of information anarchy.

Feudalism, as in the Middle Ages, can describe organizations in which business units or functional units define their own information needs and report or allow access to limited information for the rest of the corporation. In such states the central authority is weak, and the divisions have considerable strength through their own autonomy. Each "lord" or "baron" (division executive) decides what, when, and how to report to the "king" (CEO). Each develops its own special "language" and the effect fragments the organization. In some corporations, war breaks out between these feudal lords; or sometimes the leaders "arrange a marriage" for mutual benefit.

Monarchy helps explain a corporation whose leader defines the information categories and reporting structures. This leader may or may not share the information after it is collected. The CEO (monarch), or someone empowered by the CEO, dictates the information doctrine. Since power is central, each division has little control over information policy. The monarchy may vary from an "enlightened despotism" who decrees a policy of common information to "constitutional monarchy" complete with a written information Magna Carta to establish the rules and enforcement processes. However, this model is subject to the mortality of the king. "The King is dead, long live the King" may work for the United Kingdom, but in most organizations the transfer of power after a CEO steps down is defined as one of the nine crises of business (see chapter 7), right up there with a drop in stock price or market share.

Federalism is an approach to information management based on negotiation and consensus concerning the critical information needs and reporting structures. In the contemporary business environment, this information state is desirable for most organizations. This model acknowledges the importance of politics. "In contrast, technocratic utopianism ignores politics, anarchy is politics run amok, feudalism involves destructive politics, and monarchy attempts to eliminate politics through strong central authority. Federalism treats politics as a necessary and legitimate activity by which people with different interests work out among themselves a collective purpose and means for achieving it." Federalism works well in corporations with strong central leadership and a culture that supports cooperation and learning, as well as strong negotiation skills among information managers.

Davenport, Eccles, and Prusak argue that federalism and monarchy are effective models for the majority of corporations. The other information states, particularly technocratic utopianism and anarchy, are preferred by technologists, technical journals, consultants, and vendors. They suggest that information politics can be managed following this advice: select an information "state," match the information politics to your company culture, practice technological realism, elect the right information politicians, and avoid building information empires.

USING MEDIA TECHNOLOGIES

The power of public opinion became part of the strategy of large businesses with the rise of corporations during the twentieth century. At the beginning of the century, newspapers and magazines were the only mass media. Radio, TV, and film took on greater influence. Then Marshall McLuhan opened the eyes of the world to the power of communications media. Corporations have seized the opportunity to influence audiences internally and externally with technology and media ever since.

Forward thinking organizations developed strong relationships with the media, partly in response to the negative attitude toward business that followed the so-called muckrakers such as Upton Sinclair and Ida Tarbell. These journalists were reacting to a public need for information about large organizations that almost exclusively at the turn of the century held firm to the notion that what they did was not the concern of the general public.

The obvious lack of what we now know as corporate citizenship created an adversarial relationship between business and the media that continues to exist today, though the relationship between business and the press is now somewhat more symbiotic than in the past. The media depends on business for information related to the company, so an atmosphere of mutual benefit has emerged.

Broadcast media—radio and television—telephone and computer networks have changed the relationship once more. This section examines the ways in which corporations use technology and media to communicate internally and with external audiences.

Broadcast News Networks

Gone is the era in which the three national networks dominated the television screens of America. Major markets have a dozen or more stations, and when you include cable the number increases to well above fifty.

Nevertheless, the national network news still plays a major role in bringing business news to most people. Creating good relations with the national networks and their local affiliates is fundamental to an effective corporate communications strategy. Providing timely information to the news media is also part of that strategy, since the reporter has to meet a deadline. If your organization returns a call late in the day or early the next morning, the reporter is likely to say something like, "XYZ Corporation did not return our telephone call." Such a phrase, while true, appears to the viewing public as if your corporation had something to hide and was dodging the reporter's questions, when the truth may have been just the opposite—you may have been checking your facts.

Reporters work under pressure and an effective relationship with them acknowledges their deadlines in all conversations. This is particularly true when we consider that the content of business reporting on nightly news often is related to some sort of crisis or emergency. (Since chapter 7 fully discusses crisis and emergency communication, this section will concentrate on other aspects of business communication.)

Generally, corporate use of national networks is related to building corporate identity and corporate image, discussed in chapter 4. This is not to imply that television does not play an important role in major organizations. Many companies use television on a daily basis for meetings, informational sessions, training, and annual meetings. Though they use closed or business networks, the production of an interview with the vice president for marketing on what new products will be offered next year requires the same techniques as putting Larry King on the air.

Corporate television must have the same look and feel of broadcast television because the audience is video-literate and sophisticated; they also expect high production quality in the programs they view. The audience's needs drive the level of quality for corporate programs very high.

Radio

Radio in the age of television has become an "outlaw" medium. It is very personal and focused on niche markets. Certain products and services can be discussed and advertised on the radio with relative ease. For instance, condom manufacturers advertise during dating hours, such as Friday and Saturday nights on rock stations for an audience predominantly sixteen to twenty-four years old.

Radio stations appeal to smaller and smaller audiences with ever-increasing diversity. Radio advertising and sponsorship of shows is a bargain compared to television network rates. A corporation may routinely sponsor a radio broadcast of a sports or cultural event, such as the long-running Texaco opera series.

Radio is also used to inform employees about events at a local factory or corporate headquarters, in the case of natural disasters and plant closings. Radio news and talk shows are a sort of grassroots therapy session for the community.

Cable Network

Like radio, cable television has so many stations, in some areas over seventy, that its audiences are smaller and more diverse. Advertising for local businesses makes economic sense in these markets. Cable stations focus on types of information—sports, weather, financial reports, world affairs, political events in Congress, court trials, call-in talk shows.

Cable also covers business news and events more closely than the national broadcast networks because it follows the all-news format of the radio and can devote more time to business issues. Also, business-related programs comprise much more of the programming on these stations.

The infomercial, or long-form commercial, has become a popular device on cable network stations. The company buys an entire half hour or hour and sells a product but presents it as if it were a talk show or game show. Diet programs, investment schemes, automobile polish products, and kitchen counter top gadgets are some of the staples of this form. However, Ross Perot's use of the long-form format during the 1992 presidential election suggests that the form may begin to have an impact on mainstream products and audiences.

The infomercial allows for more detail and discussion, the appeal of the Perot presentations, as a way to cut through the clutter of the fifteen-second ads on network television. It also suggests that the ads appeal to an audience that receives most of its information through the broadcast media, not newspapers, books, or periodicals. Perot was less successful in his 1996 attempt at using an infomercial. Perhaps he had lost credibility the second time around.

Video and Satellite News Releases

Traditional communication with newspapers called for the circulation of a written press release usually sent by mail or fax. If the information was considered very important or particularly newsworthy, the company would hold a press conference.

Now many organizations use video and satellite technology to provide information about the company and its products and services to local news stations, the national networks, and cable companies. In effect, the corporation prepares a video news story the outlet can run in its entirety or use clips in developing its own story.

The practice has benefits for both the company and the news organization. It allows the company to provide detailed information in a visual format that it can monitor and control. It offers the news program a feature without the production costs involved in sending out a crew to the company site. Often the company can provide much more dramatic footage than the station has available or could prepare on a daily deadline schedule or budget, for instance, pictures of aircraft in flight, automobiles or other vehicles undergoing testing, or computer simulations of planned buildings within the community.

Corporations use video internally to provide information to staff and employees. Companies such as IBM have a television network that broadcasts company news daily to major sites around the world. The messages are communicated in a timely and consistent manner to all employees. Often the television monitors are located in high-traffic areas, by elevators or near the entrance to the company cafeteria. The screen may have a scrolling message in words, similar to the use of video in hotel lobbies. In addition to this video bulletin board, the monitor may offer short pieces of information from company officers, plant employees, and community leaders.

Corporate video can also be used for the orientation and training of employees, mentioned in the discussion about ways to perpetuate corporate identity.

Corporate video is used to provide important information to the community. For example, local utilities such as telephone, gas, and electric companies routinely develop information about safety and about how to cope with a natural disaster such as a flood or winter storm. Often they work together with a nonprofit organization to produce an informational video for the community.

Corporate video also is used to present product information to potential customers and current owners. Many organizations provide a "setup" video for the new buyer of a complex or technical product, along with the traditional instruction booklet. Many companies use video to present financial information in what has been called a video annual report. In both cases, the use of video meets the needs of an American population that has grown up on television and receives most of its information from the video screen, whether through a broadcast, a tape played on a VCR, or computer.

Interactive video has proven useful in providing information to knowledge workers. It works like a computer program and allows the user to select information from a menu by using a light pen, mouse, or keypad. Such systems are in use in hospitals, factories, hotels, and offices.

The combination of computers and video has opened the corporation to new media technologies such as voice mail, e-mail, and Local Area Networks (or LANs).

VOICE MAIL, E-MAIL, LAN, THE INTERNET, THE WORLD WIDE WEB

The 1980s brought a quiet media revolution to the office in the form of personal computers. Now, powerful machines and programs made it possible for one or two people to do the work of several. Spreadsheets and word processing and desktop publishing are among the most common computer applications. Larger corporations are now using the computer network as a major communications channel.

Voice mail allows computers to answer telephones and store messages, and users can call in for messages from anywhere in the world and at any time. This service, unknown only a few years ago, has become commonplace in business.

E-mail, or electronic mail, is linking computers to send messages from one computer to another. The systems have global reach through various networks such as the Internet and commercial providers such as CompuServe. The advantage of these electronic communication channels is savings of time and distribution costs. A message can be sent to a general bulletin board that anyone on the system can have access to, or to a designated distribution list, or to one person on the network. E-mail allows one to send messages tagged for urgency, or to ask for a verification of the message being received and read. In this manner, e-mail has replaced, in many organizations, the use of and need for informational memos. Using e-mail to replace paper memos and physical distribution of those documents has substantially accelerated the communication of information within organizations that use them.

Local Area Networks (LANs) function like e-mail, but consist of several computers in a particular location linked to form a computer network that allows the users to share the use of data and programs. LANs have the outward appearance of being a centralized computer mainframe setup, but the system functions more like a bundle of cells. The LAN is also a secure system because it is not connected to outside users.

The Internet and the World Wide Web came into popular commercial use after 1994. Some see tremendous growth for the Internet. Companies have built Web pages for fear of being left out of this technological revolution. The Internet may fulfill the predictions as interfaces improve, the infrastructure gets better, security becomes tighter, bandwidth becomes higher, and full motion video is added.

Skeptics see the open architecture of the Internet and the World Wide Web as the reason for its success, as well as being a built-in problem for corporations. The network was designed by the Defense Advanced Research Projects Agency (DARPA) to be able to withstand the catastrophic damage of a nuclear holocaust. Its strength is in its open nature, thus security of proprietary company data cannot be protected in this environment with high confidence. Nevertheless, almost every company, up from less than half in 1995, has an Internet address.

ORGANIZATIONS AND PEOPLE SUITABLE
FOR TECHNICAL INNOVATION

What type of person is best suited for a technical innovation? What role do expectations play in the process? Do some corporate cultures adapt to technical innovations better than others?

What type of person is best suited for technical innovation and change? You may have noticed around your organization an individual, and that person may be you, who sees the widespread changes in work processes and outcomes as a stimulating challenge. This person comes to work with a smiling face and a spring in his or her step, often arriving early and leaving late. No matter how much chaos the organization is in, this person appears to respond well to the situation.

Others in the organization respond less well to change and exhibit dysfunctional behavior. There are degrees of dysfunctional behavior related to change. For instance, examples of a low degree of dysfunction include poor communication, reduced trust, blaming, defensiveness, increased conflict with fellow workers, decreased team effectiveness, and inappropriate outbursts at the office. Moderate dysfunction includes lying or deception, chronic lateness or absenteeism, symptoms such as headaches and stomach pains, apathy, and interpersonal withdrawal. A high degree of dysfunction includes covert undermining of leadership, overt blocking, actively promoting a negative attitude in others, sabotage, substance abuse, physical or psychological breakdown, family abuse, violence, murder, and suicide.

The person who responds well to change exhibits buoyancy, elasticity, resilience—the ability to recover quickly from change. Note that such people possess a strong, positive sense of self that provides them with the security and confidence they need to meet new challenges, even if they do not have all of the answers. These people, like successful athletes, are focused on a clear vision of what they wish to accomplish, and they are tenacious in making their vision a reality. In addition, these people tend to be accommodating and flexible in the face of uncertainty and organized in the way in which they develop an approach for managing ambiguity. These people are proactive. They engage the circumstances, rather than defend against change.

The type of person I have described here is not that unusual. Such a person practices fairness, integrity, honesty, and human dignity—the principles that provide us with all of the security to adapt to change.

What role do expectations play in the change process? If, as I have suggested, all change is personal, how can understanding and managing expectations help an individual or organization through the change cycle? Everyone has made personal changes: leaving home for college, getting married or divorced, relocating to another town. Each personal change brings with it the feeling that *things* will get better. Like most of the characters in Dickens' *Great Expectations*, fame and fortune are often illusive and illusory because they neglect to consider that change is an equal opportunity for failure. A contemporary rock song puts it this way: "If you don't expect too much from me, you may not be let down."

However, it is not to lower expectations, but to *manage* them. In managing expectations, consider that in responding to positive change most people go through the following phases:

1. uninformed optimism or certainty at the start, like the joy at a wedding

2. informed pessimism or doubt—here people may quit publicly, or more destructively they will quit privately and continue to work, allowing the negative feelings to generate dysfunctional behavior

3. hope emerges with a sense of reality

4. informed optimism results in confidence

5. satisfaction closes the cycle of change upon completion

The good news is that the cycle is predictable and can be used to manage expectations by helping people prepare for the rough periods. The bad news is that most people feel they are the exception and will not follow the cycle from beginning to end.

Do some corporate cultures adapt to change better than others? The concept of corporate culture is complex, but for this discussion we can consider that it is made up of the physical things and patterns of behavior that reflect the values and beliefs and basic underlying assumptions of the corporation or organization. A culture that values the status quo may resist change, but may paradoxically be best suited to meet the challenge of change. A process culture such as a public utility or telecommunications company, may have the scope and resources to make a successful cultural change. It has the capacity to survive as the people and processes go through the cycle of change. A macho culture such as an investment bank or a movie studio, may be entirely wiped out by changes in laws or in the economic environment. AT&T and IBM are still alive, while E. F. Hutton and Drexel Burnham are not.

The survival of an organization, like the survival of an individual, also depends on its buoyancy, elasticity, and resilience—its ability to recover quickly from change. Corporations that employ such people have those organizational abilities.

THE INFLUENCE ON LANGUAGE

Often people react to new situations without fully realizing what their true feelings are; they cannot articulate their underlying understandings. In an effort to do so, the metaphors they use shape and reveal how they comprehend the events. The metaphors of change can be roughly aligned with the following four types of organizational change:

- maintenance

- developmental

- transitional

- transformational

In *maintenance,* change is equated with something being broken or poorly maintained. Change in such an environment means that something is wrong and needs to be fixed. The metaphor provokes a fix-and-maintain image, represented by agents such as a mechanic, maintenance worker, or "repair person." Ross Perot was fond of such metaphors during his campaign for the presidency: "Let's get under the hood and fix it."

In *developmental,* change builds on the past and leads to better performance over time. In this environment teamwork is the key to build and develop. The agents are often called trainer, coach, mentor, facilitator, or developer. You might hear metaphors borrowed from sports, "There is no "I" in "TEAM.""

Transitional change involves a move from one state or condition to another. For instance, an operation goes from manual to automated. The image is often one of movement and relocation, and the agents are often called planners, guides, or explorers. In such environments you might "need to create a map for unexplored territory."

Transformational change implies the transfiguration from one state of being to a fundamentally different state of being. An example might be a business or an industry that changes from a regulated monopoly to a market-driven competitive business. The image is often one of liberation and recreation, and the agents are often called visionaries, creators, or liberators. In this environment, you might "create a vision for reengineering the corporation."

In managing the language of change,

- note the word images used to describe the change;

- say what you mean; make the metaphor coincide with the literal meaning;

- describe the change using the four metaphor types to gain insight;

- align the language with people's behavior;

- use metaphors, symbols, and images to shape the way people think about change; and

- change the metaphors and images as a way to get "out of the box" and stimulate new ways of thinking.

Understanding and using the language of change can benefit everyone involved and help them perceive change as an opportunity to move forward, rather than being a threat to their well–being.

TECHNOLOGICAL IMPACT

Corporations are changing; they are reinventing, rethinking, transforming, and reengineering themselves. And with change comes chaos, uncertainty, *and renewal.* For everyone involved, change represents a threat to security, or an opportunity to move forward.

What are the forces at work in changing corporations? Five general categories of forces have emerged, including the following:

- a new sophistication in customers, or audience

- new media and technologies, or communication tools

- a more widespread ethical environment

- stronger economic factors

- new strategic alliances

A New Sophistication in Customers, or Audience

The force of the customer is felt everywhere, from consumer electronics to the use of new management tools such as Integrated Product Development (IPD) in traditionally conservative, hierarchical organizations such as the Air Force. Customers at all levels demand quality products, and they are hungry for information about the products they want and eventually purchase. They are also looking for stimulation and entertainment, which has profound implications for such fields as software interfaces and the development of the information superhighway.

New Media and Technologies, or Communication Tools

The creation of new media and technologies are the tools of change. But which innovations take hold and which do not depends not on us but on others, since we tend to be the early adapters for new tools. What determines the future of these tools in the marketplace has less to do with the elegance and value of the technology. It is really the second and third segments of adapters who do not share that "gee-whiz" enthusiasm for new technologies who determine if a technological tool takes hold or not. Geoffrey Moore's *Crossing the Chasm* explains the complexity of the forces at work in taking the innovations in technology to the customer. Now, too, the number of channels of communication available is increasing: E-mail, fax, voice mail, desktop publishing, personalized magazines and journals, and networking software and groupware. Because there are more tools and more choices, customers need more information than ever before.

Moore describes the characteristics of five categories of people in a technology adoption cycle.

1. *Innovators*—pursue new technology products; seek them out before marketing begins; place technology at the center of their lives; take pleasure in exploring new technology for its own sake; make up a small, but influential, minority.

2. *Early Adapters*—buy new products early in the life cycle, but they are not technologists; easily imagine, understand, and appreciate the benefits of new technology; relate potential benefits to their own goals; make their buying decisions on their own intuition rather than another's recommendation.

3. *Early Majority*—shares some of the early adapter's appreciation of technology, but is driven by practicality; waits to see how others do before it buys in, since it knows how fads work; requires well-

established references before it invests; makes up about one-third of the adoption cycle and is critical to the success of any product.

4. *Late Majority*—shares all of the concerns of the early majority, and more; possesses no comfort with the ability to handle a technological product; waits until a standard is established; requires lots of support from a large, well-established company.

5. *Laggards*—want nothing to do with technology for many reasons, personal and economic; buy technological products buried deep in another product so it is invisible to them, like the microchips in an automatic coffee maker; are generally not a target for high-tech approaches.

A More Widespread Ethical Environment

Since the tools of our technological age have enormous social and economic impact, the ethics of the workplace now come into play more strongly as we approach the twenty-first century. No longer can a corporation make a product and not worry or care about its impact on the community. Companies must now function as "corporate citizens." New methods of government regulation and new laws underscore the responsibility customers expect of the providers of goods and services.

Stronger Economic Factors

Competition, competition, competition has been the strongest economic factor for change in corporations. It has forced the quest for quality and efficiency as co-equal goals in a company's strategy. It has also forced the rapid growth in globalism. After all, no organization can afford to operate for long if its balance sheet is lopsided.

New Strategic Alliances

Ventures, partnerships, reorganizations, mergers, acquisitions, buyouts, reengineering, downsizing, right-sizing—these are more than buzz words; they are the codes for a workplace in tremendous upheaval. I can not think of anyone I know whose organization in the last several years has not undergone, or is undergoing, a profound change in structure or ownership. The new alliances, if managed well and communicated to all audiences efficiently and clearly, signal a new way of thinking about work in general, and about the nature of the workplace itself.

As more and more government and business partnerships emerge, replacing the role corporations such as IBM and Digital played in research and development, the need to communicate among organizations and with the general public on the meaning of these complex research efforts will grow. But in an environment of lean corporate structures and a vastly reduced government workforce, who will communicate the complex information to the public?

Taxpayers and stockholders will want to know what their hard-earned dollars are supporting. Corporations have considered this question as part of strategic planning. The new, more nimble technology development companies and partnerships with the government would do well to remember that communication to internal and external audiences is a fundamental strategic element of technological and financial success. For the near future and the next century winning must take place in the laboratory and in the market; "Wall Street," "Main Street," and "Industrial Park" are closer to one another than ever.

IMPACT OF TECHNOLOGICAL INNOVATION ON THE CORPORATION, ON PEOPLE, ON PROCESS

The way people react to change is always personal, whether they are in a corporate environment, a small town, or on a farm. To some, change means chaos and uncertainty, stimulating fear and anger. For others, the same change signals *hope and renewal*, creating excitement and anticipation.

As corporations continue to reinvent, rethink, transform, and reengineer themselves, a growing number of reports look at the impact these changes are having on people and on the process of communication within the organization. For everyone involved, change represents a threat to security, or an opportunity to move forward.

New media and technologies—the tools of communication—continue to have a profound impact on corporate communications and culture. Customers at all levels demand quality products and are hungry for information about the products they want and eventually purchase.

INFORMATION AND ELECTRONIC MEDIA

In organizations—profit and nonprofit—knowledge is power. Electronic media offered the productivity and communications tools to usher in the information age to organizations. It was simultaneously a lever to flatten hierarchical organizations and provide the means for an empowered and informed workforce. However, as Shoshana Zuboff of the Harvard Business School and author of *In the Age of the Smart Machine* (1988) told the *New York Times* (November 4, 1996, D1), "The

paradise of shared knowledge and a more egalitarian working environment just isn't happening. Knowledge isn't really shared because
management doesn't want to share authority and power." Are these the
signs of a failed revolution, or are they more likely the end of a cycle in
which the organization and the individual continue the struggle for
dominance?

With all of the innovation, empowerment, restructuring, and
promises for a bright tomorrow, organizations seem to be gravitating
back to the traditional, hierarchical model questioned in the 1920s and
1930s. Since then, and through the depression, organizations had been
working toward the realization of a human relations model, a model
first described by Elton Mayo and expanded on by Abraham Maslow,
Frederick Herzberg, and Chris Argyris.

These theorists articulated for the twentieth century the conflict
between the needs of the individual and the needs of the organization.
Then, as now, this conflict remains the irreconcilable force of the
industrial revolution, the post–industrial revolution, and the information age. Our electronic communications tools highlight the paradox. A
single person can influence the course of large organizations, such as
the case of Intel's introduction of the Pentium chip in the winter of
1994–1995. Such David and Goliath tales of organizational life certainly
make headlines. It is, after all, news. More often than not, though, it is
the organization that still wields such power and influence that most
contemporary Davids are overwhelmed almost effortlessly. Today
David can be downsized, restructured, press released, or budget cut
into submission. Or David can be worked into submission, his support
staff replaced by productivity software, groupware, and Internet access.
Recently Joe Chew contemplated the negative side of electronic
communication for an individual in his Introduction to the Special Issue
on Electronic Communication and Interaction (Chew 1994, 193):

> The opposite end of the range of possibilities is too awful to
> contemplate: combining the worst aspects of physical commuting and
> telecommuting. Seeing any time to contemplate writing and reasoned
> decision-making (insofar as the telephone, fax machine, meetings,
> and cubicle environments have left any such time) smashed into
> MTV-paced fragments by a productivity tool—if, that is, people adopt
> the tool at all.
>
> But that is too apocalyptic a vision. Plainly people are getting
> things done in spite of, or perhaps even with the help of, electronic
> interaction, so there must be ways to cope.

Tools, as every anthropologist knows from the observations of
Margaret Mead, are the artifacts of a culture. Add a new tool to an

existing culture and it changes that culture. Our media technologies now allow us to communicate anytime, anywhere. The impact of a global, twenty-four-hour workday has profound implications on our lives, as Valerie Perugini explained in her article (see the Selected Commentary at the end of this chapter) on how communication technology influences our society. Books by Bill Gates, *The Road Ahead* (1995), and Nicholas Negroponte, *Being Digital* (1995) to the contrary, the change is not always positive.

Selected Commentary

The commentary and case study selected for this chapter are from the presentations at the annual Conference on Corporate Communication at Fairleigh Dickinson University. Each of the authors focuses on a part of corporate communications theory and practice that is associated with using various types of media in a corporate environment.

Valerie Perugini discusses the impact of the ability of people to communicate anytime, anywhere, in our society. She explores both the benefits of such a capability for the disabled, the possible erosion of face-to-face communication, and the physiology of a twenty-four-hour society.

Michael Cusack's case study of the interaction of people and computers illuminates the relationship writers have with their new tools.

Anytime, Anywhere
The Social Impact of Emerging Communication Technology

Valerie Perugini

Anytime, anywhere communication. Industry analysts are writing about it, technophiles are talking about it, and advertisers are shouting it in large, bold typeface. But what does it mean, really? Cellular phones are already old news; we know that they can keep us in touch with our homes and offices virtually twenty-four-hours a day, so what is all the fuss about?

More than just mere telephone conversations, anytime, anywhere communication is the combination of computing and communication technologies which will enable portable, wireless transmission and manipulation of voice, data, images, and messages around the clock and around the globe. Just as the invention of the computer and the telephone has had profound effects on our everyday lives, so will the emerging technologies making anytime, anywhere a reality.

No one can be sure exactly how the future will look, but the phenomenon of anytime, anywhere communication may well integrate the features of today's most popular computing and communication hardware into handheld devices that will be mobile, cheap, and easy to use. Combined with their cellular cousins, the revenue from the wireless data markets in the United States alone is expected to hit $10 billion a year by the end of the decade (Kupfer 1993, 147).

This commentary by Valerie Perugini, of AT&T, was presented at a colloquium at Fairleigh Dickinson University in 1995. An updated version appears here with her permission.

THE TECHNOLOGY

Wireless Infrastructure

Computers have drastically reshaped the way we collect and distribute information. They have become so popular that we see and use them in many different parts of our lives: in our homes and where we work, and sometimes we even carry them with us. One of the drawbacks of existing computer technology, however, is that in order to make them communicate, to access databases, send electronic mail (e-mail) or data files, the user's choices are limited by location (with an available phone line) or cost (of cellular service and equipment). Cellular phones, while they have freed us from the wires for making voice calls, have not quite done the same for data, images, and messaging. This has long been the missing piece to the anytime, anywhere puzzle. These limitations will soon be conquered as technological advances overcome the barriers and competition heats up in the mobile marketplace.

One of the first tasks in this undertaking is to put the infrastructure in place to support wireless communication. Although the plans for this infrastructure are still evolving, it is expected that we will soon see radio-based, satellite, and enhanced cellular technologies at the forefront of the so-called Personal Communications Services (PCS) market. The list of players is impressive; companies like Motorola, IBM, GTE, Sprint, and AT&T are just a few of the corporations scrambling for a piece of the pie (Therrien 1993, 128–33).

Products and Services

When this infrastructure is in place, anytime, anywhere communication can become a reality that we can carry around in a pocket or briefcase. New devices and services will speed our entry into the Information Highway by giving us round-the-clock access to people and data.

Among the first devices especially designed for untethered operation is the personal communicator. Also known as a personal assistant or intelligent communicator, these gadgets are expected to marry the mobility of the cellular phone with the features and abilities of computers, fax machines, and pagers. The software being developed to support them will enable personal communicators to "handle your appointments, translate your written commands to type, send out your e-mail and faxes, and retrieve news and other information" (Eng 1994, 141–42).

Although Personal Digital Assistants (PDAs) like Apple's *Newton*, AT&T's *Eo*, and Casio's *Zoomer* have already hit the market, they all lack the usability and true mobility that will be essential to the success of the personal communicator market. One of the first of such handheld devices to really go portable is Motorola's *Envoy*, which has been touted as a product that "offers a quantum improvement in communications functions and usability over prior handheld personal digital assistants" (Hutsko 1994, 78). A relatively new entry to the market, time will tell if *Envoy* lives up to its claims.

Applications

Much of what they will do with personal communicators is the same as what they do today with phones, computers, and datebooks. They will just have the freedom to perform these functions anywhere we happen to be. For example, one of the most often cited applications for these devices is in the mobile office. Thanks to the wireless capability, people can work anywhere they choose and still have the same access to information and e-mail as they do when sitting in the office (Korzeniowski 1993, 111). In fact, the growth in the number of workers who telecommute or work at home on a full- or part-time basis since 1988 has paralleled the increase in the availability (and decrease in prices) of portable technology and the accessibility of on-line databases (Stewart 1994, 76–78).

This is just the beginning. Even now, programs are being written for these devices which will expand their usefulness in the workplace. Industry-specific services will put personal communicators in the hands of real estate agents, giving them access to multiple listing databases from the field (Hill 1994, B4). Apple is testing its *Newtons* in the hands of sales representatives and giving farmers the ability to track planting schedules, yields, and other crop information (Rebello 1994, 41). AT&T, in conjunction with Emory University in Atlanta, is developing a wireless device that lets emergency medical technicians transmit patient data to hospital-based physicians so they can begin treating patients still en route to the emergency room (Miller 1994, B2).

Software Agents

Another of the features that suppliers hope will advance anytime, anywhere communication is something called a software agent. Think of these as intelligent electronic servants which can be sent out to run errands on the various communications networks that will be available. First invented by Apple, software agent technology is a key feature of the *Magic Cap* software being created by General Magic Corp., a partnership that includes such global companies as AT&T, Motorola, Sony, Apple, and Phillips. Already, Sony and Motorola have introduced devices that utilize Magic Cap, and AT&T has brought its PersonaLink Services network on-line to support the "agent" activities (Burgess 1994, H1).

In the beginning, the agents' capabilities will be limited to activities like setting up appointments and looking up e-mail addresses. As more personal communication services and information databases become available, they will be able to order concert tickets, make airline and dinner reservations, renew a driver's license, send flowers to mom on her birthday, and shop for the best deal on ski boots. And since the agents can be directed to run these errands at any time of the day or night, the user is free for other pursuits (Burgess, H1).

Many feel that the software agent will be at the heart of value-added services that wireless companies will be trying to sell. According to an analyst from BIS Strategic Decisions, "the real pot of gold in [wireless] is not in selling the devices, but in selling communication and information services to be consumed by those devices" (Cringely 1993, 92).

Others, like University of Maryland Professor Ben Shneiderman, think that software agents will never really catch on. An expert on human interaction with computers, Dr. Shneiderman believes that "for most computer users an on-screen agent would just get in the way. People want to feel they're directly controlling the machine, not negotiating with an intermediary" (Burgess, H4).

The Future

At least for the immediate future, it seems that anytime, anywhere communication will come to us in the form of these pocket-sized, handheld devices. But what about the long term?

Author John Verity points out that computer technology is rapidly getting smaller and faster and may soon disappear altogether. "Researchers at Xerox Corp. and Olivetti are driving toward a concept called 'ubiquitous computing,' in which computing resources are embedded throughout the human environment—in appliances, digital whiteboards, and walls, or the surface of your desk, which might turn your scrawl into perfectly formatted, spell-checked text" (Verity 1994, 18). Computer scientists at Xerox's Palo Alto Research Center (PARC) agree that what they are developing is "technology so powerful it's invisible" (Wolkomir 1994, 82).

Ubiquitous computing works on the anthropological theory that in order to be successfully integrated into society, technology should be virtually invisible to the user. It all starts with the idea of taking the computer chips that are already built into many of today's appliances and automobiles and giving them the ability to communicate via radio or infrared signals. Individuals would carry similar, identifying, computer chips in their pocket or on their clothing. These devices would emit signals to receptors embedded in the environment, which are all linked to a computing network. In this way, say PARC scientists, the computer always knows who and where you are. If, for example, you were to walk down a street in Japan, the street signs might change to English as you go by; and your voice and e-mail could be accessed from virtually any display screen in the world, because the computer would be able to recognize individual users. Your own household computer will switch the lights on as you enter a room and maybe even turn on the coffeepot when it senses you are about to wake.

Although ubiquitous computing sounds like it's a long way off, the groundwork is already being laid. Many of the appliances and other mechanical devices that we use today, from coffeepots to televisions to automobiles, already have one or more microprocessors inside. The ability to interconnect all these computer chips and give them the ability to communicate with each other and with us will be the key to making ubiquity a reality (Wolkomir, 84–92).

ACCEPTANCE AND INTEGRATION

The Marketing Mission

A popular fallacy in business is that one only needs to create a product and the market will follow. And although this does occur on rare occasions, the truth is it usually happens the other way around. Building a better mousetrap doesn't automatically mean that the world will beat a path to the door.

Following its invention, a technology or technological innovation goes through a period of diffusion, wherein "an innovation is communicated through certain channels over time among the members of a social system" (McGinn 1991, 90). Whether or not the technology is accepted or rejected will depend largely on the "economic, sociological, and political features" of the society in general, including determination of whether the technology is compatible with that society's values. Today, of course, diffusion is facilitated by the marketing process which utilizes such earlier innovations as radio, television, and the printing press as the channels for communicating both quickly and to large audiences (McGinn, 91–92).

Judging by the sales performance of the first generation of personal communication devices, the marketing folks have their work cut out for them. Sales of *Newton*, *Eo*, and *Zoomer* have all fallen well short of the initial, and highly publicized, projections (Hill 1994, B1). Bell South and

IBM pulled the plug on their product, *Simon*, before its scheduled introduction in order to regroup in light of the failures of their predecessors in the market (Wildstron 1994, 20). So just how will the manufacturers and providers of the next wave of products and services get them into the hearts (and palms and pockets) of the users?

The first question is, is there really a market for the advanced devices that will make anytime, anywhere a reality? Companies like Motorola and Apple seem to think so. So does Link Resources, a New York-based consulting firm, whose recent survey shows that there is significant consumer interest in a device "that would manipulate their personal data, provide both voice and wireless data communications and connect them to their desktop computers" (Hill, B1, B6).

Marketing New Technology

The marketing of new, high-technology products and technology-based innovations presents an entirely different set of challenges than would be found if one were selling "new and improved" soap products, or even the new model year automobile. One of the things that makes introducing anywhere, anytime communication products and services different from selling soap or cars is that this technology requires consumers to change their behavior in order to use it. Rather than being a simple upgrade to a familiar product, the products and services that will support anytime, anywhere will require changes not only in the way consumers interact with technology, but also in the overall telecommunication infrastructure, requiring the establishment of nationwide (and eventually global) support networks (Moore 1991, 10–11).

How will marketers meet this challenge of bringing a previously unknown technology into the mainstream? In his book *Crossing the Chasm*, author Geoffrey A. Moore points to the Technology Adoption Life Cycle as the marketing model for introducing new products (Figure 8-1). This model illustrates the process by grouping consumers according to their reactions and buying patterns with regard to behavior-changing innovations brought on by new technology. Innovators, for example, are those who aggressively pursue new technologies, mainly because of their interest in exploring new devices and innovations. Early Adopters also tend to buy into new technologies early in the life cycle, but rather than being technology buffs like the Innovators, they are more interested in how new technologies can be used for solving business problems.

The Early Majority, while they are comfortable with and look favorably on the potential benefits of new technologies, are much more practical than the Early Adopters. Although not afraid of innovation,

Figure 8–1. Technology Adoption Life Cycle

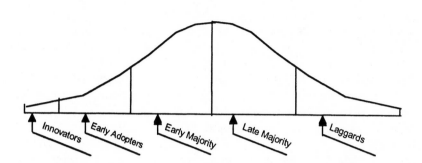

the Early Majority are reluctant to sink money into passing fads and prefer to wait until products are relatively well established before jumping in. The Late Majority, although similar to the Early Majority in many ways, are different in one significant area: members of the Late Majority do not feel comfortable with their ability to handle a new technology. Therefore, they are unlikely to purchase new products until their performance and benefits are proven and documented, the standards well established and accepted throughout an industry, and they are well supported by large companies.

Finally, the Laggards are those who don't want anything to do with new technologies and probably will never purchase them unless they become so embedded in other products that they are virtually invisible to the end user (Moore, 11–14).

Already we can see how the marketing efforts for personal communicators have progressed through this model. The Innovators rushed out to buy them, despite some acknowledged shortcomings in the technology, and Early Adopters also made purchases, probably because of innovative applications developed for particular industries, such as agriculture and pharmaceutical sales (Rebello, 41).

It would appear that sales of the initial personal communication devices have stalled, somewhere between the Early Adopters and the Early Majority. And since the latter group makes up about one-third of the entire market, new technology will never break through into the mainstream without capturing this segment and the Late Majority members who will follow.

This situation however is entirely consistent with Moore's vision of the Technology Adoption Life Cycle in that he also describes a gap, or chasm, that exists between each of the components of the life cycle which make it difficult for technology marketers to create enough momentum to cross over from one segment to the next. In short, the techniques and strategies that work on one segment are not likely to be successful with the next, simply because of the different needs and concerns of each group (Moore, 14, 17). In fact, Moore characterizes the chasm between the Early Adopters and the Early Majority as "by far the most formidable and unforgiving transition" (p. 20) in the life cycle. "This is indeed a chasm, and into this chasm many an unwary start-up venture has fallen" (p. 23). The reason these companies fail, he claims, is because they mistake the upswing in sales created by the Innovators and the Early Adopters as the beginning of mainstream acceptance of the product. According to Moore, this can be a fatal mistake. "There is something fundamentally different between a sale to an Early Adopter and a sale to the Early Majority" (p. 25).

Since the Early Majority component of the market clearly can't be ignored, how can high-tech companies take anytime, anywhere out of the chasm and into the mainstream? The first step, according to Moore, is to consider the psychological make up of the customers in each market segment. Because while Innovators are known as technology enthusiasts and Early Adopters are visionaries, the Early Majority are the pragmatists (pp. 29, 33, 41). They are simply not interested in the same things as those who have preceded them in the cycle. In order to sell to pragmatists, one must first understand what they value. What the Early Majority look for in new products is steady, incremental, process and productivity improvements and prefer not to take risks if they don't have to. When they buy, they look for quality and reliability in products and services; an established infrastructure of distribution channels; supporting products and interfaces; and a competitive market. "Pragmatists want to buy from proven market leaders because they know that third parties will design supporting products around a market-leading product" (pp. 42–45).

What is the next step for the marketing of anytime, anywhere communication? What is the right strategy for getting personal communication services into the hands of the Early Majority? Well, we are just about to see the introduction of the next generation of devices. These gadgets have upgraded functionality and portability, but also have the beginning of something near and dear to the pragmatist's heart: the establishment of industry standards and system-to-system compatibility.

Many of the devices and services initially coming to the market will utilize the *Magic Cap* operating system and *Telescript* communications software developed by General Magic Corporation. The General Magic consortium hopes to set the standard for personal communication devices with *Telescript*, software which will enable communication between a wide variety of devices, both wired and wireless. Member companies plan to solidify *Telescript*'s place in the market by introducing a variety of compatible services and software (Ziegler 1994, 83–84).

Usability

One of the reasons most often cited for the failure of the early devices to live up to expectations is that many people found them both difficult and expensive to use. Flawed handwriting recognition programs made it hard for users to enter information, and they also lacked an acceptable communication capability. The *Newton*, for example, could send faxes and electronic mail, but the user first had to find a phone line to plug it into (Wildstrom, 20). And although the *Eo* featured an attachable cellular phone, its $2,500 price tag and ungainly design put off many potential buyers. Still others point to the functionality of these devices as the main problem. "I've heard people say that ease of use is one of the key barriers, but I think that's completely wrong," says Nathan Myhrvold of Microsoft Corp. "The problem is they don't do anything useful" (Hill, B1).

As manufacturers face up to the challenge of making these products more useful, we will see enhancements and added features designed to make the equipment more value-added in the eyes of the consumer. Ease of use is another issue entirely. How does one fit technology that once required the space of a gymnasium and hundreds of feet of cable and wire into a pocket-sized device that is easy to understand and easy to use?

Donald A. Norman, author of *The Design of Everyday Things*, maintains that usability is a primary key to the widespread acceptance of any new technology. Too often, he believes, product designers ignore usability in favor of aesthetics or adding fancy (and complex) features (Norman 1998, 151). The much-heralded handwriting recognition programs on both *Newton* and *Eo* were so difficult to use that they were cited as one of the main causes of the products' downfall (Wildstrom, 20). Many consumers rethought their buying decision after seeing handwriting recognition technology lampooned in the comic strip "Doonesbury" (Arnst and Cortese 1994, 88).

Probably the most important reason this feature failed is because it didn't account for the inconsistency of the human interface. Handwriting varies significantly from person to person and, believe it or not, they have been known to make mistakes. Norman's credo is: "If an error is possible, someone will make it. The designer must assume that all possible errors will occur and design so as to minimize the chance of the error in the first place" (Norman, 35–36).

How can companies avoid making the same mistakes when they go back to the drawing board? Norman proposes four principles of good product design.

1. Visibility—The user should be able to tell, just by looking, what state the device is in and what his/her alternatives are for action.

2. A good conceptual model—The designer provides a good conceptual model for the user, with consistency in the presentation of operations and results and a coherent, consistent system image.

3. Good mappings—It is possible to determine the relationships between actions and results, between the controls and their effects, and between the system state and what is visible.

4. Feedback—The user receives full and continuous feedback about the results of actions. (pp. 52–53)

Of course, if these design rules are as simple and straightforward as they seem, how is it that manufacturers often take five or six tries to get a product design that's acceptable to the Early Majority (p. 29)? Norman maintains that it is because of the numerous pressures and constraints placed on product designers, including what he calls the "Two Deadly Temptations." These are:

1. Creeping Featurism—Where designers tend to add to the number of features/functions that a device can perform, often overwhelming the user with features that he/she doesn't need or can't figure out how to operate.

2. Worshipping False Images—Sometimes designers and users worship complexity, or the appearance of complexity, in a device. This is especially true in a society like ours, wherein individuals often value appearances, such as the appearance of technical sophistication, over functionality. (pp. 174–76)

Still other forces that work against successful design evolution are time and individuality. In many industries, even as one model is introduced its successor is already well into the design phase. This is particularly true of automobiles, where new car models are in development for years. The process does not allow for timely collection and incorporation of consumer feedback into the new designs. There is also a great deal of pressure on manufacturers and service providers to be unique, for the products they bring to the market to have an air of individuality, and for "new and improved" products to be easily distinguishable from their predecessors (pp. 142–43).

According to Norman, the most frequent reasons that designs fail are the emphasis on aesthetics over functionality, and the fact that the designers (and usually their clients) are not "typical users." There is also pressure to make things that are visually sleek, or sophisticated, or flashy, instead of usable.

> Designers go astray for several reasons. First, the reward structure of the design community tends to put aesthetics first. Design collections feature prize-winning clocks that are unreadable, alarms that cannot easily be set, can openers that mystify. Second, designers are not typical users. They become so expert in using the object they have designed that they cannot believe that anyone else might have problems; only interaction and testing with actual users throughout the design process can forestall that. Third, designers must please their clients, and the clients may not be the users. (p. 151)

Where did Apple go wrong with the *Newton*, for example? Did it fail to perform the tasks it claimed it would? Did its manufacturer misjudge the needs and wants of its intended consumer? No. The real problem, the reason that users gave the machine the thumbs down, was mostly because it wasn't easy to use, something that the designers (being so technically sophisticated themselves) might not have realized. Its highly touted handwriting recognition program was reportedly slow and inaccurate, making it difficult for users to enter information into the notepad, calendar, or phone book (Wildstrom, 20).

One might wonder, then, if early versions met with such limited success, why not give up altogether instead of going back to the drawing board? Well, history shows that such technologies often meet with resistance in the earliest days of their introduction and since there is firm belief that there is a big market for this technology, no one is ready to walk away just yet. Product designers seem to agree that with such a completely new technology, it is unlikely that the design would be perfect on the first try. In fact, it often takes several tries to get it right (Norman, 29). Commenting on the devices already on the market, research analyst Kimball Brown notes that "It will take two or three iterations before these things are any good." Andrew Seybold, publisher of a mobile computing newsletter, concurs. "The grandson of *Newton* will be a great product" (Hill, B1–B2).

What will change for the next generation? The Motorola *Envoy*, for one, will make the break from wired to wireless with the inclusion of a credit card-sized radio modem which will not only allow for smaller, lighter devices, but will replace the pricey cellular technology with less expensive radio transmission (Wildstrom, 20). Another key feature of this next generation of personal communicators is the software. Those utilizing General Magic's *Magic Cap* will bypass the unpopular handwriting recognition and allow users to simply tap an icon representing the function they wish to perform, or send messages in their own handwriting (Burgess 1994, 19, 25).

Also, in an effort to capture customers one market segment at a time, companies may begin focusing on customized applications. Apple, for instance, is regrouping and reevaluating its strategy with regard to the *Newton*. Some tactics include providing software development tools to make it easier for corporations to do their own customization, and specialized software for specific industry applications in farming, real estate, and sales (Rebello, 41).

Hopefully, having learned from past mistakes, the next generation of handheld computing devices will shed some of the less successful features of their predecessors, in favor of simplicity and ease of use. The functionality of the new devices will be leagues ahead of their forerunners as well. Instead of being fancy datebooks, the next generation will offer such advanced communication capabilities as voice and data transmission, including faxes, e-mail, and cellular phone calls (Arnst and Cortese, 88).

SOCIETAL IMPACTS

Benefits and Burdens of Technology

We can see how the issues of marketability, usability, and acceptance are inexorably linked to the concept of societal and cultural needs and values. In order to successfully market technological innovations, it is necessary to first understand the values of the group, or society, one is trying to sell to. The better one can understand how the group's members live, what motivates them, what they care about, and what they want, the easier it will be to design and market products that they will accept and adopt into their culture.

But these ideas relate to getting new technology into a society. Of even greater concern is what happens to that society after the technology has been accepted/adopted.

Since the beginning of human occupation of earth, each new technological innovation has had a hand in the development and shaping of our society. Just think of how profoundly inventions such as the wheel and the telephone have affected our everyday lives. Anytime, anywhere communication technology promises to be no different in that respect. The question is, *how* will it change our society? It is important to remember that while technology has brought us many new and wonderful things, it has not been without a price. Certainly, for everything that technology gives us, it also takes something away.

In pondering the benefits and burdens of technology, Sigmund Freud once wrote

> One would like to ask: is there, then, no positive gain in pleasure, no unequivocal increase in my feeling of happiness, if I can, as often as I please, hear the voice of a child of mine who is living hundreds of miles away or if I can learn in the shortest possible time after a friend has reached his destination that he has come through the long journey unharmed?

And although he acknowledges these benefits, Freud also points out that technology has created problems as well

> If there had been no railway to conquer distances, my child would never have left his native town and I should need no telephone to hear his voice; if travelling across the ocean by ship had not been introduced, my friend would not have embarked on his sea-voyage and I should not need a cable to relieve my anxiety about him. (Postman 1992, 5–6)

Plain and simple, any technology adopted by a society will have *"inherent and identifiable* social, political, and environmental consequence" (Mander 1991, 49). And although these consequences may be both beneficial and detrimental, the negative attributes are usually slower to appear and, even if they are known at the outset, are often concealed by the technology's proponents (p. 49).

What impacts will emerging communication technology have on our society? What benefits will it bring, what burdens will it bestow, and upon whom? What, if anything, can be done to anticipate and minimize the negative aspects of anytime, anywhere technology?

Popular opinion on this issue is sharply divided. For example, Nicholas Negroponte, Professor of Media Technology at Massachusetts Institute of Technology (MIT) and a Founding Director of the Media Lab, paints an ambitious picture of the future.

> Early in the next millennium your right and left cuff links or earrings may communicate with each other by low-orbiting satellites and have more computer power than your present PC. Your telephone won't ring indiscriminately; it will receive, sort, and perhaps respond to

your incoming calls like a well-trained English butler. . . . Schools
will change to become more like museums and playgrounds for
children to assemble ideas and socialize with other children all over
the world. . . . As we interconnect ourselves, many of the values of a
nation-state will give way to those of both larger and smaller electronic communities. We will socialize in digital neighborhoods in
which physical space will be irrelevant and time will play a different
role. (Negroponte 1995, 6–7)

Conversely, computer security expert and author of *Silicon Snake
Oil*, Clifford Stoll, presents a more cautious view.

Perhaps our networked world isn't a universal doorway to freedom.
Might it be a distraction from reality? An ostrich hole to divert our
attention and resources from social problems? A misuse of technology
that encourages passive rather than active participation? . . . Here are
my strong reservations about the wave of computer networks. They
isolate us from one another and cheapen the meaning of actual
experience. They work against literacy and creativity. They will
undercut our schools and libraries. (Stoll 1995, 2–3)

Whatever the eventual reality, it is clear that the choices we make
today will guide the evolution of this emerging technology and the
resulting impacts on our society.

Values

Back in 1965, psychologist Theodore J. Gordon, interested in the
relationship between technology and values, did a number of studies to
find out how the values held by a society affect the technology which
that society produces, and how that technology, in turn, affects a
society's values. Based on this research, Gordon developed the concept
of a feedback mechanism which exists between values and technology.
In short, he believed that the effect of any new technology on values is
circular, and that it is a society's values which bring about the creation
of the technology in the first place. Once adopted, the technology itself
becomes the catalyst for the value changes which then drive the
creation of still other technologies. This feedback mechanism between
values and technology is illustrated in Figure 8–2 (Baier and Rescher
1969, 150).

An example of this type of technology/value feedback can be
found in Freud's story about his son, who had chosen to live a great
distance away from his father. Following the invention of the steam
locomotive, passenger rail travel became popular because of those who

Figure 8–2. Feedback Between Values and Technology

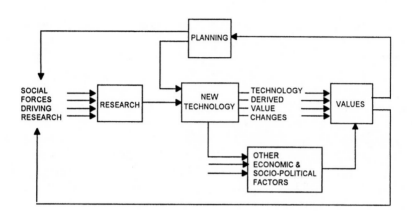

valued the challenge and adventure of travel to faraway places. However, once the railroad became an accepted means of long-distance travel, people began to realize how emotionally difficult it was to be separated from their families. Thus, the desire to keep in touch with loved ones fueled the widespread adoption of the telephone.

Gordon is quick to point out, however, that in a scenario like this one, the values were not necessarily created as the result of technology, but rather they just became more important to people because of it. That is, when people already have the things they value, there's no need to actively pursue or create technologies to attain them. In this example, people always valued family ties, but didn't need to do anything about them until the physical distance enabled by the railroad made keeping in touch a higher priority. It was this shift in priorities that brought about the acceptance of the device we know today as the telephone (Baier and Rescher 1969, 150–58).

What societal values brought on the development of anytime, anywhere communication? Perhaps it is a fondness for novelty, for things that are new and exciting. Maybe it is pride in our nation's technological superiority, or a fascination for material possessions, or just an "I want it now" sense of urgency. And if it is true that, as Gordon claims, "values apparently change to fit the world which technology presents" (Baier and Rescher 1969, 153), what value changes are in store for us as the result of all this new information technology?

Privacy

One of the first value conflicts on the horizon surrounds the issue of personal privacy in an information society. Unfortunately, the desire for privacy and the ability to control the access to information about oneself is seriously, if not irrevocably, jeopardized by advances in computer technology.

Even today, merchants electronically collect, share, and sell information about the people who buy their products and services. The U.S. Postal Service regularly sells the names and addresses in its database to direct marketing companies and supermarkets record purchases made by each customer (Branscomb 1994, 4–18). All of this data collection has been made possible by advances in computer and bar-coding technology. Merchants and businesses can record the most minute data about an individual's preferences and buying habits. This information is then stored, sorted, and sold to anyone who can afford it. For example, marketers use it to more accurately define the desired target population for specific promotions (Berry et al. 1994, 56–57).

What affect will anytime, anywhere technology have on this process? If nothing else, it may make it even easier for marketers to find out personal information and preferences, thanks to the software agents that we will use to run errands for us. Armed with credit card numbers and other personal information, these agents will cruise the Information Highway, making purchases and requesting data on our behalf. Just as they do in the supermarket when you buy groceries, it is likely that there is nothing to stop service providers and merchants from recording and using (or selling) personal information about the masters of those software servants.

What about the consumer's right to privacy? Unfortunately, big business triumphs more often than not in the courts. According to Robert S. Bulmash, president of a public advocacy group in Illinois, "existing laws regulating privacy simply aren't effective." Even longstanding laws, like the 1970 Fair Credit Reporting Act, allow for the release of financial information for "legitimate" business needs, a concept which has never been clearly defined. One thing is for sure, as data collection techniques become more sophisticated and intrusive, protecting one's privacy will become increasingly difficult (Lewyn 1994, 60–61).

The key to this issue, say many, is to put measures in place now to ensure that privacy is a consideration before all this technology gets so far advanced that it is too late. "The information industry must not become a Peeping Tom whom we must catch in the act of violating our privacy" (Branscomb, 28). Jan-Lori Goldman, director of the American Civil Liberties Union's Privacy and Technology project, agrees. "We need to realize that if we don't protect personal information on the highway up front, people won't use it" (Himelstein 1994, 134).

What is being done to protect the privacy of individuals? Some of the legislation being considered includes

1. the creation of a Privacy Protection Commission, responsible for setting privacy policy and ensuring that access to and use of electronic data is not abused.

2. the Fair Health Information Services Act, aimed at protecting the confidentiality of medical information. It establishes privacy standards and includes both civil and criminal penalties for misuse of patient data.

3. the Consumer Reporting Reform Act, which addresses access to, accuracy, and privacy of consumer credit information. It includes a provision allowing individuals to opt out of having their personal data used for marketing purposes. (pp. 134–35)

Security

While privacy issues are concerned with what is done with personal information by people or companies that obtained it legitimately, security concerns relate to keeping that data out of the hands of those who have no right to it in the first place. As information becomes more easily accessible, concern continues to grow about the ability to keep databases secure and incorruptible. When you think about software agents, which consist of mini-programs that travel through computer networks performing preselected tasks, they sound disturbingly like what we know today as computer viruses (Burgess, H1, H4).

As with privacy issues, people are asking questions about system security and the use of agents. "How can businesses ensure that a human being actually will pay the bills that mobile agents run up? How can networks prevent people from sending out agents that falsely purport to represent someone else? What authority should agents have to spend a master's money? . . . How do you define the boundaries of authority?" (H1, H4).

As we know just from reading the newspapers, so-called computer "hackers" specialize in defeating allegedly secure systems, sometimes for criminal purposes, other times just for fun. What will stop them from attaching viruses to agents as they move from place to place, or 'impersonating' another user in order to obtain information or merchandise illegally?

One of the ways currently being looked at to prevent tampering and forgery in electronic messaging is using digital signatures. This concept uses mathematical formulas and a pair of numbers called the public and private keys of an individual user to encrypt and decode messages. It is supposedly foolproof. And while the technique is already being incorporated into some software, like Lotus Notes, widespread usage is currently limited by lack of agreement over an industry standard (Wildstrom 1994, 13).

The Mobile Office

One of the most highly touted uses for anytime, anywhere is in creating the "virtual office." This means that whether an employee is on the floor of a customer's plant, stuck in a traffic jam, or sitting in the spare bedroom at the end of the hall, he or she can also be "in the office" because the office, in essence, travels wherever the employee goes. New devices and wireless networks will allow workers to make calls, send voice and data messages, and access important information from wherever they happen to be. Clerical work and routine tasks that were previously done by large staffs can now be handled by fewer workers and better computers (Kupfer, 147). This technology will not only change the way we do our work but the nature of the work itself. According to management consultant Gill Gordon, "we're on the verge of what is perhaps the most radical redefinition of the workplace since the industrial revolution, with some tremendous benefits involved" (Shellenbarger 1994, B1).

Many companies are trying out the mobile office concept, a paradigm shift brought about by a variety of influences, including compliance with the Federal Clean Air Act, reductions in administrative and operational expenses, and hoped-for increases in productivity. One of the most important goals, for many companies, is for employees to spend less time in the office and more time with their customers. Statistics show that currently "there are 25 million American workers without desks, and millions more who regularly travel in their work" (Cringely, 84). Corporate Chief Information Officer Ernest von Simson predicts that "eventually, 90% of people who are working will be tetherless" (Kupfer, 147).

Of course, dependence on mobile technology will not happen overnight. But since the introduction of cellular phones, pocket pagers, and portable PCs, the list of devotees has been steadily growing. For example, virtual office pioneer Ronald E. Compton, chairman of Aetna

Life and Casualty Co., is a firm believer in portable technology. He calls it "the best communication instrument since the papyrus. For a lot of communication, it's even better than face-to-face, because of the clarity and precision you get in writing" (Roush 1994, 148).

Other techno-converts agree. Corporate executive Myron Cohn says the thing he likes most about portable devices is that they allow him and his family to spend more time at their beach house. Says wife Nancy, "We can bring the office with us now that my husband and I are on-line" (Coxeter 1994, 147).

Despite this optimistic outlook, the long-term success of the mobile office is far from a sure thing. In fact, some feel that companies may have jumped too quickly on the bandwagon purely because of the perceived short-term financial benefits, and failed to study the lasting effects on employees and productivity. Even now, as the ranks of mobile employees are just beginning to swell, many companies are realizing that not everyone is cut out for the virtual office scenario. Following some problems with employees who could not make the adjustment, AT&T has set up a program to screen workers in advance for their suitability for the virtual office. In some cases, workers feel more pressure to perform since they are not in the office where the boss can see them. Karen Walker of Compaq cites problems with employees who are now "on the job" for 12 to 18 hours a day. She's had to ask some employees to cut their hours, saying that "your mind has to have some downtime" (Shellenbarger, B1, B4). Consultant Paul Rupert attributes this behavior to poorly defined expectations. "Many employees have only a vague sense of what is expected of them. As a result, they may be working 90 hours a week and still feel like they're falling short" (B1, B4).

In addition, working outside of the traditional 9-to-5 office schedule tends to blur the line between our work and private lives. As one technology writer puts it: "The good part is now we can do real work from the beach in Hawaii. The bad part is now we can do real work from the beach in Hawaii" (Cringely, 92).

Others will have difficulty with the isolation; the feeling of being cut off from their co-workers. "Working at home has its drawbacks. [Financial analyst and telecommuter Amy] Arnott misses sharing ideas with her co-workers" (Atchison 1994, 149). And when the feedback was received after AT&T's first Employee Telecommuting Day, one of the most frequent themes was the lack of face-to-face contact with peers. According to one employee, "People still need to see one another to keep the team environment strong." Others simply said, "I miss the socialization of the office" (Peterson 1994, 6).

Removing workers from the office environment also means that organizations are giving up some of their ability to control their activities.

But a bigger concern, according to interpersonal communication expert Robert E. Kraut, is that the absence of physical proximity of co-workers will impede the ability of the organization to be productive.

> Informal communication is needed to gain new information, clarify values, evaluate alternatives, and make decisions. It is for this reason, for example, that managers spend almost 50 percent of their work day in unscheduled meetings. Much communication in organizations results from people bumping into each other in hallways, in lunchrooms, or by the copier. . . . Informal communication supported by physical proximity serves many functions in organizations. It is frequently the basis of supervision, socialization, social support, on-the-job training, and the spread of corporate know-how and culture. Moreover, the informal communication among co-workers helps provide the major satisfaction denied to home workers—socializing and friendly social interaction. (Kraut 1989, 26)

Retired *Business Week* editor Jack Patterson echoes Kraut's assertions. "Whenever I took a stroll around the floor, I encountered other people who were—in various degrees and combinations—talented, stubborn, knowledgeable, irritating, interesting and opinionated. . . . My fellow workers and I argued a lot, but we learned a great deal from one another" (Patterson 1994, 86). The real problem with the virtual corporation, says Patterson, "is that the intangible but indispensable values I discovered at work will be lost: the sense of community, the shared goals, the spirited exchange of ideas, the pride of achievement . . . without them, I think, permanent gains in efficiency and quality will be difficult or impossible to achieve" (p. 87).

Company leaders, asserts Raychem CEO Robert J. Saldich, must find ways to confront and deal with this issue, because "man has always sought the company of people, and that will be the driving force of organization" (Hammonds 1994, 76). Those who feel left out or isolated from the human contact of the traditional work environment are not likely to be as productive as if they were in the office.

Virtual Communities

Those in virtual offices and others who are feeling isolated from human contact and interaction will find alternative ways to fill their needs for socialization. One way will be through electronic bulletin boards and virtual communities that will replace the real thing. Thanks to services like Prodigy and America On-Line, and the Internet, individuals are now able to correspond in real-time with people all over the world. These virtual communities are "bringing together people who otherwise would never meet" (Verity, 12). On-line meeting rooms and discussion groups are growing more and more popular, prompting one artist to state that "technology today is the campfire around which we tell our stories." Others describe it as a place where people "hold meetings or schmooze in on-line watering holes" (Baig 1994, 124). These on-line environments are fast taking the place of face-to-face interaction and conversation. In fact, on-line discussion groups are even challenging singles bars and fitness centers as a popular spot to find romance (Baig 1994, 128).

It is true that these on-line environments will greatly expand our access to people from all walks of life. But author Clifford Stoll cautions that many of these relationships are superficial and lack the same risks, depth, and commitment of face-to-face conversation. "Electronic communication is an instantaneous and illusory contact that creates a sense of intimacy without the emotional investment that leads to close friendships" (Stoll, 23–24). According to Stoll, these electronic communities lack the humanity and the feeling of belonging found in real neighborhoods. Computer networks, he warns, "isolate us from one another, rather than bring us together. . . . By logging on to the networks, we lose the ability to enter into spontaneous interactions with real people" (p. 58).

Disabled Persons and the Elderly

The advent of anytime, anywhere communication will have a significant impact on the lives of the elderly, shut-ins, and those with disabilities. Many of these communication technologies can be easily adapted for the handicapped and infirm, giving them the same access to information and the same ability to communicate as those without disabilities. Take Samuel Block, for example, an 83-year-old retiree who has been deaf since the age of seven. Since discovering the PC, Block has used it not only to keep in touch with his friends and four sons, but to play games and help others with their taxes (Arnst 1994, 145).

According to Professor Mary S. Furlong of the University of San Francisco, the potential benefits of information technology for older adults is substantial. The needs of this market, such as "social interaction, access to information, opportunities for entertainment and for learning," combined with the physical limitations of many of its population, are a perfect fit with many of the new devices and services that anytime, anywhere technology will offer (Furlong 1989, 145).

To illustrate, Furlong points to the success of the SeniorNet, an experimental on-line service targeted specifically at older Americans. Thanks to overwhelming participation and support from its users, she says, "Our vision for SeniorNet has changed from operating an on-line network to creating an 'electronic community' for older adults" (p. 149). The impact of communication technology is even more profound on patients confined to nursing homes, where it represents a critical link to the outside world. "Many of our residents are physically limited only," says Tim Hager, site coordinator at the Sheyenne Care Foundation. "This leaves them with alert minds and limited ability to participate in activities. SeniorNet is an excellent way for them to remain active and be continuously learning and growing. . . . We have an opportunity for the residents to reach out to those across the country to touch and be touched by the lives of others without any hindrance by their physical limitations" (p. 152).

For these same reasons, people with disabilities will also benefit. Many, like AT&T's Sue Decker, feel that emerging technology is making it easier for disabled people like herself to do their jobs. Says Decker, "This is probably the best time ever to be deaf" (Hartsfield 1994, 2).

Human Factors and the 24-Hour Society

Human factors analysts Edith Weiner and Arnold Brown tell us that although data processing capability has increased sharply over the last decade, overall productivity has not shown any great gains. Clearly, they maintain, productivity is not getting the full benefit of the new technologies being introduced. They feel that the problem lies in the fact that highly advanced technologies are being developed "without any real understanding of how people might interrelate with new technologies" (Weiner and Brown 1989, 9). In fact, the information that we can now get from machines is more than human beings can absorb. It is this overabundance of data that hampers the human ability to make decisions.

Some of the problem may be caused by technophobia. A survey done by Dell Computer Corporation reveals that 55% of the population has some level of fear or apprehension about technology. Up to one-third of those, according to clinical psychologist Michelle Weir, experience physical reactions like nausea, sweating, and dizziness (Hogan 1994, 116).

More often, says writer Richard Heygate "the real problem lies at the border between human skills and information technology" (Heygate 1994, A10). Simply put, the machines are getting more and more sophisticated and the people using them just cannot keep up. One consulting firm estimates that PC users waste "5.1 hours each week 'futzing' with their computers—learning how to use them, waiting for them to do things, checking things they do and so on. And that doesn't even measure the time wasted by employees playing games loaded on their PCs as standard equipment" (p. A10).

In his book *The Twenty-Four-Hour Society*, Harvard Professor of Physiology Martin Moore-Ede, M.D., Ph.D., points out that human beings are simply not designed for the nonstop world that anytime, anywhere technology is creating. "At the heart of the problem," says Moore-Ede, "is a fundamental conflict between the demand of our man-made civilization and the very design of the human brain and body" (Moore-Ede 1992, 5–6). We just were not built to function around-the-clock.

Moore-Ede maintains that while machines have become significantly more reliable over the years, the reliability of humans has declined. Much of this is because we have become machine-centered in our thinking, rather than human-centered. That is to say that we are focused more on the optimization of technology and equipment than human alertness and performance. "Human error has become the problem of our age because the trade-offs and compromises, made to ensure the techno-logical achievements of the modern world, have not taken into account the design specs of the human body. Creating and installing a human-centered technology to redress the balance will be one of the most important challenges of the twenty-first century" (pp. 20–21).

The problems of 24-hour operation have long existed in such envi-ronments as air transportation, medical care, factories, and nuclear plants. Anytime, anywhere communication will add yet another dimension, since round-the-clock access to information means little without the will-ingness and ability to make decisions and take action based on that data.

The fact that communication technology now enables an instan-taneous and seemingly inexhaustible supply of information also reduces, especially in crisis situations, the amount of time in which to analyze a situation and weigh alternatives before making decisions. However, when people "make decisions in the fog of fatigue, the enhanced power that technology has provided amplifies the magnitude of any errors made" (pp. 130–31). The sheer volume of data available can easily be more than a human brain is capable of absorbing and processing, especially when the element of fatigue is introduced (p. 131). It is no coincidence, according to Moore-Ede, that the most devastating industrial accidents in recent memory, like Bhopal, Chernobyl, and Exxon's Valdez, all occurred in the middle of the night (pp. 5, 6). It is because 24-hour technology does not respect the biological need for "down-time" or the circadian rhythms that govern the functions of the human body, including alertness and drowsiness cycles (pp. 11–12).

Another aspect of the technology is the fact that because the ability to send and receive information around-the-clock exists, we will be expected to make use of it the same way. Thus, information overload will only get worse as communication technology gets better. When the telephone was virtually the only method of long distance communication in business, the lines between on- and off-duty were much clearer. As technology moves into our homes and hip pockets it will become more and more difficult for people to turn it off, even when they want to. Moore-Ede describes a colleague who "makes a trip to France or Singapore, and she cannot escape. She cannot blame the postman for a delay in delivery—the sender knows when and where the missive has arrived. She has no excuse to take a break or escape— her boss expects her always to be available, to do her job, wherever she may be" (pp. 202–3).

The answer to the dilemma, says Moore-Ede, is for humans to "rethink our ways of doing things and construct a world in which we can each flourish. We cannot let technology control our lives according to its own whims" (p. 203). We can do this, he says, simply by changing our mind-set. By making a conscious decision to separate our personal and working lives, to define our schedules for work, sleep, and relaxation. "The aim is to create a work and relaxation pattern that takes care of business but also takes care of the soul—that keeps you at your best and puts technology in its place as a follower in your personal pack, not the leader" (pp. 203–4).

Others, like philosopher Daniel Dennet, agree that "information technology will ruin our lives unless we think of some radical way to get it under control" (Weiner and Brown, 10). And according to Weiner and Brown, the increasing frustration of managers inundated with so much raw data is leading to the latest occupational illness, called "techno-stress." They recommend that instead of being in such a hurry to buy into new technologies, managers should first examine not just what the technology can do, but how it fits with people (p. 11).

Global Politics

Even bigger than the impact that anytime, anywhere communication will have on individuals is the effect it will have on whole societies and cultures, and maybe even world geography.

Because it utilizes thin little wires and invisible airwaves, communication technology pays little attention to the geographic or other types of boundaries between countries, and in some cases has played a role in literally reshaping borders. There was once a time when communication across continents took the form of pen on paper, which then had to be hand-carried to its destination. Interim developments improved the process, but it was with the launch of Sputnik in 1957 that the globalization of communication took a quantum leap forward, making possible the rapid transmission of information anywhere in the world. Since then, "the convergence of computers with telecommunications . . . ever cheaper and simpler techniques for collecting and broadcasting the news, and the fax machine—has created a global arena of shared popular information that takes no notice of the lines on the map" (Wriston 1992, 129–30). Anytime, anywhere communication technology has the potential to play an ever-increasing role in the global political scenario.

Information is power. That's why repressive governments have traditionally sought to control it. Ever since Gutenberg's invention of movable type helped to erode the influence of the Catholic Church (Postman, 16–17), communication technology has continued to play a role in changing cultures and reshaping borders around the world. During the 1991 uprising in Russia, for example, the army shut down radio and television stations in an effort to cut off its citizens from the outside world. "They overlooked the fax machines, and via fax, stories of the turmoil in Moscow were handed out on the barricades" (Wriston, 174).

Another recent example comes from the Persian Gulf War, during which communication technology became nearly as big a story as the war itself. For the first time, ordinary citizens could sit in front of their television sets and see what was happening as it happened. People who were "watching live reports on CNN of the direction of incoming Iraqi Scud missiles were on the phone relaying the information as it came in to their relatives and colleagues in Saudi Arabia and Bahrain, warning them to take cover" (Moore-Ede, 131).

Thus, wireless communication technology will continue to play a part in the communication revolution by enabling instant access to information in all corners of the world. Such access, and such information, puts pressure on repressive governments because they will no longer be able to hide things like human rights abuses from the world. "While old power structures will resist this kind of outside interference, technology will render them obsolete. At the end of the day, technology will be seen to have brought effective pressures for reform." In practice, "We are thus witness to a true revolution; power really is moving to the people" (Wriston, 176).

CONCLUSION

Anytime, anywhere communication is well on its way to becoming a reality. When all is said and done, today's emerging communication technologies will be as much a part of our everyday lives as telephones and computers are today. There are, however, numerous issues to be resolved before the complete acceptance and integration of this technology can take place.

Because *communication* is the primary objective of these emerging technologies, the establishment of global industry standards for software protocols and interface capability is absolutely essential to the success of anytime, anywhere communication. To be truly user-focused, the devices and services must be designed so that the complexities of system-to-system interface are virtually invisible to the user and so messages sent from one type of device can be received by any other communication device in the wired or wireless environment.

Firm measures must be taken to address the issues of individual privacy and system security. Laws protecting the acquisition and use of information should be enacted, which include penalties for improper uses and the definition of the agency or agencies charged with the jurisdiction and responsibility for enforcing the laws regarding illegal use of information. In addition, the adoption of industry standards for data encryption and security features would not only allay the fears of many potential users, but also serve to speed up the widespread acceptance of the technology.

Also, employers who want to take advantage of the productivity gains that anytime, anywhere technology will make possible, must first come to grips with the human elements involved. For example, they will need to understand the human physiological needs for rest and relaxation, and the limitations on comprehension and decision-making abilities when these needs are not met. Clear lines should be drawn between business and personal time, meaning that the more independent employees become, the more they will need to have clearly defined job and performance objectives and expectations. Employers will also need to come up with creative and alternative ways to build a sense of camaraderie among the workers in order to take full advantage the synergies created in the group environment, such as in problem-solving and decision-making, and to keep the lines of communication open for mobile employees in order to avoid the isolation and other negative social impacts of the virtual office.

Finally, and most important, individuals in our society must take responsibility for deciding how this technology will become a part of our lives. Instead of blindly accepting that "bigger, faster, flashier" really is the best thing for us, we should be asking ourselves today what we really want from communication technology tomorrow. Will it be used to enhance our face-to-face communication or to replace it? What guidelines and boundaries will we place between our work and our personal time? How will we deal with the pace of a 24-hour society and our own physical limitations? It is only with a full understanding of the possible impacts that we can make the decisions that will help us to shape the future of both our technology and our society.

REFERENCES

Arnst, Catherine. "Tackling Technophobia." *Business Week* (Special Issue–June 1994): 145.

Arnst, Catherine, and Amy Cortese. "PDA: Premature Death Announcement." *Business Week* (September 12, 1994): 88.

Atchison, Sandra. "Amy C. Arnott." *Business Week* (Special Issue–June 1994): 149.

Baier, Kurt, and Nicholas Rescher. *Values and the Future.* New York: Free Press, 1969.

Baig, Edward C. "Ready, Set—Go On-Line." *Business Week* (Special Issue–June 1994): 124.

Baig, Edward C. "Love at First Byte." *Business Week* (Special Issue–June 1994): 128.

Berry, Jonathan, Gail DeGeorge, John Verity, and Kathleen Kerwin. "Database Marketing." *Business Week* (September 5, 1994): 56–57.

Branscomb, Anne Wells. *Who Owns Information?* New York: Basic Books, 1994.

Burgess, John. "Calling Agent 486." *The Washington Post* (March 6, 1994): H1, H4.

Burgess, John. "Tackling 'Communicator' Glitches." *The Washington Post* (February 7, 1994): 19, 25.

Chew, Joe. "Introduction to the Special Issue on Electronic Communication and Interaction." *IEEE Transactions on Professional Communication* 37, no. 4 (1994): 193.

Coxeter, Ruth. "Lloyd and Myron Cohn." *Business Week* (Special Issue–June 1994): 146–47.

Cringely, Robert X. "Who, What and Why of Wireless." *Forbes ASAP* (September 13, 1993): 84, 92.

Eng, Paul. "Smart, Useful—And They Won't Put a Sag in Your Suit." *Business Week* (May 30, 1994): 141–42.

Furlong, Mary S. "An Electronic Community for Older Adults: The SeniorNet Network." *Journal of Communication* (Summer 1989): 145, 149, 152.

Hammonds, Keith H., Kevin Kelly, and Karen Thurston. "The New World of Work." *Business Week* (October 17, 1994): 76.

Hartsfield, Ollie. "Focusing on Ability." *AT&T News* (October 1994): 2.

Heygate, Richard. "Technophobes, Don't Run Away Just Yet." *The Wall Street Journal* (August 15, 1994): A10.

Hill, G. Christian. "First Hand-Held Data Communicators Are Losers, But Makers Won't Give Up." *The Wall Street Journal* (February 3, 1994): B1, B6.

Hill, G. Christian. "Motorola, Hewlett-Packard Stake Out New Market." *The Wall Street Journal* (March 7, 1994): B4.

Himelstein, Linda. "Attack of the Cyber Snoopers." *Business Week* (Special Issue–June 1994): 134–35.

Hogan, Kevin. "Technophobia." *Forbes ASAP* (February 28, 1994): 116.

Hutsko, Joe. "Online, On the Go With Wireless Envoy." *PC World* (April 1994): 78.

Korzeniowski, Paul. "Wireless Computing is Attracting Mobile Workers." *Infoworld* (November 15, 1993): 111.

Kraut, Robert E. "Telecommuting: The Trade-Offs of Home Work." *Journal of Communication* (Summer 1989): 26.

Kupfer, Andrew. "Look, Ma! No Wires!" *Fortune* (December 13, 1993): 147.

Lewyn, Mark. "You Can Run, But It's Tough to Hide From Marketers." *Business Week* (September 5, 1994): 60–61.

Mander, Jerry. *In the Absence of the Sacred*. San Francisco: Sierra Club Books, 1991.

McGinn, Robert E. *Science, Technology, and Society*. Englewood Cliffs, N.J.: Prentice Hall, 1991.

Miller, Andy. "AT&T Testing Mobile Applications for Televised Medicine Technology." *Atlanta Constitution* (June 17, 1994): B2.

Moore-Ede, Martin. *The Twenty-Four-Hour Society*. Reading, Mass.: Addison-Wesley, 1992.

Moore, Geoffrey A. *Crossing the Chasm*. Harper Business, 1991.

Negroponte, Nicholas. *Being Digital*. New York: Alfred A. Knopf, 1995.

Norman, Donald A. *The Design of Everyday Things*. New York: Doubleday, 1988.

Patterson, Jack. "Welcome to the Company that Isn't There." *Business Week* (October 17, 1994): 86, 87.

Peterson, J. R. "Telecommuting." *AT&T News* (October 1994): 6.

Postman, Neil. *Technopoly: The Surrender of Culture to Technology*. New York: Alfred A. Knopf, 1992.

Rebello, Kathy. "Newton: Will What Fell Down Go Up?" *Business Week* (July 1, 1994): 41.

Roush, Chris. "Ronald E. Compton." *Business Week* (Special Issue–June 1994): 148.

Shellenbarger, Sue. "Overwork, Low Morale Vex the Mobile Office." *The Wall Street Journal* (August 17, 1994): B1, B4.

Stewart, Thomas A. "The Information Age in Charts." *Fortune* (April 4, 1994): 76–78.

Stoll, Clifford. *Silicon Snake Oil: Second Thoughts on the Information Highway.* New York: Doubleday, 1995.

Therrien, Lois. "It's a Mad, Mad, Mad, Mad Wireless World." *Business Week* (November 29, 1993): 128–33.

Verity, John W. "The Information Revolution." *Business Week* (Special Issue–1994): 18.

Weiner, Edith, and Arnold Brown. "Human Factors." *The Futurist* (May–June 1989): 9–10.

Wildstrom, Stephen H. "The PDA May Not Be DOA After All." *Business Week* (June 13, 1994): 20.

Wildstrom, Stephen. "Digital Signatures That Can't be Forged." *Business Week* (July 4, 1994): 13.

Wolkomir, Richard. "We're Going to Have Computers Coming Out of the Woodwork." *Smithsonian* (September 1994): 82, 84–92.

Wriston, Walter B. *The Twilight of Sovereignty.* New York: Charles Scribner's Sons, 1992.

Ziegler, Bart, and Kathy Rebello. "Reach Out and Touch Anyone, Anywhere." *Business Week* (January 17, 1994): 83–84.

Efforts to Simplify Human-Computer Communication

Michael W. Cusack

THE NATURE OF THE PROBLEM

A traditional computer scientist might tell an audience that a modern computer "boots up, configures, reads, writes, copies, and edits files, flushes buffers, creates, refreshes, kills and buries windows, arrests processes, inspects, downloads, offsets, describes and sends messages, calls and traces functions, etc., etc."

There is undoubtedly a communications gulf between the small minority who dictate how computer programs work, and the great majority who want to use computers for the production of documentation and graphics, spreadsheets, database records, scheduling, training, and advisory systems, as well as personal entertainment.

While a diminishing number of computer scientists are out of touch with the people who will eventually try to take advantage of their programming expertise, it is a problem getting technically oriented individuals to understand the needs of the ordinary user. Most developers tend to sacrifice usability for functionality. It is often left up to the user to wade through mounds of documentation or take expensive training courses in order to discover how best to use an application.

Apart from usability issues, a secondary problem which plagues human-computer communication today is that of information access.

This case study by Michael W. Cusack, of AT&T, appeared in the *Proceedings of the Fifth Conference on Corporate Communication*, May 1992, and in a slightly different form in *IEEE Transactions on Professional Communication* 36:1 (March 1993): 14–19. It appears here with his permission.

Even the smallest computers are capable of storing far more information than any user needs to access. A lightweight machine which comfortably fits into a briefcase can run spreadsheet applications, interact with multiple databases, store a large desktop publishing document complete with graphics, and communicate with the outside world via electronic mail and communications packages. Yet despite all that information so close at hand, it has become more difficult to find exactly what you need when you need it most.

Every day, massive corporate databases, news services, electronic mail, and text retrieval facilities provide subscribers with countless facts and figures. Information alone, however, is not knowledge. The problem is how to find specific information with minimal difficulty. Presentation, speed of access, and ease of use are all important. Special care is needed in constructing computer applications so that the user can easily find the required information.

EXPERT SYSTEMS AND OTHER NOTIONS

Computer scientists are not necessarily atheists. Even if they don't believe in the existence of a Supreme Being, they can always create one of their own. Just as Pygmalion made his own woman out of ivory, and Aphrodite subsequently brought her Galatea to life, many are drawn to the idea of creating intelligence outside the human body. This fascination is known to the computer world as Artificial Intelligence, an industry which borrows as much of its prowess from myth and mystique as from science.

Today, the overpromotion of Artificial Intelligence has led to unrealistic expectations, and its tendency to encourage research directed and focused on very difficult problems has kept it from becoming broadly useful. The industry also suffers from an "is-that-all-there-is-to-it" problem. Like a magic trick, once you explain an Artificial Intelligence technique, the magic is gone, often taking with it the user's confidence. For all the extravagant claims of scientific achievement, and after more than thirty years of attempting to create artificially intelligent programs in the laboratories, only the category known as "Expert Systems" has emerged as a major class of usable commercial technology.

In terms of improving human-computer communication, it is important to understand that expert system programming differs in several ways from traditional programming. While traditional programming usually implements an algorithm (an explicit sequence of steps to solve a problem), an expert system program may implement heuristics ("rules of thumb") because no algorithm exists for the problem being attacked. Expert system programming usually tackles problems that are not well defined and are very complex, so that no algorithmic solution exists. Instead, expert system programming uses reasoning techniques that have been identified by studying how people solve difficult problems.

It is not easy to create a good expert system. In the first place, there must be a human expert. An expert system cannot create expertise. It must be programmed by someone who has exhaustively interviewed an expert, or by the experts themselves.

Expert systems have been successfully deployed for many tasks in industry. The MCI Automated Money Transfer Service, for example, is a natural language system that takes free text messages from MCI International's Messaging Service for telex messages, and outputs structured versions of the message. This allows MCI's client banks to handle money orders mechanically.

Another example is the American Express Credit Authorizer, which assists authorizers in making real-time authorization decisions for credit card transactions. The system retrieves and displays the credit history along with its recommendation for approving or denying the transaction. The human authorizer makes the final decision. Cost savings through improved authorization are in the millions of dollars per year.

Probably the most successful expert system development in the world has taken place at Du Pont, where there are over 200 expert systems already running. Some of the more widely known global systems have aquired names like "Mike-In-The-Box" (the real Mike being the best engineer Du Pont has at purging a distillation column of impurities), "God-In-The-Works" (the captured expertise of an aging, irreplaceable blast furnace expert at Nippon-Kokan), and "Geoff's Book" (thousands of expert rules from the head of the top estimator at building contractor Lend Lease of Australia). At the British National Health Service, a demanding and critical evaluation task that took six experts two hours is now done (better) in nine minutes.

THE TASK OF KNOWLEDGE ACQUISITION

A human expert may need the help of a "knowledge engineer" to get his expertise encoded into rules. The knowledge engineer observes the expert at work, asks many questions, examines case studies, and looks at seemingly endless details, trying to understand the expertise so that it can be expressed in rules. This task, referred to as "Knowledge Acquisition," is considered the hardest part of building the expert system. This is because when a human expert knows something, this knowledge is often composed of feelings, rules-of-thumb, hunches—in short, unconscious or subconscious processes—as well as book learning, acquired knowledge, and well-thought-out ideas. An expert system, however, must have knowledge represented in clear, unambiguous rules that are precise, complete, and consistent.

Contemporary knowledge engineering is a job slot for noncomputer professionals. The extraction of knowledge does not necessarily require any programming skills, as long as the knowledge engineer knows the formalisms into which the knowledge must be encoded. Some companies seek bright, analytical social science and humanities majors to train as knowledge engineers.

The task of the knowledge engineer is to construct a program which has a wide base of knowledge in a restricted domain, using complex inferential reasoning to accomplish tasks which a human expert could normally be expected to achieve. Hence the triangle of the programmer, the knowledge engineer, and the expert is central to the successful application of any expert system.

Every knowledge engineer should have strong organizational skills, the ability to minimize hostility and fear on the part of the user, tact and diplomacy, empathy with his subject, persistence, and self-confidence. The knowledge engineer should understand the problem completely, undertaking comprehensive background reading where possible, surveying of in-house documentation, and discovering the location of experts.

One could argue that if nothing else came of Artificial Intelligence research but expert systems, the field would have borne abundant fruit. After all, designing and building systems that help us solve complex real-world problems is no mean feat.

BRIDGING THE GAP—INTELLIGENT APPLICATIONS

We are constantly bombarded by data that demands our attention. This data ranges from the information provided in newspapers, magazines, and television broadcasts, to stock market reports, economic projections, census data, and other items that are used in a variety of applications and analyses. Collectively, we are approaching, and have probably exceeded, the point of information glut, where we can no longer assimilate and utilize more than a small fraction of the available data. Symptoms of this general malaise are plentiful. People begin to cancel their magazine subscriptions because they no longer have time to read all the issues. Managers insist on executive summaries of the data because they don't have time to deal with all the details.

Databases, which are simply composed of records relating to a particular occurence—such as when you last visited the doctor—are extremely useful to those who constantly need to access and manipulate information. The trouble is that there is now so much information available that it is difficult to access what you need when you need it most. This is where efforts to simplify human–computer communication are most relevant. The problem of information overload is of enormous concern to the computer industry. It is hoped that by using what have come to be known as "Intelligent Applications," more people can have better access to, and use of, more kinds of information than they could otherwise.

WHAT IS AN INTELLIGENT APPLICATION?

The original motivation for databases came from computer programmers who wanted a convenient way of handling the data that was being used for their programs. In addition to this type of database (fields, records, etc.), another development was that of a textual database, which typically represents documents through citations, abstracts, and index terms.

Text databases represent a new direction in information technology. They provide text in an "on-line" or computerized form. In contrast to a conventional book, a single electronic copy of a text source may be received from many different locations in the same day. This overcomes some of the frustration that library users feel when the book that they want is currently checked out. The second effect of textual databases is that they provide a very flexible way of organizing information. In a library, books are typically ordered by subject in a linear sequence of stacks. However, with index terms, the same text may be accessed in a number of different ways.

Now that technologies such as expert systems and hypermedia have reached a stage of maturity on their own, it is possible to define an overall unifying structure for viewing these fields as parts of a blueprint for intelligent applications. Such applications would provide a common approach to the access and use of information for analysis and decision making.

The essential characteristics of an intelligent application are that it is easy to use, can handle large amounts of information in a fashion which is transparent to the user, and allows people to carry out their tasks using an appropriate set of computer applications.

The first level of architecture in the intelligent application is that of spreadsheets and graphic representation programs, which are modified so as to be compatible with the database model. The second level is the high-level user interface. This is the level with which users interact directly. This level creates the model of the task and database environment that users interact with. As such, it has to deal as much with how the user wants to think about databases as it does with how the database engine actually operates. The third and final level is the intelligent database engine. This incorporates a model that allows for an "object-oriented" representation of information that can be expressed in different ways.

By using intelligent applications, users can perform tasks involving large amounts of information that otherwise could not possibly be performed. Intelligent applications manage information in a natural way, making that information easy to store, access, and use.

"HYPER" PRODUCTS—THE ESSENTIAL INGREDIENTS

Hypertext can simply be defined as the creation and representation of links between discrete pieces of information. When this information can be graphics or sound, as well as text or numbers, the resulting structure is referred to as hypermedia.

A normal document is linear, and one tends to read it from beginning to end. In contrast, reading a hyperdocument is open–ended and one can jump from idea to idea depending on one's interests. The nearest thing to a hyperdocument that most people are familiar with is a thesaurus. A thesaurus has no single beginning or end. Each time the thesaurus is consulted, it is entered at a different location based on the word used to initiate the search. Hypertext, for example, can be thought of as an enriched thesaurus where, instead of links between words, links between documents and text fragments are available.

In many ways, hypertext and hypermedia require different ways of thinking about tasks such as text writing and searching for information. The proponents of hypermedia claim that it is more "natural" and that its associative and nonlinear nature corresponds to the way the human mind works. These claims have generally focused on the use of hypermedia as a browsing medium.

Intelligent applications which include hyperproducts, expert systems, and intelligent databases are the most tangible evidence today that the computer industry is concerned with revealing the secrets of database management and information retrieval in a manner that is obvious even to inexperienced users. Developers are clearly engrossed with the concept of a computer functioning as a super-memory which emulates the workings of the human brain, but with far more power to recollect events. Using distributed networks which may hook hundreds of databases together, users should be able to request information on any one of a myriad of subjects and receive instant feedback.

INTERFACE DESIGN—THE KEY TO SUCCESSFUL COMMUNICATION

Computer scientists value the program and how it works; designers value the picture and how it looks. This difference is the primary source of misunderstanding between computer scientists and designers, and also explains the traditional programming mentality that user interface design is of secondary importance. As a traditional developer might say to a frustrated user: "It works! That's all that matters. It's up to you to find out how to use it. Why don't you read the documentation?"

Fortunately, as computer technology has become available to more and more people in a greater variety of devices and contexts, the need for accessibility and ease of use has grown more and more pronounced. People with a greater variety of skills and points of view have become involved. Those who study thought, language, entertainment, and communication, as well as those who study algorithms, hardware, and data structure, all have a role to play in interface design.

When the concept of interface design first began to emerge, it was commonly understood as the hardware and software through which a human and a computer could communicate. As it has evolved, it has come to include the cognitive and emotional aspects of the user's experience as well. While developers and users often have differing views on how we should interact with computers, no one doubts that the best way to unleash the power of a specific application is to make the process of human-computer communication as natural as possible.

This raises the issue of just what constitutes "natural" interaction with a machine. Today, the method of communication remains essentially the same as it was when the typewriter was invented by Christopher Sholes in 1867. The standard keyboard continues, with a few exceptions, to resist advocates of technologies like "voice recognition" and "touch screen" computing. In fact, neither of these keyboard "replacement" technologies can be considered as mainstream substitutes for the keyboard until they attain a level of sophistication, low cost, and ease-of-use which drives traditional computing methods into redundancy.

The Importance of Users

Interface designers should always consider it their job first and foremost to meet the user's needs, rather than simply to implement a certain set of features or a certain interface style. The usual concerns of interface designers—creating more legible type, designing better scroll bars, integrating color and sound and voice—are all important. But they are secondary. Improving the way people can use computers to think and communicate, observe and decide, calculate and simulate, debate and design—these are primary.

Apple Corporation, who initiated the commercial use of the graphical user interface (GUI) for their Macintosh computer, had the simple aim of making interfaces more intuitive. Much of the ease-of-use of the Apple Macintosh was attributed to the correspondence between the appearance, uses, and behaviors of such interface objects as documents and folders and their real-world counterparts.

The graphical approach represented a radical departure from the way people traditionally interacted with computers, which was via character-based user interfaces. Character-based applications are easy to program and cheap to produce, and are still widely in use today. Users are often confronted by cluttered screens of text and blank spaces—or worse still, blank screens with a solitary blinking cursor—which offer little, if any, indication of what to do next. Such applications compel the user to learn a complex and somewhat arbitrary syntax.

Ease of use is of primary importance in any user interface design. It reduces training and support costs with a well-designed interface. It allows users to perform tasks more easily and reduces complaints and customer support problems. It is a more intuitive, direct means of interaction with software. However, users may not understand menu labels, may not easily identify icons, and may not remember mouse functions. Therefore, an interesting graphical user interface may promote ease of use, but is not a sufficient condition for it. After all, the graphical prowess of today's computers has encouraged the production of a plethora of unreadable graphics. There is one other step which may be taken in the attempt to ensure user satisfaction, and that is the addition of "intelligence" to the user interface.

DESIGNING AN INTELLIGENT INTERFACE

Graphical user interfaces provide a form of human–machine communication that has no direct analog in human–human communication. A graphical interface can also be intelligent over and above the extent to which it is easy or natural to use. Use of an expert system "front end" would allow users to query the system, supply information, receive advice, and so on. Intelligent interfaces to worksheets and databases, for example, can help end users interact with the systems more easily. This interface would aim to provide the same form of communication facilities provided by a human expert.

The less experienced the operator of a system, the more likely an intelligent interface is to be helpful. For example, the less accurate a typist or data entry operator the user is, the more likely such an interface is to catch mistakes that might otherwise result in bad business decisions. Similarly, a manager might be a terrible typist and be prone to making data entry errors that could prove disastrous when decisions must be made later.

HELP DESKS—A CASE IN POINT

In recent years, expert systems tools and techniques have proven effective in the automation of customer service as well as internal help desk activities. This reflects a maturation of expert system technology and the real benefits achieved by those pioneering companies that identified and pursued help desk applications in their search for uses of the technology.

In order to provide some assistance for the user operating in a real-world domain with uncertain data, expert systems can be designed to make use of stored information about similar problems, coupled with the user's general knowledge. This process, known as Case-based Reasoning, provides users with options not normally available in the expert system domain. This is achieved by using reasoning based on the applicability of historical events, called cases. A case consists of a textual problem description, a set of questions and associated answers, and a resolution. The system automatically summarizes past case information, then it selects cases relevant to the current problem, providing examples and guidance from past successful solutions.

Case-based Reasoning allows "front-line" service representatives to provide many answers that usually can only be determined by referrals to experts. These systems can automate and improve critical help desk tasks by capturing expert knowledge as documentation (using hypertext), as experience using cases.

The user interface for Case-based Reasoning systems is ideally graphical and customizable to suit the needs of the user. This is achieved by using an application (i.e., a screen design package with program links to the expert system) which lets developers add, modify, or delete icons, buttons, entry fields, windows, scroll bars, help screens, and other features on the screen. These features in turn are linked to a code which directs the expert system to perform certain actions to achieve the desired result.

The resolution to a user's problem could take a number of different forms. Depending on the category and complexity of the problem, the resolution may be one sentence, several sentences, a graphic, or sections cut from on-line documentation or training modules. The service representative will be able to read these over the phone, or use electronic mail or fax machines to respond to the user.

THE BENEFITS OF CASE-BASED REASONING

There are many business reasons supporting the development of Case-based Reasoning systems. They relieve the human expert of mundane tasks, allowing them to focus on more challenging work. This permits less-trained professionals to perform more expert work. Case-based Reasoning systems also provide intelligent tools for the experts themselves. Other benefits include greater flexibility. Maintenance has always been an expensive issue. Case-based Reasoning systems can be relatively easy to maintain because of the independent modules that are easy to change. There is better distribution of expertise, as expert knowledge is available to the entire organization and at all hours of the day. Also, consistency in decision making is assured because of the endorsement of the knowledge that is in the expert system.

Resolution of errors becomes more immediate because the Case-based Reasoning application recommends specific actions and typically justifies its recommendations. Case-based Reasoning applications can provide user-friendly help that allows users to ask why a particular question is being asked or how a particular decision was reached. This provides on-the-job-training tools to help less-skilled professionals become more expert at a task over time.

FUTURE HUMAN–COMPUTER INTERACTION

Despite a track record of success in many companies, artificially intelligent applications remain something of an enigma to the general business community. Rather than take a chance with a new technology, most companies prefer the "tried and trusted" approach of conventional system development. While the notion of using an "expert" system may be appealing, a shortage of knowledge engineers means having to bring in expensive consultants to get the job done. This route is simply not feasible at a time when budgets and jobs are being cut. It is somewhat ironic, however, that the entire premise of an "expert system" is to save the company money by releasing employees from routine chores so that greater productivity can be achieved. The uncertainty and risk inherent with such an undertaking, as well as a strong opposing lobby of traditional programmers, has slowed the development of expert systems within many companies.

Technologies such as hypermedia and graphical user interfaces have already proven their worth in terms of improved human–computer communication, and both are relatively easy to develop as well as being available commercially at low cost. These, however, are only the "visible" parts of a far more complex sphere of functionality. Emerging technologies, such as natural language applications, are becoming more sophisticated and less costly, giving nontechnical people the opportunity to exert an influence over the final appearance and functionality of a product.

As previously discussed, the emergence of Case-based Reasoning products, which use powerful expert systems but do not require any prior programming experience, can open the door to a new breed of developer. Using natural language-type interaction, graphical user interfaces, and hypermedia, this type of application is ideally suited to nontechnical personnel who want to create custom-built software applications for business.

Despite the tremendous interest in new technologies throughout the corporate world, most companies are content to adopt a "wait and see" attitude before actively pursuing the development of applications which will change the way they do business. After all, even minor movement along some new line of reasoning can lead to dramatic changes in the way people do their jobs. This makes the business of technology impact assessment even more difficult—and more critical. The focus is still on "hard" facts, like cost, because they are so much easier to quantify when studying organizational impact.

The evolution of computer technology will continue to enhance human–computer communication. Increased development of intelligent databases, hypermedia, expert systems, and natural language applications will not only make computers easier to use, but will also solve the critical problem of information overload, making it possible to find exactly what is needed when it is needed most.

Research also continues to reveal improved methods of communication. For example, it is quite possible that within the next few years government leaders will be able to talk in foreign languages directly by phone with automatic instantaneous translation between the two. New technologies continue to spring up with the ultimate goal of being simple and inexpensive enough for any member of the general public to purchase and master. Computers are found everywhere today and will continue to exert a pervading influence over our lives as we approach the next century. Efforts to simplify human–computer communication continue to move toward the ultimate goal of a universal reliance on machines to conduct routine business. On a positive note, this trend is creating opportunities for nontechnical types to become actively involved in what was once the exclusive domain of the computer scientist.

REFERENCES

Aucella, A. "Design Guidelines for Graphical User Interfaces." Presented at the Human Factors Society Conference, October 1990: 1–68.

Badler, N. "Task Communication through Natural Language and Graphics." *AI Magazine* (Special Issue–1990): 71–73.

Bailey, R. *Human Performance Engineering.* Englewood Cliffs, N.J.: Prentice-Hall, 1982.

Brand, S. *The Media Lab: Inventing the Future at MIT.* New York: Penguin, 1987.

Bryant, J. "Expert System Follow-up." *PC AI* (July–August 1990): 36–39.

Brynjolfsson, E., and T. Loofbourrow. "PC Tools." *PC AI* (September–October 1988): 31–34.

"CASE for Expert Systems." *AI Expert* (February 1990): 27–31.

Chapnick, P. "Expert Systems and People." *AI Expert* (July 1989): 5–6.

Clancy, W. "Viewing Knowledge Bases as Qualitative Models." *IEEE Expert* (summer 1989): 9–20.

Doane, S. "Design Issues for Graphical UNIX User Interfaces." *Proceedings of the Human Factors Society* (October 1990): 272–76.

Erickson, T. "Creativity and Design." In B. Laurel (ed.), *The Art of Human-Computer Interface Design.* Reading, Mass.: Addison-Wesley, 1990: 1–4.

Feigenbaum, E. A., and P. McCorduck. *The Rise of the Expert Company.* New York: Times Books, 1989.

Harmon, P. "Automating Knowledge Flow at the Help Desk." *Intelligent Strategies* (November 1990): 1–9.

———. "Object-Oriented Systems." *Intelligent Software Strategies* (September 1990): 1–6.

Harris, L. "User Interfaces for Inference-based Programs." *AI Expert* (October 1990): 42–46.

Hayes, F. "Windows Meets UNIX." *UNIX World* (November 1990): 55–58.

Hochrun, G. "Capture that Information on an Expert System." *The Journal of Business Strategy* (January–February 1990): 1–6.

Hollan, J., and M. Williams. "The Craft of Exploiting AI Techniques in Human Interface Design." *Presented at the National Conference on Artificial Intelligence* (July 1990): MA4-1–MA4-90.

Hsu, J., and J. Kusnan. *The Fifth Generation: The Future of Computer Technology.* Blue Ridge, Summit, Pa.: Windcrest, 1989.

Kim, S. "Interdisciplinary Cooperation." In B. Laurel (ed.), *The Art of Human-Computer Interface Design.* Reading, Mass.: Addison-Wesley, 1990: 31–44.

Lane, A. "What is an Expert System?" *PC AI* (November–December 1989): 20–22.

Laurel, B. *The Art of Human–Computer Interface Design*. Reading, Mass.: Addison-Wesley, 1990: xi–xvi.

Miller, B. "Expert Systems—An Introduction." *PC/AI* (September–October 1988): 26–28.

Minasi, M. "Putting Expert Systems in Their Place." *AI Expert* (January 1990): 13–15.

Mishkoff, H. *Understanding Artificial Intelligence*. Indianapolis, Ind.: Howard W. Sams, 1985.

Mountford, J. "Tools and Techniques for Creative Design." In B. Laurel (ed.), *The Art of Human–Computer Interface Design*. Reading, Mass.: Addison-Wesley, 1990: 17–30.

Nee, E. "How Apple is Losing the Interface War." *UNIX World* (October 1990): 67–71.

Parsaye, K., and M. Chignell. *Expert Systems for Experts*. New York: John Wiley & Sons, 1988.

Parsaye, K., M. Chignell, S. Khoshafian, and H. Wong. *Intelligent Databases*. New York: John Wiley & Sons, 1989.

Prerau, D. *Developing and Managing Expert Systems*. New York: Addison-Wesley, 1990.

Rheingold, N. "An Interview with Don Norman." In B. Laurel (ed.), *The Art of Human–Computer Interface Design*. Reading, Mass.: Addison-Wesley, 1990: 5–10.

Salzman, I. "Off the Shelf: A Look at Graphical Shells." *UNIX Review* 8 (7): 103–11.

Shafer, D. *Designing Intelligent Front Ends for Business Software*. New York: John Wiley & Sons, 1989.

———. "Making EIS Intelligent—How to Get Knowledge to Computerphobic Managers." *PC AI* (July–August 1990): 30–35.

———. "Intelligent Applications—How Do They Know?" *PC AI* (January–February 1991): 20–22.

Sherwood, A. "Workstation—The Emerging Alternative for AI." *PC AI* (July–August 1990): 28–50.

Tannenbaum, A. "Expert Systems: Promises and Pitfalls." *Database Programming and Design* (February 1991): 54–59.

"Text Retrieval—True Management." Delphi Consulting Group White Paper 1990: 1–16.

"Using Natural Language for Database Queries." *The Spang Robinson Report on Artificial Intelligence* (December 1990): 2–12.

Vertelney, L., M. Arent, and H. Liberman. "Two Disciplines in Search of an Interface." In B. Laurel (ed.), *The Art of Human–Computer Interface Design.* Reading, Mass.: Addison-Wesley, 1990: 45–55.

Walker, L., and P. Gerkey. "The Seven Veils of Expert Systems." *PC AI* (September–October 1988): 31–34.

Woolf, B. "Knowledge-based Environments for Teaching and Learning." *AI Magazine* (Special Issue 1990): 74–76.

Yager, T. "Open Desktop: Relief for the UNIX Wary." *BYTE* (September 1990): 176–80.

9

Corporate Communication in Global Markets

"Act local, think global" has become the business mantra of the end of the century. The simplicity of the phrase can lure the unsuspecting into a simpleminded interpretation.

Much has been said, written, and videotaped about the need to compete in global markets. And much of what has been said and written about the globalization of business emphasizes the notion that even though we may want a quick and easy method for entering markets outside of our own country, the reality is that doing business in another country can be complex and difficult.

The complexity is in large measure cultural. We understand that working in a culture or nation different from our own requires us to master these determining forces to communicate and manage effectively. In addition to a familiarity with the history, the politics, the alliances and treaties, and the art and literature of a country, an effective approach to learning about the transnational environment would also include an understanding of the following:

- language

- technology and the environment

- social organization

- contexts and face-saving

- concepts of authority

- body language and nonverbal communication

- concepts of time

Language. Doing business successfully in an international, a global, or a transnational environment demands attention to cultural, social, political, and religious practices, in addition to technical, business, legal, and financial activities.

Communication is the key to each. Real communication—not just cookbook do's and don'ts, such as not showing the soles of your shoes in Saudi Arabia, not shaking hands with a Japanese after putting something in your back pocket, always finishing the bottle when a Russian begins to toast you, or not discussing business with a Mexican on the first business meeting.

Such advice may be very interesting to read and think about, but it rarely recognizes that after the do's and don'ts run out, what do you do next? Such information is like having the pieces in a much larger puzzle, without a clear notion of the whole picture of the complete puzzle. That is where the "act local" part comes in. If you want to act local, you must be local.

In other words, understand the country you are doing business in. The first step is to make every effort you can to learn the language. Almost all nations notice your effort to learn their language. This is more than just symbolic. Language encodes culture, and making an attempt to understand the words leads to trying to understand the way that people think. Learning the language helps you also learn the way the people who speak it view their world. In addition to its power to convey information and ideas, language is also the vehicle for communicating values, beliefs, and culture.

The following examples of simple language differences are by now classics, almost clichés for international communication: General Motors' efforts to sell its Chevy Nova in Mexico. Nova sounds like the Spanish *No va*, or no go! And Ford's Pinto is Portuguese slang for a small male appendage. The popular *Bich* are Bic pens in the English-speaking world for obvious reasons.

On a deeper level, understanding the language will give you an insight into the art and literature of a nation.

Technology and the environment. The way people view technology and their environment is often culturally defined and can have an impact on international business communication. The way people view man–made work environments differs in the perception of lighting, roominess, air temperature and humidity, access to electricity, telephones, and computers.

People perceive their relationship to the physical environment differently. For some, nature is to be controlled; for others, it is neutral or negative, and for others yet it is something for man to be in harmony with. Even climate, topography, and population density have an impact on the way people perceive themselves, which has an impact on the way they communicate, their concepts of mobility, and the way they conduct business.

You certainly expect an office that is clean and relatively quiet; one with dependable lights, telephones, copiers, networked computers and E-mail, and temperature control. Be prepared to have a work environment that is different from your office. Many countries ration essential services such as electricity. Transportation and housing may be less than you expect.

The natural environment may be much hotter, colder, more humid or drier than you imagine. Daylight in northern countries may be limited in winter and almost endless in summer. Heat and rain may change the daily routine, particularly in the tropics. Be prepared to adapt.

Social organization.   Social organization, or the influence of shared actions and institutions on the behavior of the individual, has a strong impact on business communications worldwide. Institutions and structures tend to reinforce social values—the consensus of a group of people that a certain behavior has value.

For international business communications we might consider the following social structures that influence the workplace:

- kinship and family relationships
- educational systems and ties to business
- class and economic distinctions
- religious, political, and legal systems
- professional organizations and unions
- gender stereotypes and roles
- emphasis on the group or the individual
- concepts of distance and attachment to the land
- recreational activity

Each of these aforementioned areas should be the focus of background research before traveling overseas.

Some familiarity with the major works of art and literature will give you some insight into the social organization of the country you plan to visit on business.

You might find the worksheet in Table 9–1 helpful when preparing to go overseas.

Contexts and face-saving.   Contexts and face-saving refer to the way one communicates and the situation in which the communication

TABLE 9-1
Gathering Facts for a County Analysis

COUNTRY OR REGION_____

1. **National Language** Local Languages Dialects 1A. **National Symbols** Flag, Songs, Colors, Flowers, Holidays	1.
2. **National Foods**	2.
3. **Politics and Government** System of Government Political Parties Organization of Government Political Leaders Police System Military	3.
4. **Economics and Industry** Major Industries Imports/Exports Foreign Investment Industrial Development Agriculture Fishing Markets Urban and Rural Conditions	4.
4A. **Resources, Communication, and Transportation** Human Natural—Climate and Geography; Minerals Agriculture, Forests, Water Communication Infrastructure Media—Print and Broadcast Computer Network Transportation Infrastructure	4A.
5. **Arts and Culture** Painting and Sculpture Music and Dance Literature, Drama, Poetry TV and Radio Movies and Cinema Architecture Folk Arts, Crafts	5.
6. **Education** Educational Philosophy School System Colleges and Universities Vocational Training	6.
7. **Science** Inventions and Achievements Technological Infrastructure Attitude Toward Science Institutions and Laboratories Medicine and Hospitals	7.
8. **Religion and Philosophy** Modern Beliefs Folktales and Superstitions Sayings and Proverbs Myths and Legends	8.
9. **Family & Social Structure** Customs and Rituals—birth, death, marriage Social Welfare Systems	9.
10. **Sports and Games** Local Sports Children's Games Contemporary World Sports	10.

Checklist for gathering basic factual information about the country or region where you plan to work.

occurs. We refer to cultures that are high context, like the Japanese, and low context like the German. For example, a Japanese painting of a landscape will use only a brush stroke or two to represent a range of mountains, the details being left to the viewer's imagination.

On the other hand, a high-context culture would express figures and landscapes with almost photographic detail. In a low-context culture like the British, details about class and education and even the place of birth are apparent in the clothes someone wears and the accent in their conversation.

People all over the world seek to preserve their outward dignity or prestige—face-saving. Cultures, however, differ in the emphasis on it.

High face-saving cultures have the following general characteristics:

- high contexting

- indirect strategy for business communication

- toleration of a high degree of generality, ambiguity, and vagueness

- considers indirect communication polite, civil, honest, and considerate

- considers direct communication offensive, uncivilized, inconsiderate

- uses few words to disclose personal information

Low face-saving cultures have the following general characteristics:

- low contexting

- a direct strategy for business communication; confrontational

- very low tolerance for generality, ambiguity, and vagueness

- considers indirect communication impolite, unproductive, dishonest, and inconsiderate

- considers direct communication professional, honest, and considerate

- uses written and spoken words to disclose personal information

Saving face is also allied with concepts of guilt and shame. Shame is associated with high-context cultures, guilt with low. This makes sense when you consider that low-context cultures value rules and the law; breaking the law or a rule implies a transgression—sin and guilt—as a mechanism for control. High-context cultures use shame as the agent for controlling behavior through face-saving, honor, dignity, and obligation.

Concepts of authority. The concept of authority, influence, and power, as well as how power is exercised in the workplace, differs from culture to culture. For instance, in Western cultures such as the United States and Europe, power is the ability to make and act on decisions. Power for such cultures is an abstract ideal discussed and debated by philosophers and theorists from John Stuart Mill to Karl Marx.

For Asian cultures, power and authority are almost the opposite of the Western concepts. Power results from social order. Asians accept decision making by consensus and decide to become part of the group rather than its leader. Understanding the concept of power helps shape a business's communication strategy. The direct approach to communication, so effective in the United States, may prove crude and offensive in France or Japan.

Body language and nonverbal communication. Body language and nonverbal communication are just as important in international and cross–cultural communications as they are in communications within a homogeneous culture. Watch movies and TV from a country you wish to visit before you go, as well as when you arrive. This gives you some cues to appropriate nonverbal behavior.

Pay attention to kinesics (body movements), physical appearance and dress, eye contact, touching, proxemics (the space between people), and paralanguage (sounds and gestures used to communicate in place of words). Also, colors, numbers and alphabets, symbols such as the national flag, and smell are important elements in international communication.

Concepts of time. Concepts of time differ from culture to culture. In the twentieth century physicists such as Albert Einstein and more recently Steven Hawking have demonstrated that time in the physical sense is relative. For purposes of communication across cultures, it helps to consider time as a social variable.

In the Caribbean, for example, the American tourist is frustrated to distraction when asking for a cab and getting the response, "Come soon." Time is defined culturally and by shared social experience.

THE LOGISTICS OF AN OVERSEAS ASSIGNMENT

Table 9–1 offered a checklist to aid in understanding the country and culture in which you will be working. Along with that planning, a more down-to-earth plan is necessary.

Table 9–2 will help you begin planning the practical details of working in a global environment. Since you will be away from everything that is familiar to you, prepare for everything, no matter how small.

TABLE 9-2
What to Bring—Logistics

ITEM/AREA	ACTION
Documents	• Apply for passport and visas • Obtain an international driver's license
Medical	• Have a medical exam before you leave, and any necessary immunizations, including hepatitis • Obtain copies of records, X-rays, and prescriptions • Know blood type; shots • Obtain prescriptions for glasses • Have a dental exam; get dental records • See a vet for appropriate shots and certificates for your pet.
Legal	• Update your will before you go • Designate power of attorney to a responsible relative or friend
Financial	• Buy local currency for countries you will be traveling through for transportation, tips, etc. • Buy traveler's checks to cover travel expenses • Arrange financial transfer and access with your bank—mailing statements, access to safe deposit boxes, power of attorney authorization, and signature cards • Obtain lines of credit and credit card notification • Arrange with an accountant to have proper state and federal tax forms filed • Meet with your insurance agent to discuss medical, life, home, auto, fire, and accident coverage at home while you are away; discuss coverage for the country in which you will be working. • Keep receipts of all expenses related to your move
Education	• Meet with teachers and administrators to discuss tests, evaluations, transfer of records, placement in schools in the host country • Contact schools in the host city well in advance; select the school and arrange for spaces for your children
Communication	• Get a change of address kit from the post office • Notify family members of your new address and the customs requirements • Stop deliveries of newspapers, magazines, and other services • Arrange for mail and telephone service where you plan to be
Transportation	• Visit AAA for an international driver's license
Household	• Notify your utility services of your plans, and arrange to discontinue service—telephone, gas, oil, water, and electricity

SOURCE: Robert Kohls, *Survival Kit for Overseas Living*, 2d Ed.

Checklist to start planning for your overseas assignment.

WHO TO CONTACT

Before you go, become familiar with the official U.S. presence in the host country, and the structure of a typical U.S. diplomatic mission. Also, find out specific contacts from the Departments of State and Commerce:

- U.S. Commerce Department, International Trade Administration, Trade Information Center: 1-800-USA-TRADE (1-800-872-8723)

- U.S. Departments of State and Commerce, Country Desk Officers: (202) 482-3022; for a specific Country Desk Officer: (202) 647-4000

- U.S. Department of State Coordinator for Business Affairs: (202) 647-1942; fax (202) 647-5713

Table 9–3 offers some helpful contacts for doing business once you are situated in the host country.

COMMUNICATION IN THE NEW EUROPE

From the chaos and political instability that faced Europe at the end of the World War II came a movement to unite the countries that had led the world into global conflict twice in less than four decades. The concept was to link the countries economically in the hope that development of such ties would reduce the risk of going to war.

In addition, the goals of a European Community would contain nationalism that was the main cause of war in Europe, contain a dominant Germany, create a barrier against Soviet Communism, strengthen prosperity at home and in world markets, and gain a strong European voice in international affairs. Since 1950, numerous treaties, agreements, and acts have evolved into the European Union, which in 1995 was comprised of Germany, France, Italy, Great Britain, the Netherlands, Denmark, Ireland, Belgium, Luxembourg, Spain, Portugal, Greece, Austria, Sweden, and Finland.

A main trading partner of the European Community is the European Free Trade Association (EFTA), which was formed in 1960 and includes Austria, Finland, Iceland, Liechtenstein, Norway, Sweden, and Switzerland. Russia and the former Communist bloc countries of Central and Eastern Europe—Hungary, Poland, Rumania, Slovakia, Czech Republic, Bulgaria, and the countries of the Commonwealth of Independent States—are developing new relationships with one another and with the European Union.

These enormous shifts in political and economic philosophy present a business communications challenge and opportunity. As

TABLE 9-3
Doing Business Overseas—Who to Contact

KEY OFFICERS	RESPONSIBILITIES
Chief of Mission—Ambassador, Minister, Chargé d'Affaires	All components of the U.S. mission within a country, including consular posts
Commercial Officer	Assists U.S. business through arranging appointments with local business and government officials, counseling on local trade regulations, laws, and customs, identifying importers, buyers, agents, distributors, and joint venture partners for U.S. firms, and other business assistance
Commercial Officers for Tourism	Implement marketing programs to expand inbound tourism, increase the export competitiveness of U.S. travel companies, and strengthen the international trade position of the United States.
Economic Officers	Analyze and report on macroeconomic trends and trade policies and their implications for U.S. policies and programs
Financial Attachés	Analyze and report on major financial developments
Political Officers	Analyze and report on political developments and their potential impact on U.S. interests
Labor Officers	Follow the activities of labor organizations to supply such information as wages, non-wage costs, social security regulations, labor attitudes toward American investments, etc.
Consular Officers	Extend to U.S. citizens and their property abroad the protection of the U.S. government. Maintain lists of attorneys; act as liaison with police and other officials; have authority to notarize documents. The State Department recommends that business representatives residing overseas register with the consular officer; in troubled areas, even travelers are advised to register.
Administrative Officers	Responsible for normal business operations of the post, including purchasing for the post and its commissary.
Regional Security Officers	Responsible for providing physical, procedural, and personnel security services to U.S. diplomatic facilities and personnel; responsibilities extend to providing in-country security briefings and threat assessments to business executives.
Security Assistance Officers	Responsible for Defense Cooperation in Armaments and foreign military sales to include functioning as primary in-country point of contact for U.S. defense industry.
Scientific Attachés	Follow scientific and technological developments in the country.
Agricultural Officers	Promote the export of U.S. agricultural products and report on agricultural production and market developments in the country.
AID Mission Officers	Responsible for AID programs, including dollar and local currency loans, grants, and technical assistance.
Public Affairs Officer	Press and cultural affairs specialists who maintain close contact with the local press.
Legal Attachés	Serve as representatives to the U.S. Department of Justice on criminal matters.
Communications Programs Officers	Responsible for the telecommunications, telephone, radio, and diplomatic pouches, and records management programs within the diplomatic mission; maintain close contact with the host government's information/communications authorities on operational matters.
Information Systems Managers	Responsible for the post's unclassified information systems, database management, programming, and operational needs; provide liaison with appropriate commercial contacts in the information field to enhance the post's systems integrity.
Animal and Plant Health Inspection Service Officers	Responsible for animal and plant health issues as they impact U.S. trade and in protecting U.S. agriculture from foreign pests and diseases; expedite U.S. exports in the area of technical sanitary and phytosanitary (S&P) regulations.

SOURCE: Department of State Publication 7877, 1993

U.S. Mission, Key Officers and Their Responsibilities: A Wide Range of Help and Information for U.S. Citizens In-country barriers to trade are removed, the natural barriers of distance, culture, and language that have kept people apart for centuries again begin to play an important role in business transactions.

In the European Community, particularly since the fall of the Soviet Union, is a group of "Europeans." These are business professionals from all over Europe who tend to share a cultural and belief system that has more in common with their international business counterparts in America or Asia. What they share with one another is often more than what they share with their own countrymen—taste in art, literature, music, recreational activities, cars, homes, and attitudes towards work and money. Thus what has emerged is a "global professional."

For example, an advertising executive in France or England can function within the professional context almost anywhere in the world because of the commonality of activity. What has happened to almost all of the business professions is something that engineers have known and practiced for years—technical expertise translates well across many borders.

The business professional has emerged as a European class, often very well versed in the language and culture of the political nations he or she is working in and with. Other nations can hope to achieve this ideal of the international attitude and ability that Europeans have developed over centuries of trade.

COMMUNICATION AND THE PACIFIC RIM

For Americans doing business with nations of the Pacific Rim we can add to the difficulties of language and culture the added differences in context and face–saving, discussed earlier. Context in communication usually refers to how much influence the situation exerts on meaning for the participants. Context can come from the impact of silence, from unspoken words, from inflection and tone of voice, from gestures, from timing of events, and from form rather than substance.

Low-context cultures, such as those in Germany and the United States, place a high emphasis on explicit communication, the law, and contracts. They rely on verbal communication, tolerate relatively little ambiguity, and place reduced emphasis on personal relationships and face–saving.

High-context cultures, such as those in Japan and Latin America, place a high emphasis on personal relationships, present information indirectly and often ambiguously or through nuance, and act at all times to preserve one's prestige or outward dignity—to save face. The word, the laws, and contracts are seen as less important than the bindings of personal relationships.

In the high-context cultures of the Pacific Rim, business communicators from low-context cultures such as the United States will be
confronted with controlled use of silence, or communication through
intuition. The Japanese have elevated such meaningful silences to an art
form and call it *haragei*. *Hara*, or literally "belly," is the English equivalent of heart or center of one's being; the center of feelings, courage, and
understanding, as well as the wisdom gained through one's experience.
Haragei is the opposite of the argument or verbal confrontation so
common to the business communication of Westerners.

Another concept in the high-context cultures of the Pacific Rim is
the Korean *kibun*, or moods or feelings. Koreans are very sensitive to
maintaining harmony and go to what Westerners consider great lengths
to maintain their own kibun as well as everyone else's. The concept
plays a role in the aversion of most Asian Pacific Rim nations to bring
bad or unpleasant news. It is also related to an unwillingness to say
"no" directly as a way to save face.

In high-context cultures the differences between the surface truth
and reality may be much more important than in low-context cultures
that often make no such distinction. The Japanese use the terms *tatemae*
and *honne*. Tatemae is the facade of a structure like a building, and
honne is one's true voice, what one really thinks and feels. Every
culture has such concepts to some degree. Even a quick scan of most
European novels of the last century or the works of American novelist
Henry James reveal the richness that exists in the difference between the
public expression and the private thoughts of individuals.

The status of the Pacific Rim as an economic and a political force
requires corporations of any size to develop a business and communications strategy that meets the business challenge effectively. Making a
strong and conscious effort to understand the concepts of contexting
and face–saving is essential for any effective assignment in almost every
nation of the Asian Pacific Rim.

COMMUNICATION WITH DEVELOPING COUNTRIES

Americans doing business in developing countries should make every
effort to understand the cultures, customs, and language of the people
they are communicating with in those nations or regions. While
working and talking to people in developing countries, make no
excuses about being from another culture. Chances are they know a lot
more about you from movies, books, and mass media than you know
about them. Many of the business professionals were educated in the
United States and are more likely of a higher social class than most of
their countrymen.

Developing countries may appear to have disadvantages compared to some of the advanced economies of the world. But remember, they often have a rich artistic, religious, and cultural heritage that should be the focus of your building a business relationship with them. The economy of many developing countries may be built on many families or on sole proprietor companies. They can therefore compete in a global economy because in their small companies the flexibility and lack of bureaucracy give them a comparative advantage.

Since they might also know English, you may show your interest in them by at least reading their literature in translation, being aware of their cultural and artistic accomplishments, and making an effort to learn their language.

But also be proud of who you are. Nothing seems less genuine than a foreigner who seems to "go native" at the expense of his or her own culture.

To communicate in a global environment, the understanding of contexts, situations, languages, cultures, and motives should prove an appropriate and a valuable approach to almost any new culture. In short, make every effort to understand your audience's needs and expectations.

COMMUNICATION TECHNOLOGIES OVERCOME BARRIERS OF TIME AND SPACE

Working in a global environment underscores the importance of some communication media. Technologies such as satellites and E-mail have increasingly replaced the telex, the fax machine, and the telephone in international business.

It is common in some technology-based companies to have groups from all over the world work on projects around the clock. These professionals and technicians are connected to one another by computer networks. For example in New York, one group will work on a project. At the end of the work day, it will pass the job to another group on the computer network in Los Angeles. In this way, the work is distributed around the world and around the clock, overcoming the communication barriers of time and space.

Technological advances in communication have created the global business environment that challenges us today.

Europe and the European Union

Michael B. Goodman

Europe has been historically the site for most overseas work. The nations of Europe have been and are global partners and adversaries and leaders in world trade. No matter what part of the world you are from, Europe figures into the mix in some strong way.

Doing business in Europe would seem on the surface a no-brainer. History, culture, and often language all point toward an equitable arrangement. But pay special attention to the differences, for the misconception of similarities like the subtle differences among members of the same family can often grow into disputes and blocks to economic partnerships. Take for example the case of a Detroit-based diesel manufacturer's European CEO. He delegated responsibility to set up a program in Zurich to create a European team after acquiring several of its parts suppliers. The person had been successful in Detroit and as a teacher in Cairo, but with an abrasive style.

> The Europeans call him an *Arbeitstier*—a "work animal"—because he always works late. He never joins the staff for a leisurely lunch, preferring to eat a sandwich at his desk. He still can't speak even rudimentary Swiss German . . . On top of that [his] wife is unhappy in Zürich because she misses her job, and their daughter is upset because she's having trouble applying for U.S. colleges from the school she's attending. (Adler, Gordon, "The Case of the Floundering Expatriate," *Harvard Business Review* [July–August 1995]: 166)

The essay is from Michael B. Goodman's *Working in A Global Environment: Understanding, Communicating, and Managing Transnationally*, Piscataway, N.J.: IEEE,1995.

This highlights, according to Fons Trompenaars, author of *Riding the Waves of Culture* (1993), a common misunderstanding of the challenges involved in managing in Europe. Creating an effective team there means more than helping people adjust to another business model. It requires commitment and the selection of people who are not only excellent technically, but also understand the organizational and behavioral forces at work. Europeans manage by objectives, apply total quality principles, survey their employees and customers. But often the person sent from the United States to do these things is a subject matter expert, with little or only a surface knowledge of the context of the foreign environment. Working together overseas requires a deep understanding of the differences in local cultures. "It's amazing what can be achieved when one makes a business issue out of intercultural experiences. Increasingly, international managers realize that they can gain competitive advantage by understanding cultural differences. Technologies can be copied quickly. Intercultural competence cannot be copied; it must be learned" (*Harvard Business Review* (July–August 1995): 38).

In understanding cultural differences and working in Europe and the European Union, consider: the impact of World War II on Europe, the nature of work and their bureaucracy, the economic nature of the European Union (EU) and its policies, their attitudes toward business activities, rules and regulations necessary to do business there, and the political tensions that are inherent there.

THE IMPACT OF WORLD WAR II ON EUROPE

Wars, particularly recent ones, play a profound role in shaping the way Europeans think, and by extension, the way they think about business. The absolute devastation and destruction brought on by World War II left almost the entire continent in ruin, financially exhausted and in despair. Leaders within Europe, and throughout the world, felt that in an atomic age to continue the cycle of war and destruction put the entire world at risk.

On the other hand, a Europe at peace would point to prosperity. One approach to forging the peace in an era of increasing military tension brought on by the Cold War with the Soviet Bloc was through economic cooperation. In April 1951 the European Coal and Steel Community was established between Germany and France. By placing these adversaries in cooperation over the raw material of war, this was to be a model of cooperation in other areas. Figure 9–1 offers an overview of important treaties and events that led to the evolution of the European Union.

DATE	EVENT
1951	• Signing of the Treaty of Paris establishing a European Coal and Steel Community (ECSC)
1957	• Signing of the "Treaties of Rome" establishing the European Economic Community (EEC) and the European Atomic Energy Community (EAEC)
1968	• The Community becomes a customs union, import and export duties abolished among members
1973	• Denmark, Ireland, and the United Kingdom join the European Community
1979	• The European Monetary System (EMS) comes into operation
	• First direct elections to the European Parliament
1981	• Greece joins the European Community
1984	• Second direct elections to the European Parliament
1986	• Spain and Portugal join the European Community
	• The Single European Act amends the Treaties of Paris and Rome
1989	• Third direct elections to the European Parliament
1990	• Germany reunited after the fall of the Communist regime in the East
1993	• Treaty of Maastrict on European Union sets goals for a frontier-free Europe, economic and monetary union, and social and political union
1995	• Austria, Finland, and Sweden join the European Union

SOURCE: Various European Community Publications

Figure 9–1.
Events since World War II have resulted in the European Union
as a major economic entity.

Membership in this trading and economic partnership began in 1959 with Belgium, France, Germany, Italy, Luxembourg, and the Netherlands; added in 1973 were Denmark, Ireland, and the United Kingdom; Greece joined in 1981; in 1986 Spain and Portugal; and in 1995 Austria, Finland, and Sweden. The list could expand since Hungary, Poland, Cyprus, Malta, and Turkey have applied to join. And the end of the Cold War has prompted the EU to draw up plans to include in its single market Bulgaria, Czech Republic, Hungary, Poland, Rumania, and Slovakia. Other possibilities include association agreements Estonia, Latvia, and Lithuania. Figure 9–2 is a recent map of the European Union.

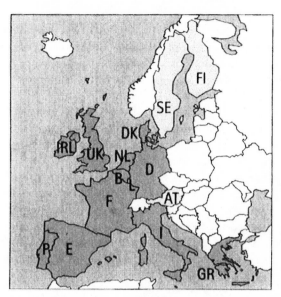

SOURCE: European Union, Luxembourg, 1997

Figure 9-2.
The European Union has evolved into more than an Economic Union to
become a global social and political force.

THE NATURE OF WORK AND THEIR BUREAUCRACY

Now as most Americans you are wondering why so much discussion of history and politics? Precisely that. Key to understanding local actions in Europe is to understand the history and political and social forces that are at work there today, but also over the course of the previous centuries. That's right, centuries. In some countries like England, the tradition of democracy goes back to the Magna Carta, whereas Germany's current democratic structure is based on America's and is the result of the American influence after World War II in rebuilding Europe.

Also, in many technically based companies, and in most of the Western world for that matter, fundamental shifts are taking place in the way people, organizations, and governments operate. Downsizing, reinventing, reengineering, and restructuring are replacing hierarchical structures and process cultures with organizations focused on the work and the outcomes of work, rather than the perpetuation of the structures of work.

Bureaucracy, a French word, has the world over become synonymous with delay, endless paperwork, diffused authority and responsibility, frustration, and added expense in time and money. No matter how much the world is streamlining processes and government, bureaucracy remains a fact of life. It may be a little more responsive and friendly in some countries of Europe, and more efficient and helpful in others, but it is still the way things get done in Europe.

It is a good idea to learn the regulatory bodies and organizations in the country you are in and treat their rules as you would the rules and laws in your own country. Obey them, and if you think they are unfair, then join others in your industry to influence a change. Bureaucracy responds well to groups of organizations and countries. Remember that a nation that has a rich and long history sees your immediate need for change from a much different perspective. Keep in mind that the current negotiations on the Uruguay Round of the General Agreement on Tariffs and Trade (GATT) began in 1987 and the implementation of the agreements started in 1995. The goal is to discipline trade-distorting practices such as tariffs and subsidies.

THE ECONOMIC NATURE OF
THE EUROPEAN UNION AND ITS POLICIES

Europe has traditionally been the largest market for the export and import of U.S. goods and services. When compared with Japan in 1992, according to the U.S. Department of Commerce, Europe imported almost $200 billion and exported slightly less to the United States for a balance of +$3.5 billion. By contrast, U.S. exports in the same period to Japan were approximately $75 billion, with much greater imports for a balance of –$38.3 billion. Put simply, trade with Europe is vast and for the most part equitable.

Though the relationship with Western Europe is profitable and friendly, care must still be taken in doing business there, as our case cited earlier demonstrates. Current trends in Europe toward a European Union and a Single Market within that Union have shifted power away from any single dominant country in Europe to the structures of the EU. As internal policy, the power in most of the member countries now includes a European Union presence in the form of the European Council and the European Court of Justice.

The first step in creating a single market was to create a frontier-free single market so "goods, services, people, and capital move unhindered across" the borders of member countries. To bring this about the effort throughout the Maastrict Treaty has as its goal to remove the physical, technical, and fiscal barriers to trade. Efforts are clearly a long way toward achieving these goals with the most evident the border crossings which now funnel EU citizens one way, and all the rest another. Transport of goods within the EU is now much more efficient since the single market allows freer movement within the EU.

Internally the efforts for deregulation and reform, as they are in much of the world, continue within the EU. To have regulations on the quality of goods and services uniform throughout the EU has fallen largely on the committees and working groups within the political arm of the EU. Figure 9–3 shows the relationship of member governments to the EU. Knowing the layers of political power in Europe is fundamental to your understanding of the power of any regulating body there. In Europe, agencies or committees or working groups set the policy and stipulate the standards for such things as electrical appliances, videotape, or the purity of beer.

RULES AND REGULATIONS NECESSARY TO DO BUSINESS THERE

To put the political and bureaucratic perspective into focus, regulations such as ISO 9000 have an enormous impact on corporations doing business with the members of the EU. If your organization does not meet ISO standards, you cannot do business in any EU member country. Think of it. Miss the standard, and your product or service, no matter how good, cannot find its way into what is now one of the three largest markets in the world, and if the expansion continues as we mentioned earlier, the world's largest market.

Those standards are developed in Working Groups that are part of the permanent bureaucracy of the EU in Belgium and Luxembourg. Organizations of international groups such as the IEEE often advise and contribute to the setting of technical standards for the EU. Increasingly, these ISO standards are becoming the world standard. It is another example of how the economy has become more and more global.

U.S. and Japanese companies stand to gain from the efforts to create a single market in Europe since both are better at and more flexible in restructuring their operations. For instance, General Motors can now consolidate its automobile operations by designating one site for electrical parts to serve all of its EU operations and replacement parts, rather than having sites in each member state as before.

Along with the advantages for those companies who think globally and make the effort to work with their European partners and customers, some systemic problems remain for U.S. business. For instance, gaining access to power. In short, who do you lobby? Other systematic problems include: creating effective organizations that work in the EU; gathering accurate information; becoming an effective player in a changing Europe; striking a balance between marketing at national and EU levels.

THE EUROPEAN DECISION MAKING PROCESS

National Parliaments—Elected —Form Governments	
National Governments —Appoint EU Representatives	

EUROPEAN COUNCIL
• Heads of Gov't.
• Foreign Ministers
• Comm. Pres.
• VP of Comm.

COUNCIL OF MINISTERS
(Decides)
• Comm. of Permanent Reps.
• Ambassadors
• National Civil Servants
• Working Groups

THE COMMISSION
20 Members
• Executive Functions
• Proposes Actions

23 Directorates General

Economic and Social Committee

Committee of the Regions

EUROPEAN PARLIAMENT
• Members Elected
• Represent National Gov'ts.
• Discuss Actions
Functions:
• Supervisory
• Legislative
• Budgetary

COURT OF JUSTICE
• Ensures EU law is interpreted and applied correctly (European "Supreme Court")

COURT OF AUDITORS
• Checks accounts against authorized budgets

SOURCE: *Working Together—The Institutions of the European Community.* European Community, Brussels, 1994

Figure 9–3.

Working in Europe demands an understanding of the EU as another political and bureaucratic force.

Particular industrial sectors need to meet the challenge of changing methods for standards, testing, and certification. Environmental and consumer protection issues need to be addressed, as well as the changes in public procurement. Industrial policy, competition, and subsidies, as well as social issues and work rule, add to the considerations in doing business in Europe.

EUROPEAN UNION ATTITUDES TOWARD BUSINESS ACTIVITIES

Business attitudes in Europe are different than ours, but people with similar educational, class, and professional backgrounds tend to share a great deal internationally. To support this notion that you share more with an engineer from Coventry, England, or Frankfort, Germany, than you do with an auto mechanic in Minneapolis, let's look at *Tomorrow's Company: The Role of Business in a Changing World* (London: RSA, 1994). This report by the Royal Society for the Encouragement of Arts, Manufactures, & Commerce (RSA), the British equivalent of The Conference Board, challenges business to meet worldwide competition through an inclusive approach.

> In an inclusive approach success is not defined in terms of a single bottom line, nor is purpose confined to the needs of a single stakeholder. Each company makes its own unique choice of purpose and values, and has its own model of critical business processes from which it derives its range of success measures. But tomorrow's company will understand and measure the value which it derives from all its key relationships, and thereby be able to make informed decisions when it has to balance and trade off the conflicting claims of customers, suppliers, employees, investors, and the communities in which it operates. (*Tomorrow's Company: The Role of Business in a Changing World*, 1)

They maintain that the forces of global competition are making change necessary. Complicating factors are rising population and consumption putting pressure on natural resources, rapid changes in technology changing employment patterns, changes in people's aspirations, the rise in pressure groups, and reduced public confidence in governments and other institutions. To compete internationally, a company needs a supportive operating environment. A shared vision and common agenda among business, government, and the community is key to meeting the challenge of competition.

Winners in this international arena maintain their "license to operate" by achieving a high level of support from everyone they contact directly or indirectly. Such companies must learn and change rapidly, inspire new levels of skill and creativity in its people, and develop a shared destiny with customers and stakeholders. Traditional measures of success, financial performance, and returns to shareholders, must not continue as the only purpose of business. All a company's relationships must be included in its definitions and measures of success. The report emphasizes that tomorrow's company has clear values and purpose, defines relationships consistently, is part of a wider system, recognizes its dependence on relationships, recognizes the need for tradeoffs among stakeholders, and understands the need to measure and communicate its performance in all its relationships.

If the RSA report sounds familiar, it is because the issues and the dialogue are about global business. These concerns transcend borders and geographic regions. They recognize, as Europeans have for centuries, that the world is a small place. Relationships and partnerships are needed for success.

THE POLITICAL TENSIONS THAT ARE INHERENT THERE

Finally, many non-European capitalists continue to be surprised by the relative harmony between business and government, compared with the relatively adversarial relationship found in the United States. Europe has had a long mercantilist tradition in which the interests of private companies and the state can be in harmony. Add to this the prominence and maturity of government long before the rise of big business and industrial organizations. Bureaucrats saw no threat since they were charged with the public welfare. By contrast, big business appeared in the United States before big government, and relations are often strained and even hostile.

The Maastrict Treaty and the movement toward a single market are manifestations of the European effort to remove some of the inefficiency, cost, poor service, and uncreative habits that have emerged from comfortable relations between business and government. But to compare capitalism in Europe and the United States only in terms of economic efficiency and performance would lead to misunderstanding.

> Given a choice between better profits and higher dividends on one hand, and the social stability represented by high employment rolls on the other, Europeans have usually chosen stability. Up to now, [they] have been willing to accept the overhead burden this choice imposes by paying higher prices and accepting lower returns . . . Economic outcome, for both companies and individuals, [is] more tightly "bunched" than [it is] in the United States and Japan. And most Europeans would sacrifice the possibility of an unrestricted

business environment that rewards a few with extreme wealth for the reality of many more people with comfortable incomes. (Henzler, Herbert. "The New Era of Eurocapitalism," *Harvard Business Review* (July–August 1992): 62)

The history of Europe with wars, revolutions, and vicious labor disputes helps a non-European begin to understand why they emphasize stability. Their history of the long-term costs of unrest and violence make any short-term price seem a bargain.

Afterword

As a boy growing up in Dallas, my father took me with him to the farmer's market. There we stopped regularly at my uncle's warehouse. He was usually in the back with his employees cutting the bananas from the stalks as they were unloaded from the railroad cars. He had a stub of an unlit cigar in his mouth, wearing a coarse apron and leather work gloves. One morning while we were there a salesman asking to see the owner of the company was directed to the back. I'll always remember the salesman's confused and startled expression when my uncle looked up, took off a glove, and extended his hand. There was no doubt my uncle was the boss no matter how he looked.

A lot more has changed in corporate America than the way we ship and warehouse bananas. But the fundamentals of clear, concise communication with customers, employees, and vendors remain constant.

Communicating effectively requires

- an ability to write and speak cogently;

- an understanding of corporate environments and cultures;

- an ability to build and maintain a substantial corporate image;

- knowledge of a corporation's role as a citizen;

- good relations with the media;

- being prepared for a crisis;

- an understanding of information and technology; and

- a willingness to compete in a global marketplace.

I hope each chapter's discussions, commentaries, and case studies in this book have provided the information that is necessary for you to meet the communications requirements of the complex corporate environment today and into the next century.

Further Reading

1. OVERVIEW OF CORPORATE COMMUNICATION

Argenti, Paul. *Corporate Communication*. Homewood, Ill.: Irwin, 1995.

Branscomb, Anne Wells. *Who Owns Information?* New York: Basic Books, 1994.

Browdy, E. W. *The Business of Public Relations*. New York: Praeger, 1987.

Conducting Research in Business Communication. Ed. Patty Cambell, et. al. Urbana, Ill.: Association for Business Communication, 1988.

Cushman, Don, and Sarah King. *Communicating Organizational Change*. Albany: State University of New York Press, 1995.

Falsey, Thomas. *Corporate Philosophies and Mission Statements: A Survey and Guide for Corporate Communicators and Management*. Westport, Conn.: Quorum Books, 1989.

Goodman, Michael B. *Corporate Communication: Theory and Practice*. Albany: State University of New York Press, 1994.

Hayakawa, S. I. *Language in Thought and Action*. New York: Harcourt Brace, 1978.

Jackson, Peter. *Corporate Communications for Managers*. United Kingdom: Pitman, 1987.

Kinneavy, James L. *A Theory of Discourse*. Englewood Cliffs, N.J.: Prentice-Hall, 1971; Norton (paper), 1980.

Lavin, Michael. *Business Information: How to Find It; How to Use It*. 2d ed. Phoenix, Ariz.: Oryx Press, 1987/1992.

Lewis, Philip. *Organizational Communication*. 3d ed. New York: Wiley, 1987.

McGinn, Robert E. *Science, Technology, and Society*. Englewood Cliffs, N.J.: Prentice Hall, 1991.

Moore, Geoffrey. *Crossing the Chasm*. New York: Harper Business, 1991.

Negroponte, Nicholas. *Being Digital*. New York: Knopf, 1995.

Norman, Donald A. *The Design of Everday Things*. New York: Doubleday, 1988.

Postman, Neil. *Technopoly: The Surrender of Culture to Technology*. New York: Knopf, 1992.

Robinson, Judith. *Tapping the Government Grapevine: The User-Friendly Guide to U.S. Government Information Sources*. Phoenix, Ariz.: Oryx Press, 1988.

RSA Inquiry—Tomorrow's Company: The Role of Business in a Changing World—Interim Report, The Case for the Inclusive Approach. London: RSA (Royal Society for the Encouragement of Arts, Manufactures & Commerce), 1994.

Ruch, William V. *Corporate Communication*. Westport, Conn.: Quorum Books, 1984.

Schramm, Wilbur. *The Process and Effects of Mass Communication*. Urbana, Ill.: University of Illinois Press, 1954.

Shannon, Claude, and Warren Weaver. *The Mathematical Theory of Communication*. Urbana, Ill.: University of Illinois Press, 1949.

Stoll, Clifford. *Silicon Snake Oil: Second Thoughts on the Information Highway*. New York: Doubleday, 1995.

Swindle, Robert, and Elizabeth Swindle. *The Business Communicator*. Englewood Cliffs, N.J.: Prentice-Hall, 1985.

Thayer, Lee. *Communication and Communication Systems*. Homewood, Ill.: Irwin, 1968.

Organizations Related to Corporate Communication

American Association of Advertising Agencies (666 Third Ave., New York NY 10017)

American Marketing Association (310 Madison Ave., New York NY 10017)

Center for the Advancement of Applied Ethics, Carnegie Mellon University (Pittsburgh PA 15213)

International Association of Business Communicators (870 Market Street, San Francisco CA 94102)

International Communication Association (P.O. Box 9589, Austin TX 78766)

Public Relations Society of America (33 Irving Pl., New York NY 10003)

Society of Professional Journalists (53 West Jackson Blvd., Suite 731, Chicago IL 60604)

Speech Communication Association (5105-E Backlick Rd., Annandale VA 22003)

Women in Communications Inc. (2 Colonial Pl., 2101 Wilson Blvd., 4th Floor, Arlington VA 22001)

2. CORPORATE COMMUNICATION PRACTICE

Annual Report Trends. Boston, Mass.: S. D. Warren, 1982.

Cato, Sid. "Best Annual Reports" *Chief Executive* (October 1994): 26–33.

————. *Sid Cato's Newsletter on Annual Reports.* Kalamazoo, Mich.: Cato Communications, 1994.

Code of Professional Standards for the Practice of Public Relations. New York: Public Relations Society of America (PRSA), 1988.

Cutlip, Scott, Allen Center, and Glen Broom. *Effective Public Relations,* 6th ed. Englewood Cliffs, N.J.: Prentice-Hall, 1985.

Fast, Julian. *Subtext: Making Body Language Work.* New York: Viking, 1991.

Fink, Steven. *Crisis Management: Planning for the Inevitable.* New York: AMACOM, 1986.

General Motors Public Interest Report (Annual). Detroit, Mich.: General Motors Corporation (Annually since 1970).

Goodman, Michael B. *Write to the Point: Effective Communication in the Workplace.* Englewood Cliffs, N.J.: Prentice-Hall, 1984.

Graphis Annual Reports 4. Zürich: Graphis Press, 1994.

Graphis Corporate Identity 2. Zürich: Graphis Press, 1994.

The Handbook of Executive Communication. Ed. John Louis DiGaetani. Homewood, Ill.: Dow Jones-Irwin, 1986.

IABC Code of Ethics. San Francisco: International Association of Business Communication. n.d.

Kahane, Howard. *Logic and Contemporary Rhetoric: The Use of Reason in Everyday Life.* 6th ed. Belmont, Calif.: Wadsworth, 1992.

Kanter, Rosabeth Moss. *The Change Masters: Innovation for Productivity in the American Corporation.* New York: Simmon, 1983.

Lesley's Handbook of Public Relations and Communications, 4th ed. Philip Lesley, Ed. Englewood Cliffs, N.J.: Prentice-Hall.

McLuhan, Marshall. *Understanding Media: The Extensions of Man.* New York: McGraw-Hill, 1964.

Meyers, Gerald. *When It Hits the Fan: Managing the Nine Crises of Business.* Boston: Houghton Mifflin, 1986.

Morris, Desmond. *Body Talk: The Meaning of Human Gestures.* New York: Crown, 1994.

Pocket Pal. 13th ed. International Paper Company, 1988.

Pratkanis, Anthony, and Elliot Aronson. *Age of Propaganda: The Everyday Use and Abuse of Persuasion.* New York: W. H. Freeman, 1992.

"PRSA Task Force: Public Relations Body of Knowledge Task Force Report," *PR Review* 41:1 (spring 1988): 3–40. An update of the PR Body of Knowledge is scheduled for November 1993 publication.

Tannen, Deborah. *Conversational Style: Analyzing Talk Among Friends.* Norwood, N.J.: Ablex, 1984.

———. *You Just Don't Understand: Women and Men in Conversation.* New York: Ballentine Books, 1991.

Tufte, Edward P. *The Visual Display of Quantitative Information.* Cheshire, Conn.: Graphics Press, 1983.

———. *Envisioning Information.* Cheshire, Conn.: Graphics Press, 1990.

———. *Visual Explanations.* Cheshire, Conn.: Graphics Press, 1997.

Van Gundy, Arthur. *Techniques of Structured Problem-Solving,* 2d ed. New York: Van Nostrand Reinhold, 1988.

On Communication Research

Anderson, J. A. *Communication Research: Issues and Methods.* New York: McGraw Hill, 1987.

Frey, L., R. Botan, and C. H. Friedman. *Investigating Communication: An Introduction to Research Methods.* Englewood Cliffs, N.J.: Prentice-Hall, 1991.

Rubin, R. B., A. M. Rubin, and L. J. Piele. *Communication Research: Strategies and Sources.* Belmont, Calif.: Wadsworth, 1993.

3. CORPORATE COMMUNICATION AND CORPORATE CULTURE

Berne, Eric. *Games People Play.* New York: Grove Press, 1964.

Deal, Terrence E., and Allan A. Kennedy. *Corporate Cultures: The Rites and Rituals of Corporate Life.* Reading, Mass.: Addison-Wesley, 1982.

"Does the Baldrige Award Really Work?" *Harvard Business Review* (January–February 1992): 126–47.

Fayol, Henri. *General and Industrial Management* (trans). London: Pitman, 1916/1949.

Handy, Charles. *Understanding Organizations*. London: Penguin Books, 1976/1993.

Hofstede, Geert. *Cultures and Organizations*. London: Harper Collins, 1991/1994.

Kanter, Rosabeth. *Men and Women of the Corporation*. New York: Basic Books, 1977.

Katzenstein, Gary. *Funny Business: An Outsider's Year in Japan*. Englewood Cliffs, N.J.: Prentice-Hall, 1990.

Kidder, Tracy. *The Soul of a New Machine*. New York: Avon Books, 1981.

Malcolm Baldridge National Quality Award. National Institute of Standards and Technology, U.S. Department of Commerce, n.d.

Mamet, David. *Glengarry Glen Ross*. New York: Grove Weidenfeld, 1984 Pulitzer Prize-winning play, 1981; movie version, 1992.

"Organizational Culture: Techniques Companies Use to Perpetuate or Change Beliefs and Values." United States General Accounting Office Report GAO/NSIAD–92–105. Washington, D.C.: GAO, February 1992.

Ott, J. Steven. *The Organizational Culture Perspective*. Pacific Grove, Calif.: Brooks/Cole, 1989.

Ouchi, William. *Theory Z: How American Business Can Meet the Japanese Challenge*. Reading, Mass.: Addison-Wesley, 1981.

Peters, Tom, and Robert Waterman. *In Search of Excellence*. New York: Harper and Row, 1982.

Sathe, Vijay. *Culture and Related Corporate Realities: Texts, Cases, and Readings on Organizational Entry, Establishment, and Change*. Homewood, Ill.: Irwin, 1985.

Stewart, James B. *Den of Thieves*. New York: Simon & Schuster, 1991.

Symbols and Artifacts: Views of the Corporate Landscape. Pasquale Gagliardi, Ed. Belgirate, Italy: ISTUD-Instituto Studi Direzionali, 1990.

Taylor, Frederick. *The Principles of Scientific Management*. New York: Norton, 1911.

Thomas, R. Roosevelt. *Beyond Race and Gender: Unleashing the Power of Your Total Workforce by Managing Diversity*. New York: AMACOM, 1991.

"Women at Work," *Management Review* (March 1992). Issue devoted to women's issues in changing corporate cultures.

Corporate Culture in the Movies and on TV

L.A. Law, NBC

Murphy Brown, CBS

Network, MGM, 1976

Roger and Me, Warner Brothers, 1989

Tucker, LucasFilm, 1988

Wall Street, 20th Century Fox, 1987

4. CORPORATE IDENTITY

Falsey, Thomas A. *Corporate Philosophies and Mission Statements: A Survey and Guide for Corporate Communicators and Management.* Westport, Conn.: Quorum Books, 1989.

Garbett, Thomas. *How to Build a Corporation's Identity and Project Its Image.* Lexington, Mass.: Lexington Books, 1988.

Graphis Annual Reports 4. Zürich: Graphis Press, 1994.

Graphis Corporate Identity 2. Zürich: Graphis Press, 1994.

Gray, James G. *Managing the Corporate Image: The Key to Public Trust.* Westport, Conn.: Quorum Books, 1986.

Roalman, Arthur R. *Investor Relations Handbook.* New York: American Management Association, 1974.

Winter, Elmer L. *A Complete Guide to Preparing A Corporate Annual Report.* New York: Van Nostrand Reinhold, 1985.

5. CORPORATE CITIZENSHIP AND SOCIAL RESPONSIBILITY

Adelson, Andrea. "Controversy Over the Body Shop Has Put a Spotlight on Socially Responsible Investing," *The New York Times* (September 16, 1994): D6.

Amba-Rao, Sita C. "Multinational Corporate Social Responsibility, Ethics, Interactions and Third World Governments: An Agenda for the 1990s," *Journal of Business Ethics* 12 (1993): 553–72.

Anderson, Jerry W., Jr. *Corporate Social Responsibility.* Westport, Conn.: Quorum Books, 1989.

Angelidis, John P., and Nabil A. Ibrahim. "Social Demand and Corporate Supply: A Corporate Social Responsibility Model," *Review of Business* 15 (1993): 7–10.

————. "Corporate Social Responsibility: A Comparative Analysis of Top Executives and Business Students," *The Mid-Atlantic Journal of Business* 29:3 (December 1993): 303–14.

Arnott, Nancy. "Marketing with a Passion," *Sales and Marketing Management* (January 1994): 64–71.

Avishai, Bernard. "What is Business's Social Compact?" *Harvard Business Review* (January–February 1994): 38–48.

Brody, E. W. *The Business of Public Relations.* Westport, Conn.: Praeger, 1987.

Bulkeley, William, and Joann Lublin. "Ben & Jerry's New CEO Will Face Shrinking Sales and Growing Fears of Fat," *The Wall Street Journal* (January 10, 1995): B1, B4.

Business Ethics—The Magazine of Socially Responsible Business (bimonthly).

Council of Better Business Bureaus, Inc., National Advertising Division, National Advertising Review Board Procedures (Amended 7-1-90).

Derr, Kenneth. "Goodbye, Grip and Grin," *Across the Board* (September 1993): 28–31.

Donaldson, Thomas, and Thomas Dunfee. "Toward a Unified Conception of Business Ethics: Integrative Social Contracts Theory," *Academy of Management Review* 19:2 (April 1994): 252–84.

Dreifus, Claudia. "Passing the Scoop: Ben & Jerry," *The New York Times Magazine* (December 18, 1994): 38–41.

Elliott, Stuart. "Selling Underwear, and Ideas: New Signs are Turning Times Square Into an Issues Forum," *The New York Times* (September 9, 1994): D15.

The Foundation Directory. New York: The Foundation Center. Annual.

Foundation Giving (see Renz).

Friedman, Milton. "The Social Responsibility of Business Is to Increase Its Profits," *The New York Times Magazine* (September 13, 1970): 32–33, 122–26.

Garbett, Tom. *How to Build a Corporation's Identity and Project Its Image.* Boston: Lexington Books, 1988.

General Motors Public Interest Report (published annually since 1971). Detroit: General Motors.

Goldberger, Paul. "Philip Morris Calls in I.O.U.'s in the Arts," *The New York Times* (October 5, 1994): A1, C14.

Gupta, Udayan. "Cause-Driven Companies' New Cause: Profits," *The Wall Street Journal* (November 8, 1994): B1.

Henricks, Mark. "Doing Well While Doing Good," *Small Business Reports* (November 1991): 28–38.

Herbert, Bob. "When Kids Say 'Enough!'" *The New York Times* (July 13, 1994): A19.

The Home Depot Corporate Social Responsibility Report 1993. Atlanta, Ga.: The Home Depot.

Jackson, Kevin. "Global Distributive Justice and Corporate Duty to Aid," *Journal of Business Ethics* 12 (1993): 547–51.

Kruckeberg, Dean, and Kenneth Starck. *Public Relations and Community: A Reconstructed Theory.* Westport, Conn.: Praeger, 1988.

Lager, Fred "Chico." *Ben & Jerry's: The Inside Scoop—How Two Real Guys Built a Business with a Social Conscience and a Sense of Humor.* New York: Crown, 1994.

L'Etang, Jacquie. "Public Relations and Corporate Social Responsibility: Some Issues Arising," *Journal of Business Ethics* 13 (1994): 111–23.

Lowengard, Mary. "Community Relations—New Approaches to Building Consensus," *Public Relations Journal* (October 1989): 24–30.

Mack, Charles S. *Lobbying and Government Relations: A Guide for Executives.* Westport, Conn.: Quorum Books, 1989.

Marquis, Chalmers. Schering-Plough Executive Lectures, Fairleigh Dickinson University, Fall 1993.

Mitchell, Russell, and Michael Oneal. "Managing by Values: Is Levi Strauss' Approach Visionary—or Flaky?" *Business Week* (August 1,1994): 46–52.

Nichols, Martha. "Does New Age Business Have a Message for Managers?" *Harvard Business Review* (March–April 1994): 52–60.

Ono, Yumiko. "Advertisers Try 'Doing Good' to Help Make Sales Do Better," *The Wall Street Journal* (September 2, 1994): B8.

Owen, Crystal, and Robert Scherer. "Social Responsibility and Market Share," *Review of Business* 15:1 (Summer/Fall 1993): 11–16.

Pinkston, Tammie S., and Archie B. Carroll. "Corporate Citizenship Perspectives and Foreign Direct Investment in the U.S.," *Journal of Business Ethics* 13 (1994): 157–69.

"Public TV: A Public Debate." Sponsored by the Center for Communication, November 15, 1994, New York, N.Y.

Reder, Alan. *In Pursuit of Principle and Profit: Business Success Through Social Responsibility.* New York: G. P. Putnam's Sons, 1994.

Renz, Loren, and Steven Lawrence. *Foundation Giving: Yearbook of Facts and Figures on Private, Corporate and Community Foundations.* New York: The Foundation Center, 1994.

Rifkin, Glenn. "PBS Seeks to Widen Its Prime-Time News With New Quiz Show," *The New York Times* (September 12, 1994): D6.

Roddick, Anita. *Body and Soul.* New York: Crown, 1991.

———. "Corporate Responsibility," *Vital Speeches of the Day* (December 1993): 196–99. Also reprinted in *New Statesman & Society* (December 17/31, 1993): 54–55.

Rowland, Mary. "Investing Your Principles," *The New York Times* (October 16, 1994): 15.

RSA Inquiry—Tomorrow's Company: The Role of Business in a Changing World— Interim Report, The Case for the Inclusive Approach. London: RSA (Royal Society for the Encouragement of Arts, Manufactures & Commerce), 1994.

Schneider, Keith. "Exxon is Ordered to Pay $5 Billion for Alaska Spill—A Record for Pollution—Jury Awards Punitive Damages to 34,000 Alaska Residents—Company to Appeal," *The New York Times* (September 17, 1994): 1, 10.

Sebastian, Pamela. "Charitable Wineries Ask for More Than Thanks," *The Wall Street Journal* (October 21, 1994): B1, B10.

Shaw, Bill, and Frederick Post. "A Moral Basis for Corporate Philanthropy," *Journal of Business Ethics* 12 (1993): 745–51.

Smith, Craig. "The New Corporate Philanthropy," *Harvard Business Review* (May–June 1994): 105–16; Responses from readers, *Harvard Business Review* (July–August 1994): 142–44.

Stevenson, Richard. "Body Shop's Green Image Is Attacked," *The New York Times* (September 2, 1994): D1, D6.

Treaster, Joseph. "School Poll Finds Harsher View of Drugs," *The New York Times* (July 13, 1994): B4.

Wilson, Jan. "Public Television: How It Can Fit Into Your Marketing Plan," *A. N. A/The Advertiser* (Winter 1992): 21–24.

Research Centers

Center for the Advancement of Applied Ethics, Carnegie Mellon University

Center for Communication, New York, N.Y.

Center for Corporate Community Relations, Boston College

Center on Philanthropy, Indiana University

The Foundation Center, New York, N.Y., and branch offices in major cities across the United States

6. CORPORATE COMMUNICATION AND MEETING THE PRESS

Corrado, Frank M. *Media for Managers.* Englewood Cliffs, N.J. : Prentice-Hall, 1984.

Evans, Fred J. *Managing the Media: Proactive Strategies for Better Business–Press Relations.* New York: Quorum Books, 1987.

Herman, Edward S. *Beyond Hypocrisy: Decoding the News in an Age of Propaganda, Including the Doublespeak Dictionary.* Boston: South End Press, 1992.

McKibben, Bill. *The Age of Missing Information.* New York: Random House, 1992.

Moore, David W. *The Super Pollsters: How They Measure and Manipulate Public Opinion in America.* New York: Four Walls Eight Windows, 1992.

Parenti, Michael. *Make-Believe Media: The Politics of Entertainment.* New York: St. Martin's Press, 1992.

Parry, Robert. *Fooling America: How Washington Insiders Twist the Truth and Manufacture the Conventional Wisdom.* New York: William Morrow, 1992.

Postman, Neil, and Steve Powers. *How to Watch TV News.* New York: Penguin, 1992.

Ridgway, Judith. *Successful Media Relations: A Practitioner's Guide.* New York: Ashgate Publishing, 1984.

Stratford, Sherman. "Smart Ways to Handle the Press," *Fortune,* June 19, 1989: 69–75.

7. CORPORATE COMMUNICATION AND CRISIS

Barton, Laurence. *Crisis in Organizations: Managing and Communicating in the Heat of Chaos.* Cincinnati, Ohio: South-Western, 1993.

Burak, Patricia. *Crisis Management in a Cross-Cultural Setting.* Washington, D.C.: NAFSA Washington, 1986.

Fink, Steven. *Crisis Management: Planning for the Inevitable.* New York: AMACOM, 1986.

Huyler, Jean W. *Crisis Communications and Communicating About Negotiations.* New York: AMACOM, 1981.

Mazarr, Michael. *Improving International Crisis Communications: Final Report of the Study Group on Crisis Communication*. CSI Studies, 1991.

Meyers, Gerald C. *When It Hits the Fan: Managing the Nine Crises of Business*. Boston: Houghton Mifflin, 1986.

Wisenblit, Joseph Z. "Crisis Management Planning Among U.S. Corporations: Empirical Evidence and a Proposed Framework," *Advanced Management Journal* (Spring 1989): 31–41.

On Green Issues

Adelson, Andrea. "Controversy Over the Body Shop Has Put a Spotlight on Socially Responsible Investing," *The New York Times* (September 16, 1994): D6.

Aeppel, Timothy. "Green Groups Enter a Dry Season as Movement Matures," *Wall Street Journal* (October 21, 1994): B1, B4.

Bendz, Diana. "Green Products for Green Profits," *IEEE Spectrum* (September 1993): 63–66.

Biddle, Michael, and Ray Mann. "Recipe for Recycling," *IEEE Spectrum* (August 1994): 22–24.

Cavanaugh, H. A. "Will Customers Pay for Renewables? PCS Launches 'green-power' Program," *Electrical World* (October 1993): 19–20.

Chambers, Catherine, Paul Chambers, and John Whitehead. "Environmental Preservation and Corporate Involvement: Green Products and Debt-for-Nature Swaps," *Review of Business* 15:1 (Summer/Fall 1993): 17–21.

Cockburn, Alexander, and Jeffrey St. Clair. "After Armageddon: Death and Life for America's Greens," *The Nation* (December 19, 1994): 760–65.

Council on Economic Priorities, Benjamin Hollister et al. *Shopping for a Better World*. San Francisco: Sierra Club Books, 1994.

Council on Economic Priorities 1993 Report. Various research reports and pamphlets from 1988 to 1994.

Crede, Karen. "Environmental Effects of the Computer Age," Master's thesis. Madison, N.J.: Fairleigh Dickinson University, 1994, in *IEEE Transactions of Professional Communication* (March 1995).

Davis, Joel. "Strategies for Environmental Advertising," *Journal of Consumer Marketing* 10:2 (1993): 19–36.

———. "Good Ethics is Good for Business: Ethical Attributions and Response to Environmental Advertising," *Journal of Business Ethics* 13 (1994): 873–85.

Dillon, Patricia. "Salvageability by Design," *IEEE Spectrum (August 1994):* 18–21.

Frause, Bob, and Julie Colehour. *The Environmental Marketing Imperative: Strategies for Transforming Environmental Commitment into a Competitive Advantage.* Chicago: Probus, 1994.

General Motors Environmental Report. Detroit, Mich.: General Motors, 1994.

"Guides for the Use of Environmental Marketing Claims: The Application of Section 5 of the Federal Trade Commission Act to Environmental Advertising and Marketing Practices," Federal Trade Commission, July 1992.

Hawken, Paul. *The Ecology of Commerce: A Declaration of Sustainability.* New York: HarperCollins, 1993.

Holusha, John. "From Firewood to Environmental Empire in 14 Years," *The New York Times* (June 26, 1994): F7.

———. "Recycled Material Is Finding a New and Lucrative Market," *The New York Times* (October 8, 1994): 1, 41.

IEEE Spectrum. "Special Report—Environment, Green Electronics," 31:1 (August 1994): 18–31.

"Institute of the Packaging Professionals Packaging Reduction, Reuse, Recycling & Disposal Guidelines," Herndon, Va.: Institute of the Packaging Professionals, 1993.

International Paper. *1993 Annual Report.* Purchase, N.Y.: International Paper, 1994.

———. "1993–1994 Environment, Health and Safety Progress Report," Purchase, N.Y.: International Paper, 1994.

———. "A Commitment to Environment, Health and Safety Excellence," Purchase, N.Y.: International Paper, 1993.

———. "Corporate Issues: The Chlorine Controversy; Corporate Position on the Environment; Food Packaging; Life-Cycle Assessment; Source Reduction for Green Packaging," Purchase, N.Y.: International Paper, n.d.

———. "Forest Stewardship—Issue Briefs," Purchase, N.Y.: International Paper, 1994.

———. "Paper Making, Pulp Bleaching and the Environment—Issue Briefs," Purchase, N.Y.: International Paper, 1994.

Kevles, Daniel. "Greens in America," *The New York Review of Books* (October 6, 1994): 35–40. Essay/review on seven books on the environment.

"Letters to the Editor: Many Sportsmen are Environmentalists," *The Wall Street Journal* (August 11, 1994): A13.

Maddox, Bronwen. "Campaigners All At Sea: Are Environmentalists in Danger of Extinction?" *Financial Times* (November 12/13, 1994): 1, 13.

McDaniel, Stephen, and David Rylander. "Strategic Green Marketing," *Journal of Consumer Marketing* 10:3 (1993): 4–10.

McDougall, Gordon. "The Green Movement in Canada: Implications for Marketing Strategy," *Journal of International Consumer Marketing* 5:3 (1993): 69–87.

McMath, Robert. "Keeping Precious Rainforest, and Themed Products, Green," *Brandweek* (October 11, 1993): 34–35.

Moffett, Matt. "Kayapo Indians Lose Their 'Green' Image," *The Wall Street Journal* (December 29, 1994): A6.

Olin, Dirk. "Environment: Shake, Rattle, and Clank—As the Sierra Club Starts to Lurch, Does the Nation's Oldest Green Group Need an Overhaul?" *Outside* (January 1995): 15–16.

Ottman, Jacquelyn A. *Green Marketing: Challenges & Opportunities for the New Marketing Age.* Lincolnwood, Ill.: NTC Business Books, 1993.

Perry, Tekla. "'Green' Refrigerators," *IEEE Spectrum* (August 1994): 25–30.

Powell, Cheryl. "The Green Movement Slows Demand for Ecofurniture," *The Wall Street Journal* (September 2, 1994): B1, B2.

Protzman, Ferdinand. "Germany's Push to Expand the Scope of Recycling," *The New York Times* (July 4, 1993): F8.

RSA Inquiry—Tomorrow's Company: The Role of Business in a Changing World. London: RSA (Royal Society for the Encouragement of Arts, Manufactures & Commerce), 1994.

Rubin, Charles T. *The Green Crusade: Rethinking the Roots of Environmentalism.* New York: The Free Press, 1994.

Stevenson, Richard. "Body Shop's Green Image Is Attacked," *The New York Times* (September 2, 1994): D1, D6.

Stipp, David. "Cities Couldn't Give Away Their Trash; Now They Get Top Dollar From Recyclers," *The Wall Street Journal* (September 19, 1994): B1, B9.

Testin, Robert, and Peter Vergano. *Packaging in America in the 1990s: Packaging's Role in Contemporary American Society—The Benefits and Challenges.* Herndon, Va.: Institute of Packaging Professionals, 1990.

Thayer, James. "EC's Green Audit Makes Manufacturers See Red," *The Journal of European Business* (November–December 1993): 62.

Walley, Noah, and Bradley Whitehead. "It's Not Easy Being Green," *Harvard Business Review* (May–June 1994): 46–52. Responses in "The Challenge of Going Green," *Harvard Business Review* (July–August 1994): 37–50.

8. CORPORATE COMMUNICATION AND TECHNOLOGY

Audiovisual Handbook. Santa Ana, Calif.: Toastmasters International, n.d.

Bittner, John R. *Broadcasting and Telecommunications.* Englewood Cliffs, N.J.: Prentice-Hall, 1985.

Chew, Joe. "Introduction to the Special Section on Electronic Communication and Interaction," *IEEE Transactions on Professional Communication* 37:4 (1994): 193.

Corporate and Organizational Video. Alan Richardson, Ed. New York: McGraw-Hill, 1992.

Cowan, Robert A. *Teleconferencing.* Reston, Va.: Reston, 1984.

Davenport, Thomas H., Robert Eccles, and Laurence Prusak. "Information Politics," *Sloan Management Review* (Fall 1992): 53–65.

Gates, Bill. *The Road Ahead.* New York: Viking, 1995.

Gross, Lynne S. *Telecommunications: An Introduction to Electronic Media.* Dubuque, Iowa: William C. Brown, 1989.

Marlow, Eugene. *Managing Corporate Media.* White Plains, N.Y.: Knowledge Industries, 1989.

Meadow, Charles T., and Albert Tedesco. *Telecommunications for Management.* New York: McGraw Hill, 1985.

Moore, Geoffrey. *Crossing the Chasm.* New York: Harper Business, 1991.

Morton, M. S. Scott. *The Corporation of the 1990s: Information Technology and Organizational Transformation.* New York: Oxford University Press, 1991.

Negroponte, Nicholas. *Being Digital.* New York: Knopf, 1995.

Norman, Donald. *The Design of Everyday Things.* New York: Doubleday, 1988.

Singleton, Lux A. *Telecommunications in the Information Age.* Cambridge, Mass.: Ballinger, 1986.

"Special Report: E-Mail—Pervasive and Persuasive," *IEEE Spectrum.* 29:10 (October 1992): 22–34.

Stoll, Clifford. *Silicon Snake Oil: Second Thoughts on the Information Highway.* New York: Doubleday, 1995.

Van Nostrand, William. *The Nonbroadcast Television Writer's Handbook.* White Plains, N.Y.: Knowledge Industry, 1983.

———. *The Scriptwriter's Handbook.* White Plains, N.Y.: Knowledge Industry, 1989.

9. CORPORATE COMMUNICATION IN GLOBAL MARKETS

Adler, Gordon. "The Case of the Floundering Expatriate," *Harvard Business Review* (July–August 1995): 24–40.

Axtell, Roger. *Do's and Taboos Around the World*, 3d ed. Compiled by the Parker Pen Company. New York: Wiley, 1993.

Background Notes. Washington, D.C.: Department of State (published annually).

Barbee, George, and Mark Lutchen."Local Face, Global Body," *PW Review* (Spring 1995): 18–31.

Barnlund, Dean C. *Communicative Styles of Japan and America: Images and Realities*. Belmont, Calif.: Wadsworth, 1989.

Business America: The Magazine of International Trade. Washington, D.C.: U.S. Department of Commerce (published biweekly).

Copeland, Lennie, and Lewis Griggs. *Going International: How to Make Friends and Deal Effectively in the Global Marketplace*. New York: Random House, 1985.

Culture Grams. Provo, Utah: Center for International Studies, Brigham Young University. Set of ninety-six cultures.

Department of State Publication 7877. Washington, D.C.: 1993.

Destination Japan: A Business Guide for the '90s. Washington, D.C.: U.S. Government Printing Office, 1991.

Directory of American Firms Operating in Foreign Countries. New York: World Trade Academy Press (annual).

Directory of Foreign Firms Operating in the United States. New York: World Trade Academy Press (annual).

Doyle, Edward. *How the United States Can Compete in the World Marketplace*. New York: IEEE, 1991.

Edwards, Mike. "A Broken Empire: After the Soviet Union's Collapse," *National Geographic* 183:3 (March 1993): 2–53.

"Enterprise Funds," GAO/NSIAD-94-77. Washington, D.C.: 1994.

Europe: The Magazine of the European Community. Washington, D.C.: EC Delegation to the United States (ten times per year).

Europe: World Partner—The External Relations of the European Community. Luxembourg: Office for Official Publications of the European Communities, 1991.

The European Community 1992 and Beyond. Luxembourg: Office for Official Publications of the European Communities, 1991.

The European Community in the Nineties. Washington, D.C.: EC Delegation to the United States, 1992.

European Union. Luxembourg: Office of Official Publications of the European Communities, 1994.

Export Programs: A Business Directory of U.S. Government Services. Washington, D.C.: U.S. Department of Commerce, 1994.

Ferraro, Gary. *The Cultural Dimension of International Business,* 2d ed. Englewood Cliffs, N.J.: 1994.

Former Soviet Union. GAO/GGD–95–60. Washington D.C.: 1995.

Frederick, Howard. *Global Communication and International Relations.* Belmont, Calif.: Wadsworth, 1993.

Gannon, Martin. *Understanding Global Cultures.* Thousand Oaks, Calif.: Sage, 1994.

Goodman, Michael B. "The Special Section on Professional Communication in Russia: An American Perspective," *IEEE Transactions on Professional Communication* 37:2 (June 1994): 90–91.

———. *Working in a Global Environment: Understanding, Communicating, and Managing Transnationally.* New York: IEEE, 1995.

Haglund, E. "Japan: Cultural Considerations," *International Journal of Intercultural Relations* 8 (1984): 61–76.

Hall, Edward T. *Beyond Culture.* New York: Doubleday, 1976.

———. *The Dance of Life.* Garden City, N.Y.: Anchor/ Doubleday, 1987.

———. *Hidden Differences: Doing Business with Japan.* Garden City, N.Y.: Anchor/Doubleday, 1987.

———. *The Hidden Dimension.* New York: Doubleday, 1966.

———. *The Silent Language.* New York: Doubleday, 1959.

Hall, Lynne. *Latecomer's Guide to the New Europe: Doing Business in Central Europe.* New York: American Management Association, 1992.

Henzler, Herbert. "The New Era of Eurocapitalism," *Harvard Business Review* (July–August 1992): 57–68.

Hodgson, Kent. "Adapting Ethical Decisions to a Global Marketplace," *Management Review* (May 1992): 53–57.

Hofstede, Geert. *Cultures and Organizations.* London: HarperCollins, 1991.

International Business Practices. Washington, D.C.: Commerce Department (#003–009–00622–8).

Kohls, Robert. *Survival Kit for Overseas Living*, 2d ed. Yarmouth, Me.: Intercultural Press, 1984.

Lawrence, Paul, and Charalambos Vlachoutsicos. "Joint Ventures in Russia: Put the Locals in Charge," *Harvard Business Review* (January–February 1993): 44–54.

Moore, Geoffrey. *Crossing the Chasm: Marketing and Selling Technology Products to Mainstream Customers*. New York: Harper, 1991.

Noël, Emile. *Working Together—The Institutions of the European Community*. Luxembourg: Office for Official Publications of the European Communities, 1994.

"North American Free Trade Agreement: Assessment of Major Issues." GAO/GGD–93–137 A & B. Washington, D.C.: 1993.

"North American Free Trade Agreement: Structure and Status of Implementing Organizations." GAO/GGD–95–10BR. Washington, D.C.: 1993.

Pagell, Ruth, and Michael Halperin. *International Business Information: How to Find It, How to Use It*. Phoenix, Ariz.: ORYX, 1994.

Piet-Pelon, Nancy, and Barbara Hornby. *Women's Guide to Overseas Living*. Yarmouth, Maine: Intercultural Press, 1992.

Rowland, D. *Japanese Business Etiquette: A Practical Guide to Success in the Global Market Place*. New York: Praeger, 1986.

Semler, Richardo. "Who Needs Bosses?" *Across the Board* (February 1994): 24.

Terpstra, V., and K. David. *The Cultural Environment of International Business*. Cincinnati: South Western, 1985.

Tomorrow's Company: The Role of Business in a Changing World. London: RSA (Royal Society for the Encouragement of Arts, Manufactures & Commerce), 1994.

Trompenaars, Fons. *Riding the Waves of Culture: Understanding Cultural Diversity in Business*. London: The Economist Books, 1993.

Victor, David. *International Business Communication*. New York: HarperCollins, 1992.

Weiss, Stephen. "Negotiating with 'Romans'," *Sloan Management Review* (winter 1994): 51–61.

Information Resources

The European Union: Washington, D.C., (202) 862-9500; New York City, (212) 371-3804.

U.S. Commerce Department, International Trade Administration, Trade Information Center, 1-800-USA-TRADE (1-800-872-8723).

U.S. Department of State Coordinator for Business Affairs, (202) 647-1942; fax, (202) 647-5713.

U.S. Departments of State and Commerce, Country Desk Officers, (202) 482-3022; for a specific Country Desk Officer, (202) 647-4000.

Index of Essay and Case Authors

Index